Resurrecting Dr. Moss

NORTHERN LIGHTS SERIES

William Barr, general editor ·
Copublished with the Arctic Institute of North America

ISSN 1701-0004

This series takes up the geographical region of the North (circumpolar regions within the zone of discontinuous permafrost) and publishes works from all areas of northern scholarship, including natural sciences, social sciences, earth sciences, and the humanities.

No. 1 · **Nunavik: Inuit-Controlled Education in Arctic Quebec** Ann Vick-Westgate · Copublished with the Katutjiniq Regional Development Council

No. 2 · **Many Faces of Gender: Roles and Relationships through Time in Northern Indigenous Communities** Edited by Lisa Frink, Rita S. Shepard, and Gregory A. Reinhardt · Copublished with University Press of Colorado

No. 3 · **New Owners in their Own Land: Minerals and Inuit Land Claims** Robert McPherson

No. 4 · **War North of 80: The Last German Arctic Weather Station of World War II** Wilhelm Dege, translated and edited by William Barr · Copublished with University Press of Colorado

No. 5 · **Writing Geographical Exploration: Thomas James and the Northwest Passage 1631–33** Wayne K.D. Davies

No. 6 · **As Long as This Land Shall Last: A History of Treaty 8 and Treaty 11, 1870–1939** René Fumoleau

No. 7 · **Breaking Ice: Renewable Resource and Ocean Management in the Canadian North** Edited by Fikret Berkes, Rob Huebert, Helen Fast, Micheline Manseau, and Alan Diduck

No. 8 · **Alliance and Conflict: The World System of the Inupiaq Eskimos** Ernest S. Burch · Copublished with the University of Nebraska Press

No. 9 · **Tanana and Chandalar: The Alaska Field Journals of Robert A. McKennan** Edited by Craig Mishler and William E. Simeone · Copublished with University of Alaska Press

No. 10 · **Resurrecting Dr. Moss: The Life and Letters of a Royal Navy Surgeon, Edward Lawton Moss, MD, RN, 1843–1880** Paul C. Appleton, edited by William Barr

Resurrecting Dr. Moss

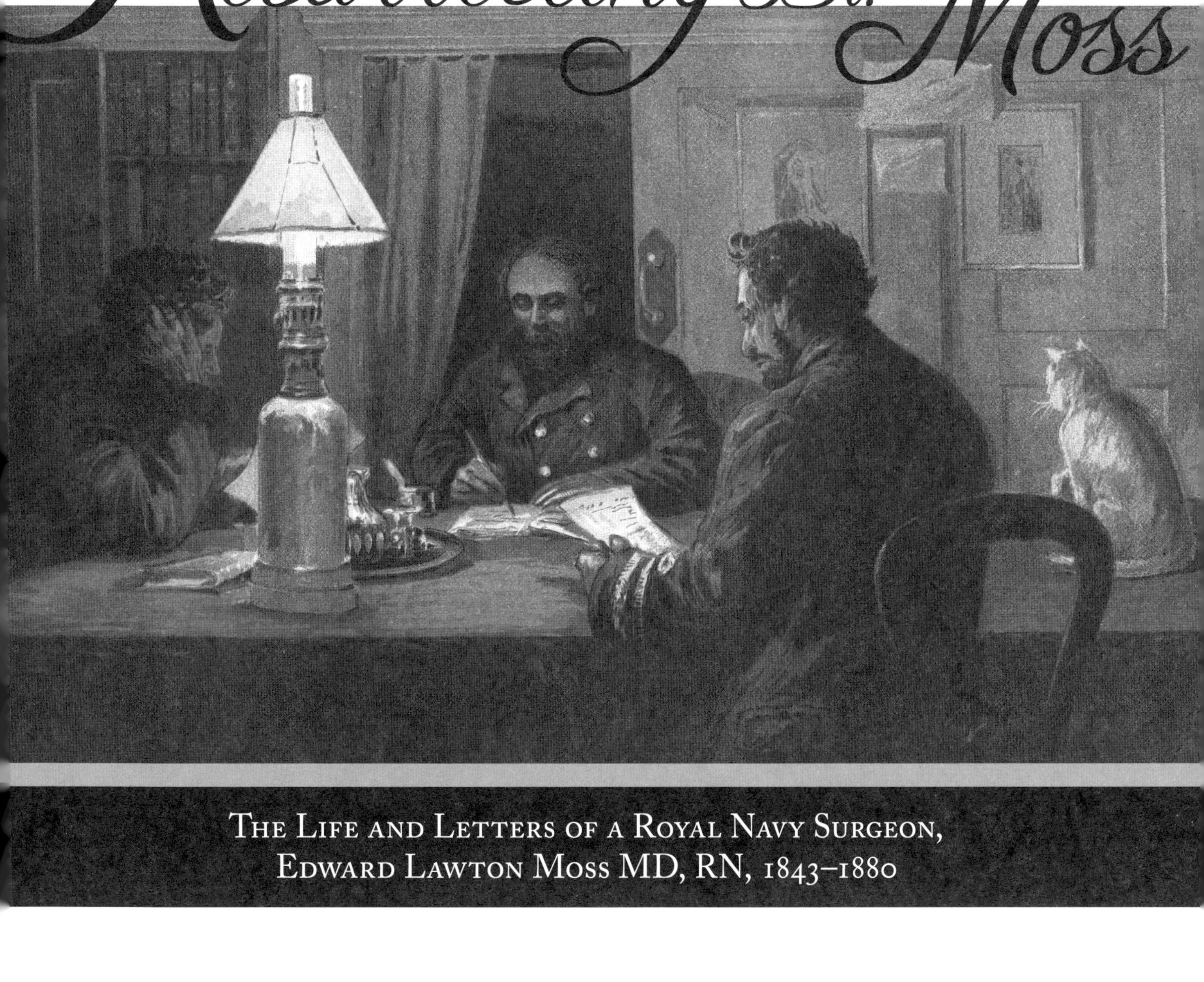

The Life and Letters of a Royal Navy Surgeon, Edward Lawton Moss MD, RN, 1843–1880

Paul C. Appleton

Edited by William Barr

University of Calgary Press
2500 University Drive NW
Calgary, Alberta
Canada T2N 1N4
www.uofcpress.com

LIBRARY AND ARCHIVES CANADA CATALOGUING IN PUBLICATION

Appleton, Paul C. (Paul Campbell), 1930-2006.
Resurrecting Dr. Moss : the life and letters of a Royal Navy surgeon, Edward Lawton Moss MD, RN, 1843-1880 / Paul C. Appleton ; edited by William Barr.

(Northern lights series ; no. 10)
Co-published by the Arctic Institute of North America.
Includes watercolours by Edward L. Moss.
Includes bibliographical references and index.
ISBN 978-1-55238-232-5

1. Moss, Edward L. (Edward Lawton). 2. Moss, Edward L. (Edward Lawton)—Correspondence. 3. Great Britain. Royal Navy—Medical care—History—19th century. 4. Medicine, Naval—Great Britain—History—19th century. 5. Arctic Expedition (1875-1876). 6. Arctic regions—Discovery and exploration—British. 7. Hospitals, Naval and marine—British Columbia—Esquimalt—History—19th century. 8. Great Britain. Royal Navy—Surgeons—Biography. 9. Great Britain. Royal Navy—Surgeons—Correspondence. 10. Ship physicians—Great Britain—Biography. 11. Esquimalt (B.C.)—Biography. I. Barr, William, 1940- II. Moss, Edward L. (Edward Lawton) III. Arctic Institute of North America IV. Title. V. Series.

V64.G72M68 2008 359.3'45092 C2008-903009-5

The University of Calgary Press acknowledges the support of the Alberta Foundation for the Arts for our publications. We acknowledge the financial support of the Government of Canada through the Book Publishing Industry Development Program (BPIDP) for our publishing activities. We acknowledge the financial support of the Canada Council for the Arts for our publishing program.

Canada Council for the Arts Conseil des Arts du Canada

Printed and bound in Canada by Kromar Printing Ltd.
This book is printed on 80lb Cougar Opaque and 80lb Starbrite Dull paper

Cover design, page design and typesetting by Melina Cusano

This book is dedicated to
Paul Appleton's grandchildren:

Jerrel, Maggie and Wesley Arai, and Vance Appleton

Table of Contents

List of Illustrations X

List of Colour Plates XI

Acknowledgments XIII

Editor's Preface XV

Chapter 1: Guildford, Surrey – "The Letter" 1

Very brief introductory chapter setting the stage for the narrative. Correspondence between Thomasina Moss and Robie Louis Reid relating to the life of her late husband.

Chapter 2: Dublin, Ireland – "Edward" 5

Brief description of Edward Moss's Quaker family, early life and education. Reasons for joining the Navy in 1864.

Chapter 3: Portsmouth – "The Royal Navy" 9

Brief look at the state of the Royal Navy and the Medical Department between 1860 and 1880.

Chapter 4: Haiti – "For the Honour of the Flag" 13

Moss is posted to HMS *Bulldog* – the "*Bulldog* Affair" – his description of firefight and blowing up the ship at Cape Haitien, Haiti. Moss's role during the fight. Analysis of the episode – "brilliant piece of fighting" or "reckless gunboat diplomacy"?

Chapter 5: HMS *Simoom* – "Service Afloat" 21

Brief chapter describing his travels and life aboard a troopship between 1866 and 1870, based on letters to his mother.

Chapter 6: Portland, Dorset – "Service Ashore" 29

Moss is posted to Portland Sick Quarters, Portland, UK. Letters to his mother during next eighteen months reveal his character and personality. Doubts about marriage and career. During outbreak of smallpox, his energy and diligence brings him to the attention of his superiors.

Chapter 7: British Columbia – "A Change of Course" 45

In January 1872, Moss is appointed to Esquimalt, British Columbia, tasked with reopening and renovating the Royal Navy Hospital serving the Pacific fleet. The prospect of more time ashore leads him to propose marriage to Thomasina Mary Dugdale. Narrative of trip to Victoria – arrival on Queen's birthday – story of first year at Esquimalt. Marriage at San Francisco, March 1873.

Chapter 8: Esquimalt – "His Own Master …" 53

Description of hospital complex – Moss works to bring the facility up to par – letters home about his work, life, and impressions of Vancouver Island.

Chapter 9: Esquimalt Hospital – "Do No Harm" 65

Victorian medical practices and the hospital based on Moss's detailed annual reports to the Admiralty. Descriptive sample of a number of cases and treatments used.

Chapter 10: Vancouver Island – "The Best of Times" 77

The young couple enjoy what amounts to an extended honeymoon as they settle into the life of the community. Social life and activities – story of an exciting hunting adventure (later published in England). Birth of Ada, their first child. Surprise telegram from the Admiralty asking Moss if he will volunteer for the 1875 (Nares) Arctic Expedition. Moss's response.

Chapter 11: England – "The Arctic Expedition" 93

Background of the new polar initiative – purpose and goals – planning the expedition – Edward's anticipated role. The new "polar fever" – high public expectations.

Chapter 12: Greenland – "To the Shores of the Polar Sea" 99

Grand public send-off from Portsmouth. Letters describing voyage along Greenland coast and through Baffin Bay to Ellesmere island – adventures – difficulties with ice – success in reaching the polar sea. *Alert* finally stopped by ice near present-day Alert Bay.

Chaper 13: Floeberg Harbour – "Polar Winter" 105

A narrow escape – Preparations for winter – problems on fall exploration parties – Edward's role and duties. Life in winter quarters – winter routines, work, and amusements. Preparations for spring polar attempt.

Chapter 14: Markham and Parr – "Daring to Do All …" 117

Commander Markham leads polar party. Leaving the ship – brutal weather and sledging conditions – immediate difficulties – Moss's assistance – slow progress – declining health of men. Refusal to recognize signs of scurvy – achieving "farthest north." Death on the ice. Moss leads rescue party. Questions about Markham's leadership. What did he know and when did he know it? Another death at the ship.

Chapter 15: Aldrich and Beaumont – "Hearts of Oak" 133

Lieut. Aldrich explores NW coast of Ellesmere island – problems – brutal travelling conditions – belated recognition of scurvy – journey to safety. Beaumont explores NE Greenland coast – appearance of scurvy – refusal to quit – rescue and more deaths at Polaris Bay. Scurvy aboard ships – Nares decides not to stay another year. Trip back to England – significance of expedition for Canada.

Chapter 16: London – "Feet of Clay?" 141

Welcome home – public honours and tributes. Moss receives Arctic Medal and promotion. Rapid appearance of criticism of expedition leadership– attacks in press over deaths and massive scurvy outbreak. Calls for parliamentary inquiry into leadership and planning, medical decisions, scurvy outbreak. Moss's testimony. Origins and treatment of scurvy – conclusions about the expedition.

Chapter 17: Kingston, Ireland – "Brief Interlude" 157

Leave and half-pay in Ireland. Writing "*Shores of the Polar Sea*" – review of book. Moss writes scientific articles. Birth of second daughter. Posting to HMS *Research* in the fall of 1878.

Chapter 18: Beshika Bay, Turkey – "Letters from Troy" 161

Russo-Turkish War – British response. Moss meets archaeologist Heinrich Schliemann – overnight visit to the dig. Letters home describe adventure and lucky escape. Conclusions about Schliemann and Troy. Friendship with Schliemann – return to England in 1879.

Chapter 19: HMS *Atalanta* – "The Perils of the Sea" 175

History of repairs and refit of a forty-three-year-old ship, HMS *Atalanta*, to replace HMS *Eurydice*, a similar training ship lost at sea. Problems with the refitted ship. Moss goes back to sea on *Atalanta* in November 1879. Letters home – hatred of gales – disappointment with career. Thoughts of future retirement – possible return to Victoria. Difficult voyage to West Indies. Appearance of yellow fever aboard ship. Advice to captain triggers decision to leave for England earlier than planned. Poignant last letter to daughter.

Chapter 20: London, April to June 1880 – "*Atalanta* Feared Lost" 185

Leaving for home – terrible gales sweep the North Atlantic – many ships lost. In April, rumours and speculation about possible loss of overdue *Atalanta*. Navy searches for ship. Questions about safety/stability, condition of ship and experience of crew. Sailor's opinions about ship. Thomasina gives birth to a son. Ship officially declared lost, with 280 men and boys, in May.

Chapter 21: Whitehall, London – "The Last Inquiry" 195

Calls for official investigation into loss of *Atalanta*. Parliamentary debates – mandate of Committee – testimony of Admiralty Lords and others. Review of decision to refit a forty-three-year-old sailing ship – conflicting testimony by surviving crew and others. Conclusions of Inquiry Committee. My conclusions – a cover up by the Admiralty. Concluding remarks.

Epilogue 206

Colour Plates 209

Notes 225

Bibliography 233

Index 239

List of Illustrations

H.M.S. *Bulldog*, aground and under fire from shore batteries, Cape Haitien, Haiti, 23 October 1865 (*Illustrated London News*). p. 17

Dr. Edward Moss, ca. 1872. Photographer G. Schroeder, Dublin (British Columbia Archives, No. G-07634). p. 47

Mrs. Edward Moss, née Thomasina Dugdale, 1873. Photographers Bradley and Rulofson (British Columbia Archives, No. G-07616). p. 48

Front of Dr. Moss's quarters, Royal Naval Hospital, Esquimalt, 1873 (British Columbia Archives, No. H-00104). p. 57

Rear of Dr. Moss's quarters and officers' sick bay, Royal Naval Hospital, Esquimalt, 1872 (British Columbia Archives, No. A-03091). p. 60

Dr. Moss on the hospital pier, Royal Naval Hospital, Esquimalt, 1873 (British Columbia Archives, No. H-00105). p. 75

Black bear shot by Dr. Moss, Vancouver Island, July 1874 (University of British Columbia, Special Collections Archives). p. 82

Black-tailed buck in velvet, shot by Dr. Moss, Vancouver Island, July 1874 (University of British Columbia, Special Collections Archives). p. 83

Discovery in Discovery Bay, in winter (Nares, *Narrative of a Voyage to the Polar Sea,* 1878). p. 106

Alert stopped by ice off Cape Prescott on her way north, August 1875 (Nares, *Narrative of a Voyage to the Polar Sea,* 1878). p. 107

Alert at Floeberg Beach, spring 1876 (Nares, *Narrative of a Voyage to the Polar Sea,* 1878) p. 119

Lieutenant Beaumont's sledge party about to leave *Discovery,* April 1876 (Library and Archives Canada, No. C52572). p. 121

Alert nipped near Cape Beechey, Robeson Channel, August 1876 (Nares, *Narrative of a Voyage to the Polar Sea,* 1878). p. 137

H.M.S. *Atalanta* (*Illustrated London News*). p. 177

List of Colour Plates

St. Mark's Church, Blue Mountains, Jamaica, February 1867, painted by Dr. Moss, during his service in the Caribbean on board HMS *Simoom* p. 209

Sea-cliffs, Trinidad, painted by Dr. Moss during his service on board HMS *Simoom.* p. 210

Ruined temple, Aiyina Island, near Athens, painted by Dr. Moss during his service in the Mediterranean on board HMS *Simoom.* p. 211

Part of the ramparts of Maiden Castle, Dorset, the largest Iron Age fort in Europe, dawn, 2 July 1871, visited by Dr. Moss, during his service at Portland Sick Quarters. p. 212

One of Moss's hunting camps near Comox, Vancouver Island, September 1872. p. 213

Alert and *Discovery* at Godhavn, Disko Island, on their way north, 10 July 1875 (Moss, *Shores of the Polar Sea).* p. 214

Alert in winter quarters, seen from among the grounded floes on her seaward side, March 1876 (Moss, *Shores of the Polar Sea*). p. 215

Alert in winter quarters, seen from astern; the rudder has been unshipped and hung across the stern to prevent it from being damaged by ice pressures. December 1875 (Moss, *Shores of the Polar Sea*). p. 216

Morning prayers and inspection under the tent housing on the deck of HMS *Alert;* the deck has been covered with snow for insulation (Moss, *Shores of the Polar Sea*). p. 217

At Floeberg Beach, northern Ellesmere Island the officers of HMS *Alert* enjoy the companionable warmth and comfort of the ship's wardroom, in striking contrast to the winter cold and darkness outside (Moss, *Shores of the Polar Sea*). p. 218

Alert in winter quarters, soon after the sun returned, March 1876; in case the ice moves out the ship is moored to anchors embedded in the beach (Moss, *Shores of the Polar Sea*). p. 219

The combined western and northern sledge parties (Markham's and Aldrich's) struggling through chaotic pressure ridges on their way to Cape Joseph Henry, 8 April 1876 (Moss, *Shores of the Polar Sea*). p. 220

Markham and the other three members of the northern party still capable of walking, on their return to *Alert*, 14 June 1876 (Moss, *Shores of the Polar Sea*). p. 221

Alert and *Discovery*, homeward bound in Kennedy Channel, off Cape Constitution, 20 August 1876 (Moss, *Shores of the Polar Sea*). p. 222

Landscape at Hisarlik (Troy), painted by Moss during a visit to Schliemann's dig, November 1878. p. 223

Map of the area of operations of the British Arctic Expedition, 1875–76 p. 224

The author, Paul Appleton (right) with Nigel Moss (Dr. Moss's great grandson) and his mother, Mary Moss, 2005(?).

photo, courtesy Mr. Nigel Moss.

Acknowledgements

As series editor of the Northern Lights Series I am enormously indebted to Mr. Nigel Moss, Mr. Jeremy Moss and Mrs. Mary Moss for their unfailing cooperation, careful proofreading of the text and suggestions for corrections, and especially for making available a selection of Dr. Moss's paintings still in the possession of the family. I also wish to thank Mrs. Dolores Appleton for providing the photograph of her husband and for her continuing keen interest in the production of the book, and also Mrs. Ruth Ralston of Victoria, B.C. who did some preliminary editing. Finally I am grateful to Mr. Cameron Treleaven of Aquila Books, Calgary, for the loan of a copy of Dr. Moss's book, *Shores of the Polar Sea,* from which some of the illustrations were scanned.

Editor's Preface

The name Edward Lawton Moss has long been familiar to Arctic historians and to Arctic bibliophiles because of his personal account of the British Arctic Expedition of 1875–76, led by Captain George Strong Nares, the goal of which was the North Pole, and on which Moss served as one of the surgeons. Moss's book, *Shores of the Polar Sea: A Narrative of the Arctic Expedition of 1875–76*, is quite rare, and now retails for upwards of US$2,500. While Moss's narrative provides a useful counterpoint to the other contemporary narratives on the expedition, the book is particularly memorable for the inclusion of a collection of striking chromolithographs based on Moss's watercolours. His publishers, Marcus Ward of London, also published sixteen of these chromolithographs separately as a folio, also much sought after by Arctic bibliophiles.

Until now, however, little has been known about Moss himself, and we are enormously indebted to the late Mr. Paul Appleton for having compiled a full, well-researched biography, relying heavily on Moss's own letters. It covers vastly more than the Arctic expedition. It ranges from the "*Bulldog* Affair" of 1865, in which HMS *Bulldog* (on which Moss was serving) was blown up by her own captain to prevent her from falling into the hands of Haitian rebels after she had run aground while under fire from shore, to details of the history of the "Old R.N. Hospital" on Esquimalt Naval Base, Vancouver Island, now a Parks Canada Heritage site, of which Moss was in charge from 1872 to 1875.

Appleton's coverage of Nares' Arctic expedition is well-researched and is illustrated by a selection of Moss's watercolours. The expedition was notorious for the fact that Captain Nares had to cut the expedition short after only one year (it was expected to last at least two years) because of a severe outbreak of scurvy. Dr. Moss was called upon as an expert witness during the subsequent official enquiry into this unfortunate development and Appleton has taken the opportunity to examine this aspect of the expedition in considerable detail.

Moss's life was tragically cut short. He had the misfortune to be serving on board the Royal Navy's training ship HMS *Atalanta*, which disappeared with all hands (280 men and boys) in 1880, while heading home from Bermuda. Moss was only thirty-seven years old. His death was all the more tragic in that his wife, Thomasina, was pregnant with their third child. Here, too, Appleton has skillfully woven the details of the subsequent official enquiry into the loss of the ship into his biography of Moss.

In short, Paul Appleton has crafted a rich, detailed biography of a very promising young Victorian naval surgeon, and both the University of Calgary Press and the Arctic Institute of North America were delighted when he thought fit to submit his manuscript for publication in January 2006. Unfortunately, however, Paul Appleton died on 29 March 2006. We at the Arctic Institute and at the Press were pleased to be able to assure his widow Dolores Appleton that we would be happy to proceed with publishing the book, and I, as general editor of the Northern Lights series, was happy to be able to handle the usual editorial details and to contribute this brief preface. Footnotes that I have compiled are identified by (WB) to distinguish them from those contributed by Paul Appleton.

William Barr
Senior Research Associate
Arctic Institute of North America

1: Guildford, Surrey

"The Letter"

The letter arrived at the home of Thomasina Mary Moss on a warm autumn day in 1927. A short time later she picked it up at the front door and walked out into the back garden of her modest home on Shalford Road at Sheen, on the margin of Guildford, Surrey. Sitting down at her favourite bench beside the apple tree espaliered along the fence, Thomasina examined the envelope quizzically. From the return address she could see that it was from someone named Reid, living at Vancouver, British Columbia, Canada, but that information conveyed nothing particular to her. Who in the world was this Reid person, and what was this about? After all, it was fifty-two years since she had lived on the West Coast of Canada. Besides, she didn't know anyone in Vancouver. It was Victoria, or more precisely, the small community of Esquimalt on Vancouver Island, where she had lived those many years ago. Curious to solve the mystery, she quickly opened the envelope and began to read the letter.

Although Thomasina probably did not realize it at the time, the writer was a very prominent Vancouver lawyer, and while the law was Robie Louis Reid's very successful vocation, history, and most particularly the collection and preservation of Canadiana, was his passion. At the time of his correspondence with Thomasina Moss he was well on his way to amassing a personal library of some nine thousand books and half that number of pamphlets relating to British Columbia, the Klondike, and the Maritimes, where he had been born and educated. Ultimately this vast collection would be donated to the University of British Columbia, forming the major portion of their Special Collections Department when it was created. Reid was on the Board of Governors at the time of his correspondence with Thomasina Moss and would later become a Fellow of the Royal Society of Canada (1936) and President of the British Columbia Historical Association (1937).[1] It was in the role of local historian and collector that Reid had written to Thomasina Moss. He had come upon a brief note about her late husband, Surgeon Edward Lawton Moss, MD, RN, in a memoir of early Esquimalt. The note had piqued Reid's curiosity, and he had somehow tracked her down to find out more about her late husband and their life in early Esquimalt.[2]

As Thomasina sat in her garden, letter in hand, that morning in 1927, the memories of Esquimalt and those first years of her married life were awakened, bringing back mental images of what had been, both for herself and for Edward, the best and most carefree time of their lives. For a few moments she found herself transported back more than a half-century and over six thousand miles from England to the headquarters of the Pacific Station of the Royal Navy. Some weeks later she sat down at her writing desk and penned the following reply to Robie Reid's letter.

Dear Mr. Reid,

I am very sorry your letter has not been answered before, but my elder daughter suddenly had to go into a nursing home for an operation & I being an old lady of 84 depend a great deal on her for help in things of this nature. I am thankful to say that she is well again.

My husband was a naval surgeon sent out by the Admiralty in the early part of 1872 to open and put in working order Esquimalt [Naval] Hospital. It had been closed for some time and required a great deal of repair. I joined him early in 1873. At that time all the ships on the Pacific Station came up to Esquimalt, & Dr. Moss had all the medical stores and supplies for them. Late spring and summer was always a busy time & very gay, especially if the Admiral's ship was in [port]. Sometimes we had four or five ships at a time and the hospital was full. All the sick were sent there instead of being kept on board. From what I hear I do not think you can imagine now what it was like in those days; no railway or motor car! Not many hotels in Victoria. My husband & I went everywhere on horseback or hired a 'buggy.' The bush all round Esquimalt was very thick, the pine [fir] trees grand, a great deal of the country was unexplored they said. Game was plentiful of all kinds. My husband shot two rather large black bears & several deer, & 14 raccoons, not far from the Hospital. They were making havoc with a farmer's turkeys. Two kinds of grouse & three kinds of quail were abundant.

Mr. Trutch was Lt. Governor, Mr. O'Reilly (his brother-in-law) was one of the judges, Bishop Hills & the Rev. F. Tribble his Chaplain, and Mr. Innes in charge of the naval yard are some of the people I remember. Just as I arrived in 1873 the islands of San Juan had been given over to America, much to British regret. The marines from there were all quartered in our kitchen & servant's room, which adjoined our part of the house, to await passage to England. I had like everyone else a Chinaman as servant [and] a capital one he was. He could turn his hand to anything and served us most faithfully. I am enclosing a few photographs taken 73–74; many that I have are too faded. My husband's sketches are lovely, but it is the colouring – the excellence in that – they are all watercolours and would be nothing photographed.

His writing was all medical or scientific. The only book he wrote was on his return from the Arctic Expedition of [18]75, *The Shores of the Polar Sea* (now out of print). He wrote nothing about Vancouver. I send you a pen and ink sketch made after a bear hunt; and also an account of the "Twin Sisters." They were two beautiful [fir] trees and there was much consternation when they were cut down. All my recollections are of Esquimalt. Dr. Moss got orders in Jan. 75 to join the Arctic Expedition then about to start and we left Jan. 28th by steamer to San Fran then across to New York, [and on to] Queenstown, [Ireland] Feb. 21st.

We hoped we might go back and settle in Victoria later in life, we loved it so much, but Dr. Moss was appointed to HMS *Atalanta* in 79 – left Bermuda Jan. 80 – no trace of ship or crew was ever heard again! I forgot to say that we had a good deal of snow both winters I was out there. I wish I could give you more information. I will look through some of my papers & if I find anything of interest I will write again, or if you like to ask any questions [I] will try to answer. If you are at any time in London and care to see the sketches, Guildford is within easy range. Come and see them. I have just written as I remembered, so please excuse such a rambling account.[3]

Thomasina Moss's response to Reid's request initiated further correspondence that provided details for Reid's article "Memories of an Esquimalt Pioneer," published in the *Vancouver Province* in October 1928. After Reid sent her a copy along with a book about early Victoria in January of 1929, she provided more information about the years she and her late husband had spent there.

How exceedingly kind of you to send me this book & I heartily thank you. It will be of great interest to me, all the people and memories it brings back. Mrs. O'Reilly I saw on some of her visits to England. Her little daughter 'Pops' and Mr. Trutch were patients of my husband. I am so glad you were able to get a copy of *The Shores of the Polar Sea*. I wish you could see the originals, his colour and atmosphere was so beautiful, the letterpress & black and white drawings also. The book was only published a few months before he was lost.

It is time I said how pleased I was with the little article you put in the paper. Mr. James Anderson of Victoria saw it and wrote to me. He thinks he is the only one living we knew out there who knew my husband. Well I should have told

Guildford, Surrey

> you, I went out from Ireland and was married at San Francisco in 73. My elder daughter was born in Esquimalt. I brought her home overland at three months. My second daughter was born in Ireland, my son in Southsea two months after his father was lost. He is an army doctor – saw much service in the war. Forgive me for telling you my family history. I hope Mrs. Reid has quite recovered her health. With all good wishes for the coming year, and again many thanks.[4]

Of course Thomasina Moss had really told Reid very little about her husband or about their years at Esquimalt and Victoria. Still, she had provided him with enough information to embellish a brief newspaper reminiscence, and for his purposes that was sufficient. He had preserved a small part of the province's local history along with some sketches, early photographs, and a rare copy of a book written by a naval officer who had taken part in the last great British polar expedition of the century. Nevertheless, Reid's short article was important, for the threads it contained would eventually lead someone else to pursue deeper research and document the life and times of a man whose all too short life is very worthy of resurrection and remembrance.

It is a narrative that begins at Dublin in 1843.

2: Dublin, Ireland

"Edward"

Edward Lawton Moss, first-born son of William Moss, MD, and Teresa Moss (*née* Richardson), came into the world at Dublin, Ireland, ten days before Christmas 1843, nearly ten months after his parents had exchanged their marriage vows in a small rural church not far from the city. In 1906 his eighty-eight-year-old mother recalled the wedding in a memoir dictated to one of her daughters.

> We were married … at the Kilternan Church by the Reverend Lenden Bolton. It was a novel sight when three Quaker bonnets made their appearance in the group attending the bride. All of the Moss family were baptized into the Established Church, now the Church of Ireland, but three sisters and one brother had joined the Society of Friends. Taking their place at the communion table they joined in the service. The church was full of the country people, many of them were Roman Catholics. Snow fell as we drove to my father's house, two Irish miles from the town. After déjeuner and when the bride cake was cut in due form my father-in-law came. It was pleasant to see the two old men, one white-haired and the other very bald, take hands and sing an old song about their good name: "From my youth have I kept it unsullied by blame, and it still from a spot shall be free."[1]

Whether non-conformist Quakers or members of the Church of Ireland, the Anglo-Irish Moss, Lawton, and Richardson families were all middle-class members of the Protestant elite that had ruled Ireland for generations. Some among Edward's extended family were landowners, respectable gentry, while others had risen from various skilled trades to become well-to-do business people. The Lawtons had built the cotton mill at Kilternan and through marriage and inheritance this venture had passed into the hands of the Moss family. On the other side, Teresa Moss's father, John Richardson owned a fairly modest farm at Kilgobbin, not very far from Kilternan. The Richardsons and at least some members of the Moss family had been converted to the Society of Friends and were members of a small but influential group of Quakers who lived in and around Dublin.

Teresa, Edward's mother, appears to have been a strong-willed woman with a good education, being well schooled by Quaker, Unitarian, and Presbyterian schoolmistresses and tutors. All three of these non-conformist denominations were ahead of their time in favouring education for women, and Teresa's schooling included more than just the three R's and the usual household arts and skills expected of a gentlewoman in her day. Around the age of six she was sent to live with an aunt in Dublin to receive her education, and in her early teens she was permitted to attend classes in science and mechanics, electricity, geology, and physiology – this at a time when, to use her own words, "girls were not supposed to know such things."[2]

During her sixteen years of married life, Teresa Moss gave birth to six children: Edward Lawton, William Richardson, Richard Jackson, Amelia Jane, Phoebe Anna, and Mary Teresa, born in 1854, five years before her father's death at age forty-seven. Although nothing is known about Edward's relationship with his father, he certainly had a strong bond with his mother and the family appears to have been closely knit. As an adult, one of the things Edward disliked most about his life in the Navy was being away from them for long periods of time.

The lot of William Moss and many other young medical practitioners in Dublin at the time of his marriage was not particularly enviable, for aside from a relatively thin upper crust, the city seethed with a huge population of the poverty-stricken and indigent. As a result, paying patients were not easily come by for a young doctor.

However, when the Poor Relief (Ireland) Act was passed at Westminster in 1838, poor law unions were established throughout the country, and then, after an epidemic of typhus in 1840, the Medical Charities Act was passed at Westminster.[3] This provided some minimal compensation for doctors who chose to treat the poor, and for a time William Moss was medical officer for the South Dublin Poor Law Union in addition to serving as a visiting physician at the Dublin Dispensary. Together these positions supplemented his initially meagre practice enough to provide a measure of financial stability.

Funding for the workhouse system (for the poorhouse unions were really workhouses) was minimal. Doctors who worked among the sick poor did so with little official recognition or adequate compensation and at enormous risk to their own health. In 1842, during the parliamentary committee hearings prior to the passage of the Medical Charities Act, William Stokes and James Cusack, two of the most influential and respected Dublin medical men of their generation, produced figures that showed that the mortality rate among Irish doctors was twice that of army officers, with about one-quarter of them ultimately dying as a result of their occupation.[4] Being a physician could be a dangerous occupation in those times.

To make matters worse, Ireland entered into the most tragic time in her troubled history a few years after Edward's birth. The potato crop had failed before, but never had it failed for three years in a row as it did in 1846, 1847, and 1848. During those bitter years three of the Four Horsemen of the Apocalypse – Famine, Pestilence, and Death – stalked Ireland, swinging a sharp and wide scythe across the land with scarcely any interference. In fact, these rapacious destroyers were aided and abetted by many of the great and the powerful in Ireland as well as England, men who were almost blind, deaf, and dumb in the face of the terrible realities savaging the urban poor and the peasantry. Two or more million Irish, mainly the Catholic peasants, but mostly the poorest of the poor, would die or be forced to emigrate before the Three Horsemen moved elsewhere in the world to continue their terrible work.

Along with the failure of the potato crop came the ever-present diseases that arose out of poverty, malnutrition, and poor sanitation. Typhus was a terrible killer among doctors as well as patients – one out of thirteen doctors working with typhus patients succumbed to the same disease that was killing those whom they were treating. Equally murderous was cholera, which the Royal College of Physicians in London, as well as the Board of Health in Dublin, still thought (almost unbelievably) to be a non-contagious disease.[5] It arrived in England in 1848 and the following year spread to Ireland with especially devastating effects.

By then William Moss had left the South Dublin Union to take charge of the Cholera Hospital. In her 1906 memoir Teresa Moss described that time in their lives:

> The medical duties were most arduous. It was incessant fighting with death. The cholera carts went round, calling at every house marked with a red cross, with two men in white overalls who would carry out the bodies and take them to a deep pit dug for that purpose and sprinkled a little earth over. Cots also carried by two men in white took those who were attacked in the street to the Hospital. I once went there with my husband, outside the hospital the poor sick people lay on the ground waiting admission; two of our intimate friends called in the morning, not thinking that much was amiss [with their health]; but after they left my husband told me that they would die that night, and so it was.
>
> Fever followed the cholera, so sheds were erected for accommodation. This charge was also given to my husband who was overworked, and in the middle of this anxious time, suddenly in the morning I awoke with one violent spasm and trying to rise fell on the floor, sinking at once into collapse.[6]

Teresa Moss had been attacked by the dreaded Asiatic Cholera, though fortunately she survived, and to the end of her days maintained that "under God, my dear husband saved my life." Although William Moss also made it through the cholera and typhus outbreaks, he did not emerge from the famine years unscathed. Shortly after his wife's illness, in spite of being exhausted from overwork, he answered an emergency call to resuscitate a man who had fallen into the nearby River Liffey. Afterwards he returned home chilled to the bone and feverish and was later diagnosed as suffering from rheumatic fever. A sea voyage and rest cure in a warmer climate was prescribed and with a friend he took a tour of Spain, Italy, and Sicily. He returned much improved several months later, but his previously robust health never returned, gradually declining over the next several years until he passed quietly away at home in 1859, probably of congestive heart failure.

Her husband's death was a serious blow for Teresa, who was now left alone to raise a brood ranging from five to fifteen years of age. William Moss's early death also came at a crucial time for his oldest son and probably changed the course of Edward's life by affecting his choice of careers.

Shortly after his father's death, Edward began his higher education at Dublin's Royal College of Science, a few blocks away from his home, where he took courses in the natural and physical sciences – mainly Physics, Chemistry, Geology, Zoology, and Botany. This was followed by medical study at the Royal College of Surgeons (Ireland) and then at the ancient and prestigious University of St. Andrews in Scotland, where he obtained his MD. According to the records of the Royal College of Surgeons, which granted his licence to practise on December 9, 1862, just a week prior to his twenty-first birthday, his practicum included twenty-seven months in attendance at the City of Dublin Hospital.

At the RCS (I) Moss studied Anatomy and Physiology, Practical and Descriptive Anatomy, Chemistry, Theory and Practice of Surgery (and of Physic), Materia Medica, Midwifery, Diseases of Women and Children, Medical Jurisprudence, Botany, Hygiene, and Ophthalmic and Aural Surgery. It is not known what subjects Moss studied at St. Andrews, but it is certainly safe to say that he received as good a medical education as was possible at the time.

He does not seem to have entered a medical practice in Ireland after graduation. There were likely few good opportunities there in any case, and of course he was very young: at twenty-one he was just at the minimum age to become licensed. Emigration to America was an alternative, and after his graduation Edward apparently spent almost two years there before returning home in 1864. Perhaps, given his youth or limited financial resources, the idea of setting up a medical practice in America did not work out as he had hoped or expected. In any case, not long after returning to Ireland he applied to become a medical officer in the Royal Navy.

3: Portsmouth

"The Royal Navy"

Although Edward Moss's motives in joining the Royal Navy can only be speculated upon, they were undoubtedly mixed. Perhaps the main incentive was the modest but regular income offered by the Medical Branch, thereby allowing him to give his mother some financial help. Joining the Navy must have appeared to be the best alternative given his circumstances, and private practice would still be an option sometime in the future if he chose to leave the service.

Most of the Royal Navy medical officers during Moss's day were surgeons rather than physicians, so Edward's MD gave him something of a career advantage. In those times, unlike today, surgeons were not specialists and were less well educated than physicians. The Navy always assigned them to service afloat, never to regular service ashore. On the other hand, as a fully qualified physician, Moss could expect to be placed in charge of a naval hospital at some point in his career, and perhaps a permanent shore appointment would ultimately come his way if the bureaucrats in the medical department found him worthy. The rank of Staff Surgeon was virtually certain; that of Fleet Surgeon very likely after about fifteen years. With diligence and some luck he might even rise to the level of Deputy Inspector of Hospital and Fleets and retire with a relative rank and salary equivalent to that of a Lieutenant-Colonel in the Army.

The Navy might also provide some opportunities for Moss to pursue his scientific interests, for naval doctors had long been encouraged – and often specifically recruited – to carry out botanical, zoological, medical, and other scientific research. Moss would certainly have been well aware that some of the foremost scientists of the century had been naval surgeons. Sir Joseph Hooker, close friend of Charles Darwin, and destined to become the Director of the Royal Botanical Gardens at Kew, served as a surgeon and botanist with James Ross on the latter's Antarctic voyage of 1839–43. The great naturalist and explorer

Sir John Richardson was also a naval surgeon for almost fifty years, serving with both the Parry (1819–22) and Franklin (1825–27) Arctic expeditions. By 1847, although he had long been ashore and was then chief medical officer at the great Haslar Naval Hospital near Portsmouth, Richardson was placed in command of the first (1848–49) expedition sent out to determine Franklin's fate.[1] During this long career, Richardson contributed immensely to knowledge in the natural sciences, particularly in ichthyology and the fauna of the Arctic and Antarctic regions.

Thomas Huxley, the famous agnostic naturalist and protagonist for Charles Darwin's new theory of evolution, also began his career as a surgeon in the British Army, and many other less well known but important men of science followed a similar career path. There can be little doubt that Edward Moss would have been acquainted with the careers and accomplishments of such notable figures, and we can be confident that as a young man he hoped to achieve a measure of distinction by taking the same route. At twenty-one years of age, all things are likely to seem possible, given determination, opportunity, and a bit of luck.

The lot of the medical officer in the Navy was beginning to improve around the time Moss entered the service. The Medical Department (and the Assistant Surgeons and Surgeons) had badgered the Admiralty for improved rank, status, and pay for many years, and, as a result, Assistant Surgeons were finally granted commissioned officer status in 1855. However, in spite of these improvements a career in the Navy was still not very attractive to most young physicians. Even after 1866, when the Admiralty finally adopted other reforms that gave the Assistant Surgeon equality with his counterpart in the Army as well as an improved promotion and retirement policy, the Medical Department did not always find it easy to recruit qualified doctors.[2]

Nevertheless, change was in the air when Moss entered the Royal Navy, albeit slowly, for tradition and practice in the great and powerful institutions of state do not adapt quickly to new ideas or methods. The great "wooden walls" of Lord Nelson's day were gradually giving way to steam-and-sail-driven vessels like HMS *Warrior* (1860), the first armour-clad warship in the world to be built entirely out of iron, and paddle-wheel gunboats like HMS *Bulldog*, or steam-driven sloops like HMS *Alert* were now becoming commonplace. Edward Moss was destined to have extremely memorable experiences serving on each of the latter two vessels.

Young Doctor Moss was joining the Navy near the beginning of a great transition. Gunnery, for example, was certainly changing. Smooth-bore cannons were rapidly being replaced by more deadly and accurate rifle-bored or breech-loading guns firing powerful explosive shells instead of cannon balls. But change did not always come easily. Many of the old admirals, as obsolete as the great wooden flagships they loved so well, did not give way without complaint and resistance. To quote James Morris, in *Heaven's Command: An Imperial Progress*; "It [change] progressed in a welter of argument, admiral against admiral, newspaper critic against naval spokesman, and if [the Navy's] professional ideas changed slowly, its gnarled, stubborn and ornate style was more resistant still."[3]

The practice of military medicine was also changing. In the sixth decade of the nineteenth century, medical theory was on the verge of what would become known as the "era of scientific medicine," and the Medical Branch of the Navy was adopting most of the new theories and practices that were coming into vogue. In this they were following in the path of civilian medical and social reformers who for years had cajoled and pressured government to initiate a variety of laws intended to improve the health of the nation. This was particularly the case in the area of sanitary reform.[4] The importance of cleanliness and adequate ventilation (the latter arising from the "miasmic" or tainted air theory) along with stress on the importance of a healthy diet was shifting medical practice towards prevention rather than attempted cure alone. This was the mantra espoused almost religiously by the Medical Branch of the Navy. In 1865, for example, naval surgeon Alexander Rattray expressed the prevalent ethic in his annual report to his superiors when he wrote that "To prevent is often not only easier, but in vastly more cases more credible to the physician than to cure sickness. The former should be his principal aim and study."[5] Carbolic acid was the flavour of the day, and when a new device (the carbolic steam-spray) was introduced around 1865, it drastically reduced deaths following surgery, particularly when used in conjunction with chloroform, which had been used in the Navy since 1852. Quinine was regularly prescribed for tropical diseases after 1854, and inoculation for smallpox became standard practice in the sixties. The issuing of regulation uniforms after 1857, combined with enforcement of rules requiring that clothing should be scrubbed and changed regularly, helped to reduce the incidence of louse-borne typhus aboard ship. An improved and more balanced diet was also provided for the men in the lower decks, resulting, as one might expect, in better overall health among naval seamen. Scorbutus (scurvy), once the bane of the sailor on any long voyage without fresh provisions, was now seldom seen in the Navy. Among the general public it was widely (if erroneously) believed to have been entirely vanquished by better diet and the regular use of antiscorbutics such as lemon or lime juice.[6]

The focus on improved diet and better personal hygiene, together with adequate ventilation and sanitation, may not seem very revolutionary. However, today there is widespread agreement that during the third quarter of the nineteenth century these, rather than new medicines or medical discoveries, did more to improve public health than anything else prior the general acceptance of Lister's germ theory.[7] Clearly they were the *right* things to do, and to their credit the physicians who ruled over the Medical Department did their best to implement them both aboard ship and at the shore hospitals.

In other ways medical practice in the Navy remained much as it had been earlier in the century, particularly in terms of medication. In 1868 over a hundred "medicinals" were issued as part of the standard kit provided to medical officers. Quite a few of them remain familiar today, still in use or among the naturopathic and alternative remedies available in drug or health food stores. Some, such as fulminate of mercury or arsenic for example, were in fact toxic, and others less than benign unless careful attention was paid to dosage.

To what extent naval surgeons could safely ignore Admiralty instructions and recommended treatments in favour of new or different methods based on their own experience or knowledge is not entirely clear, though it is likely that they were allowed a good deal of latitude as long as the results appeared to support their methods. On the other hand, as Edward would eventually discover, there were circumstances when particular medications or treatments were mandated from above and medical officers changed them or ignored them at their peril.

Edward Lawton Moss began his military service at Portsmouth, entering at the rank of Acting Assistant Surgeon. Unlike the youthful cadets or seamen who were accepting the "Queen's shilling" for service before the mast, he did not undergo any basic training. His service records reveal that he was borne for only a week on the books of Lord Nelson's great flagship HMS *Victory* – today still a major tourist attraction at the Portsmouth Dockyard, though no longer afloat.

On March 7, 1864, Edward was posted to his first ship, the paddle-sloop HMS *Bulldog*, serving on the West Indies Station. Although much less grand than *Victory*, she was no less significant symbolically. Some months later, while aboard this small gunboat at Haiti, the youthful doctor would undergo trial by fire during an experience that he would look back to with pride for the rest of his life.

4: Haiti

"For the Honour of the Flag"

In the spring of 1864, Edward Moss joined the gunboat HMS *Bulldog*, commanded by Charles Wake. *Bulldog* was on the Royal Navy's West Indies Station, tasked with keeping an eye on the many and varied British interests in the region. Edward soon discovered that the West Indies, although enticingly beautiful and exotic, could also be dangerous, for not long after joining the ship he was stricken with yellow fever, the disease most dreaded by men serving in the tropics or sub-tropics. Fortunately he survived, but ironically it would be the appearance and fear of the same disease aboard another ship that would precipitate a chain of events that would lead to his tragic death many years later.

Bulldog's duties in the West Indies were much the same as the many other gunboats standing watch across the expanse of Empire. James Morris accurately summed up the main role of the British Navy during the years when Edward Moss was in the service:

> It became more and more of an imperial force … increasingly concerned with the protection of the imperial sea routes, the suppression of subversion, showing the flag and awing the natives. Much of its energy was invested in gunboat diplomacy, that ubiquitous instrument of imperial prestige, which required the dispersal of innumerable small vessels in every corner of the world.… They might be required at any moment for the most diverse duties: shelling recalcitrant tribesmen, embellishing consular fêtes, scaring off pirates, rescuing earthquake victims, transporting friendly potentates.[1]

What came to be known as the "*Bulldog* Affair" fits the above description extremely well. This astonishing example of attempted gunboat diplomacy took place during one of the many revolutionary insurrections and coups that have characterized the political life of Haiti throughout most of its troubled history.

In 1859 the restive country came under the control of Fabré Geffard, who soon faced increasing opposition from a rebellious cabal led by one Sylvain Salnave. By October 1865 Salnave was in control of the fort at Cape Haitien, and his armed schooners had recently broken a long government blockade, thereby allowing him to restock the fort with arms and powder. Once this was accomplished Salnave was emboldened, sending his ships along the coast to intercept vessels believed to be bringing supplies to the government forces, and generally creating as much trouble as possible for Geffard.[2]

It was a confrontation at sea between *Bulldog* and the armed schooner *Volderogue* (which the rebels had captured a few weeks earlier and re-named the *Providence*) that provoked the *Bulldog* Affair. Shortly after this incident, Wake steamed to the Cape and dropped anchor in the harbour within earshot of the rebel ships. Apparently some government officials and supporters had taken refuge in the British consulate at Cape Haitien and the Salvanists, after breaking into the building, seized some of Geffard's supporters and took them away for execution. These brutal murders, though certainly to be deplored and condemned, were not really any of Captain Wake's business. However, when it was coupled with a perceived threat to the life and limb of British citizens, he viewed it with distaste and growing anger. This, along with the taunting he was being forced to endure from the two rebel ships anchored nearby, was twisting the lion's tail, so Wake decided to teach his rebel tormentors a lesson. He would ram and sink the *Volderogue* and its companion vessel and thus rid himself of these pests. As things turned out, this bold move proved to be a fatal mistake.

The earliest of surviving letters from Edward Lawton Moss to his mother was written about two weeks after the Cape Haitien incident. It provides a vivid description of the fire-fight that erupted as a consequence of Wake's action, as well as a brief view of Edward's role in helping to relieve the suffering of the wounded.

HMS *Aboukir*
Port Royal, Jamaica
Nov. 8th, 1865

Dear Mama,

I hope this letter reaches you before the news it contains is known in Ireland. The good news should be told first, and that is I am *almost* certain of being home in five months, perhaps in four & that I am quite safe and well. You see from the address above that I no longer write from the *Bulldog*. We left our ship on the 23rd of October, but I must begin to tell you the events that have crowded in on each other since I wrote to you from Cape Haitien. The revolutionary party that hold the Cape were victorious in several engagements, both on land and sea, and sent an armed flotilla of schooners to the entrance of this harbour, captured one of the president's ships and drove the others away. The blockade thus broken they received plenty of arms & powder. Growing bolder they sent their ships to cruise the coast, and one day we saw them steaming after and firing into a small steamer carrying the English flag. Captain Wake immediately interfered and we found that the small steamer had a right to our flag & that she had mailbags on board bound for us. Captain Wake therefore told the revolutionary ships that if they touched her he would sink or take them. When we came to our anchorage at Cape Haitien, we were received with insults. Letters of remonstration were left unanswered, the Captain and all of us threatened with assassination if we landed, and finally they broke into the English Consulate, took away the refugees and afterwards shot them. The Captain then resolved to teach them to respect our flag, & the European residents having left the place, the *Bulldog* opened fire on their forts and ran straight for a steamer of theirs called the *Volderogue*, with the intention of running her down as that procedure did not necessitate loss of life, whereas firing into her would [have done]. When about 40 yds. from the steamer the *Bulldog* ran on a bank of soft coral rock and remained immovable. Meanwhile the forts on shore found our range and shot after shot tore through us. We were exposed to the fire of six [gun] batteries besides the steamer and armed schooners. The latter were sunk by our fire in a few minutes and after an hour almost every gun in the forts was overthrown. During that time we had three men killed & five wounded severely, and our boats had picked up the remainder of the crew of the [rebel] steamer. I had the satisfaction of doing what I could to relieve the sufferings of the victims on both sides. A constant fire was kept up from the *Bulldog*, for the [rebels] on shore worked with great courage and perseverance, remounting their guns as fast as they were knocked down. Our large gun was dismounted and removed four times, the third time a large piece broken off it & they managed to fire from it again before another shot dashed it to pieces.

At sunset all hope of getting the ship off the bank was lost. The tide had fallen, there were 13 shot holes plugged in the water line, the engines had been struck and one shot had entered a boiler, the rudder was injured, the rigging shot away, and the hull they say struck about 50 times. All the shot and shell was expended and no means of defending the ship was left. Fresh cannon were being brought to bear upon us, and the Captain resolved to take to the boats that were left seaworthy and blow the ship up.

We left at 11½ on Monday night Oct. 23. The Captain stayed last and lit the fuse and in a few minutes the *Bulldog* blew up. I should have said that our wounded were put on board an American ship of war that was there. We [then]

went to a part of the coast that was owned by the President and after some delay he sent us all here in one of his ships of war. We must remain here until the admiral holds an enquiry into the matter. The general opinion is that Captain Wake did his duty, and some say he will get the CB [Knight Commander of the Bath] for his courage in attacking such a strong place, but the misfortune of getting on shore made a great difference in the affair.

I need not say that nearly all I had was blown up in the poor old ship, [but] the Admiralty will give me compensation for the loss. I ought to be very thankful that I was not touched, for I was on deck a great part of the time. Indeed the number hurt was wonderfully small considering the way the ship was riddled. We performed two amputations during the action. All the wounded are now at the Naval Hospital here and are doing well. I am glad to say that we have not had anything to do with quelling the insurrection here, but it is all over now & I hope they will not hang any more of the poor wretches. There is only one way of managing them or the [Irish] Fenians, viz. send them all out of the country.

I received your letter dated Sept. 30 and one from Willy dated October 10th since I came on board.... This letter is for him as well as you. I could only write one to Ireland and I knew I owed you the first news of my safety, after the action and its consequences. It is possible that I may be appointed to another ship out here but it is most likely they will send all of us home. Indeed the Admiral may decide that the Court of Enquiry should be held in England and that we all must be present. The Admiral, Sir James Hope, is expected here in about 14 days....

I am sending a rough sketch of Cape Haitien to the *Illustrated London News* and it is possible they may put it in.

Your Affectionate Son,
Edward L. Moss [3]

The story of the firefight and the scuttling of HMS *Bulldog* was, as Edward hoped, featured in the *Illustrated London News* on December 9, 1865, together with an outstanding rendition of the battle, based on the young surgeon's sketch. Moss correctly anticipated the public's attitude towards Commander Wake's actions in the face of the Salvanist insult to British honour and property. As he also expected, the Lords of the Admiralty were less than ecstatic over the loss of a perfectly good ship and the death of four men under circumstances that appeared to suggest recklessness more than bravery, so in January 1866 a court-martial was convened in England. Both the commander and the navigator received reprimands and Wake was temporarily removed from command, though his headstrong action did not harm his career in the long run, for he retired some years later with the rank of Vice-Admiral.

H.M.S. *Bulldog,* aground and under fire from shore batteries, Cape Haitien, Haiti, 23 October 1865. Illustrated London News.

About two weeks after the hearings, the popular magazine *Punch* portrayed a smiling Admiral Punch happily handing his sword back to Captain Bulldog. The cartoon was accompanied by twenty stanzas of doggerel titled THE POUNDING OF PORT-HAYTIEN: (A Fo'k'sle Ballad by a Bulldog). The final stanza summed it all up as far as the anonymous author was concerned:

> Here's three cheers for Captain Wake, and while we sail the sea,
> May British Bull-dogs always find Captains as stout as he,
> That's all for biting when they bite, and none for bark and brag,
> And thinks less about courts-martial than the honour of the flag.[4]

Was this, as well as the earlier sketch of Bulldog in action, also a product of Edward Moss's pen? Quite possibly. He certainly had literary inclinations and wrote some very similar doggerel a few years later when he was in Esquimalt, British Columbia.

Moss was among those who were called to testify at the *Bulldog* inquiry, and his report, titled "Actions and Destruction's at Hayti" [*sic*] was submitted along with the other documents that were put into evidence. He was also questioned about the injuries and treatment of the ten men who became casualties during the altercation, reporting that during the battle three of the wounded had died after surgery and a fourth died three days later when complications forced him to endure a second amputation. One of Moss's descriptions of the injuries and surgical procedures is sufficient to graphically illustrate what the young doctor had to cope with under fire.

> On the morning of October 23 we went into action at Cape Haitien and shortly after the ship grounded Mr. Painter, Boatswain, was struck by a round shot … [that] … had torn the soft parts of the outer and back part of the left thigh, fracturing the bone close to its centre. The haemorrhage was rapid and [though] amputation through the greater trochanter was at once performed, he never recovered from the shock of the injury and died about an hour after he was struck.

For Edward, the *Bulldog* experience must have been tinged with a certain degree of ambivalence. On the one hand, he could take well-deserved pride in his exemplary conduct under heavy fire; on the other hand, the failed surgical efforts of the two medical officers must have been discouraging to him. They had done their best, but it had not been enough.

Depending on the point of view the *Bulldog* affair can be seen as either a brilliant bit of naval fighting or a debacle arising out of a very questionable attempt at gunboat diplomacy – both views have been put forward by historians. Not surprisingly, Moss ascribed to the former interpretation, and his letter home describing the incident was preserved by his mother and his family, part of a proud military heritage that has been passed down through the generations. However, Moss's interpretation of the events that led up to the battle diverges significantly from some other accounts, particularly on the matter of British intervention in Haitian affairs. In *Written in Blood: The Story of the Haitian People, 1492–1971*, Robert and Nancy Heinl state that on the October 18, 1865, the British steamer RMS *Jamaica Packet*, chartered by the Haitian government, was engaged in running munitions and reinforcements into the Cape Haitien area. This was the "small steamer flying the British flag" Moss referred to in his letter. According to the Heinl account, the *Volderogue* pursued and attempted to board the British ship before Wake intervened to warn her off. Undoubtedly the trashing of the British vice-consulate at Cape Haitien as well as the seizing and execution of President Geffard's supporters was retaliation on the part of Salnave's men for perceived British meddling in Haitian affairs.

Two weeks after the destruction of *Bulldog*, two other British warships, HMS *Galatea* and HMS *Lily*, openly and vigorously aided the government in actions that broke the revolt and forced Salnave to flee the country. This produced a temporary respite for Geffard, but the Salnavists soon resurfaced and toppled the regime in 1867. In part (or so it is claimed) the re-emergence of strong support for the rebels was based on Haitian anger at Geffard for turning to the British for assistance in his effort to defeat a popular nationalist opponent. The Americans had made the diplomatically wise decision to stay on the sidelines during the trouble at Cape Haitien. When Wake asked the commander of the American warship SS *de Soto*, anchored nearby, to tow *Bulldog* off the reef, Captain Walker refused "to interfere as an ally in a war so recklessly begun,"[5] though later he did send boats to take off the wounded before Wake scuttled his ship.

Historical interpretations about what really happened at Cape Haitien may be at odds, but there was never any doubt in Edward Moss's mind that Captain Wake had acted appropriately in spite of running aground and losing his ship. For Moss, the "*Bulldog* Affair" was carried out in the bold spirit of the immortal Lord Nelson. Forever etched into his memory, both the spirit and the image of HMS *Bulldog* re-emerged on the Arctic ice-floes just over a decade later when Edward, commanding a support group for the main polar expedition parties, named his eight-man sledge after his first ship.

5: HMS Simoom

"Service Afloat"

Early in February 1866, after his testimony at the inquiry, Edward was posted to the 1,980-ton troopship HMS *Simoom*, to serve under Captain Thomas Lethbridge and Surgeon Arthur McKenna. This four-hundred-horsepower iron-clad sail and steam frigate, built at Portsmouth in 1860, became his home for the next four years. Life aboard *Simoom* proved to be a peripatetic and often boring existence interspersed with brief stays at exotic or interesting ports of call and a welcome return to England at least once a year.

Simoom's 1866 log provides a typical example of the annual routine. It shows that she left Portsmouth in February and did not return to England until the following March. The itinerary that year began with a trip to Kingstown, Ireland, where Edward had an opportunity to visit his family for a day or two. Then, after picking up or disembarking troops, it was off for Malta, Gibraltar, and across the North Atlantic to St. Andrews in New Brunswick before moving on to Halifax, Nova Scotia, where troops of the Royal Artillery and the 17th Regiment were dropped off at the end of May. Two weeks later she left for the West Indies, stopping at Barbados, Trinidad, and St. Vincent before crossing the ocean to Sierra Leone and Gambia. From there the troopship was sent back to Belize (British Honduras) on the Caribbean coast of Central America before again crossing the Atlantic to Portsmouth, where the crew took leave in March 1867. The ship then underwent a refit before leaving in June to ply the Gibraltar-Halifax circuit for five months before returning to England again. The spring and early summer of 1868 was spent in the Mediterranean, and from July to October in home waters before sailing to the Azores, Gibraltar, and Halifax, where the ship and crew spent Christmas before returning home. Much the same itinerary was followed in 1869.[1]

Unfortunately, details of Edward's life during the *Simoom* years are sparse. The medical journals from *Simoom* have not survived, so little can be said about Moss's medical work at the time. However, a few letters were kept by his mother, and these provide some insight into his life at the time. The first was written sometime in 1866, probably not long after his appointment to *Simoom*.

> Dear Mother,
>
> I owe you a letter, here it is, but you will find but little in it. We have no news about our probable future. I see the 'Guards' are to come here from Dublin, but they will hardly send us for them as we are rather small. Our Canadian trip will depend on Mr. Motley. If he goes in for making England pay £4,000,000,000 for the Alabama claims, we will take the troops out as fast as we can go. The Americans are enlarging their fleet and the spirit of the country seems to be in favour of war.... I also received a very flattering note from Mrs. Wake, and Captain Wake actually paid me a visit. An ordinary captain would consider it rather beneath him to visit anyone of less than his own rank.
>
> I intend to go to London in a few days, perhaps on Thursday. If I could get 10 days leave I would pay Willy a visit, though the cost would be something, & we are almost certain to call at Liverpool and Kingstown before we go on the Canadian or West Indian & African trips. No naval medical officers are to be sent this time to the North Sea affair. I will stand a good chance next year if any go. They will not go far north and will not be away more than 5 months. I intend to get Richard to draw £20 at regular half yearly intervals for you. It will be much better than sending it irregularly. I have some money now, but will not send it over until the end of the month because I might run short, it is but a small sum too, and I do not like to make two or three additions to take the place of one. I forgot my German book when I left home.[2]

The "*Alabama* Affair" was a very serious irritant between "Mr. Motley" (Uncle Sam) and England during and after the Civil War. The *Alabama*, built in Liverpool for the Confederacy – supposedly as a merchant ship – was mainly manned by British seamen. In 1862 she was fitted with guns and for the next eighteen months cut a wide swath across the Atlantic and the Caribbean, seizing and sinking dozens of Union merchant ships before being cornered and sunk off the French coast by a Union warship. The ensuing dispute over damages for the maritime losses was serious, for the Americans held the British responsible for knowingly allowing the *Alabama* to be converted to a warship for the Confederacy. In the Canadian colonies there were genuine fears that the grievance would be used as a pretext for an American invasion. It was one among several issues that were bringing the defence of British North America to the fore at the time – others being the Fenian Raids in 1866, unrest among the Métis in the West, and general concern over growing American expansionist sentiment in the wake of the Civil War. The *Alabama* claims[3] were not settled until 1871, when Prime Minister Gladstone formally expressed regret over the affair and agreed to pay £3¼ million in damages – a capitulation widely viewed by the British public as a national humiliation.[4]

In a second letter, probably written in 1868, when the *Simoom* was at the Royal Dockyard at Woolwich on the Thames, Edward told his mother about his visits to King's College and St. Bartholomew's, two of London's most prestigious hospitals.

"I have been up in town all day watching the practice of the great metropolitan hospitals," he wrote:

> Like all else over here they are on a grand scale, and their wards are as comfortable as hospital wards could be. I was struck by the attention paid to minor comforts, flowers on the ward, neat pictures on the walls, well polished and washed floors, etc. The mantelpieces in King's College Hospital have illuminated texts in the stonework such as 'Surely he hath borne our grieves and carried our sorrows,' 'daughter be of good cheer' and others equally suitable. The House Surgeon at St. Bartholomew's kindly introduced me to the Surgeons & I saw a great many operations – some of the new ones for the removal of deformities are truly wonderful even to a Surgeon. Many [patients] that I saw today would a few years ago either have died miserably or lived in still greater misery. Now they sit up in bed happy with the hope of returning health.
>
> Amongst the operations was one of amputation of the thigh on a little boy about 13. It was very affecting to see the poor little fellow flushed with painful excitement, speak to the [anaesthetic] operator, then shut his eyes, clasp his hands, and receive the chloroform.[5]

An earlier letter home that year was begun on August 30 at Malta, and finished at Gibraltar two weeks later. Malta had long been the headquarters of the Mediterranean fleet. The Maltese islands had come into British hands in 1802, when they helped the Maltese expel the French, who had seized the islands from the Knights of St. John in 1798. After the end of the Napoleonic Wars, the Maltese were reluctant to see the Knights (who had ruled them since the time of the Crusades) return to govern them, and apparently asked to remain under British protection. That, of course, suited the British government very well. In 1814 the Treaty of Paris formally confirmed British sovereignty and Malta became the key strategic base for British naval control of the Mediterranean Sea, and later the Suez Canal, for the next century and a half. Today the magnificent Grand Harbour at Valletta mainly hosts cruise ships and yachts instead of the great British fleet that was usually stationed there in Moss's time. One can easily imagine Edward, during one of his periodic visits to Malta, sitting with sketchbook in hand on the ramparts of the massive fort dominating the harbour.

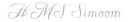

After a wonderfully good passage we arrived here six days ago and were agreeably surprised to find the island free from Cholera. It is the height of the Maltese summer and the thermometer has been 100° and upward in the shade. It has been 88 [degrees] frequently in my cabin and as no rain has fallen for many months and they have been badly off for water, indeed some could not even do washing. Today however, the usually dark violet sky was overcast and a violent thunderstorm with torrents of rain passed near us. I saw one of the redoubts of Fort Ricasole about 400 yards from us struck with lightning it made the stones and dust fly from the wall as if a shot struck it.

I went into Valletta and it was quite strange to see the waterfalls pouring down the streets of endless steps.... You asked me about the new regulations about the month's leave, it of course applies to me, but there is a paragraph saying 'if the exigencies of the service will permit.' I suppose they will permit sometimes. At present there is a very great want of Surgeons, one ship has none, and it seems likely she will go to the Red Sea to prepare the way for the Abyssinian Expeditions. I should not mind going with a naval brigade up the country but I don't think they will send me. We have had great fun every Sunday morning in the lukewarm water of the harbour. I swim a mile before breakfast regularly. It is safe because we get a boat to follow us – a boatswain will pull for hours for 6p.

Gibraltar Sept. 15

We have just come in and our letters were sent on board before we came along side the pier. I have received yours dated August 26 & it is just possible I will receive Richard's. We leave here tomorrow morning at 12 and till then I am as usual free, the ship will not see much of me in the intermediate time. There is a splendid library here and a billiards room close to it so I am all right.... I have done you a sketch of Malta as you asked me. Before you hear from me again I will probably have called at Montreal, for there will be difficulty getting leave.

Captain Lethbridge told me the other day that it seemed probable that we should have something to do in the Abyssinian affair bringing stores to Alexandria or something of that sort. An order has arrived here to buy 5,000 mules for the expedition. It is thought that it will not be necessary to assert absolute violence & that when our troops appear on the tyrant's land that the captives will be given up. I should like very much to have a chance to go into a country as wild and unknown as Abyssinia is, I think. I would almost give up a month's leave to go. You asked me whether the regulation about a month's leave would apply to me. It does, but I have had a month's leave this year already. However, I should not be surprised to get a short leave at Christmas or about

> then. The ship will require repairs, about two months in [dry] dock when she gets to England and if she goes with stores to Abyssinia she will require nearly three months.
>
> I received the letter you were anxious should not go astray. It told me about S. E. but the cause of all the mischief was not mentioned until the letter I received this morning. The circumstance will be an extra safeguard for me, for I would readily run the risk of being accepted & having a wife, or being refused and having a title to Bedlam.[6]

The "Abyssinian Affair" that Edward referred to was one (among many) of Queen Victoria's "Little Wars" during the last third of the century, and a strange war it was indeed. The troubles started with an unanswered letter. Apparently the Emperor wrote to the Queen to suggest the two of them form an alliance against his Moslem neighbours, whom he claimed were oppressing the Christians. He waited in vain for a reply. Perhaps the letter just vanished into the bowels of the bureaucracy, was lost en route, or was simply ignored. In any case the lack of a response enraged the despotic ruler of this "wild and unknown country," so he imprisoned and tortured the British Consul, holding him – along with about sixty other Europeans – as hostages. Eventually, after some bungled diplomatic efforts to obtain their release, the British government gave the Emperor an ultimatum and prepared for war against the "King of Kings and Chosen of God" in the event it was rejected.

In 1868, after the Emperor refused to release the hostages, an army of some thirteen thousand British and Indian troops crept into Abyssinia with a supply train of thirty-six thousand camels, elephants, and mules. This astonishingly colourful and diverse military force reached the Emperor's mountain stronghold (the fortress of Magdala) in mid-April and soon forced the enraged ruler to capitulate and release his prisoners. To avoid the humiliation of capture he committed suicide with a pistol that had been sent as a gift to him by Queen Victoria in happier times.[7]

Had Edward been asked to volunteer for the expedition, he would have relished the opportunity to participate in what he obviously thought would be more of an adventure than a real war.

Moss's letters to his mother during this period of his life reveal a good deal about the young surgeon. They were generally serious, and often mundane, but sometimes they were quite philosophical and occasionally tinged with wry wit or irony. Most importantly they provide glimpses into his daily life, his interests, and his religious inclinations – though of course, they remain only isolated "snapshots" – a limited and one-sided selection of his correspondence kept by his mother or other members of the family. In the following one, written from Portsmouth in September 1869, he attempted to explain some of his religious views.

Dear Mother,

I intend to send a small sum home after we leave – it has been reduced by buying a new cap, a pair of shoes & trousers & getting a new lining to my old yellow coat. We have no definite information about our next trip. If the Cape people [South Africa] choose to pay for the 9th Regiment we will not go, but if we hear from the next Cape mail that they will *not* support them (as is expected) we will go and bring them home. There will be two or three short trips about the coast of England first. The time of year is most favourable for a voyage to the Cape & I for one would like to go.

I am well occupied here. I am off duty every second evening and then I go for a swim off Southsea Bank [Portsmouth] then back to dinner, and after dinner a quiet read. I suppose Richard will let me know when he has an answer. What do you mean by his borrowing money? [this latter sentence crossed out] It does not do to live in advance of one's means, though 'live while we live' is the motto for men, now we each have about 25 years to get through in the best way we can, that is to say in the way that will leave the least fear of death, for fear of death there must be as long as our feelings are not stronger than our reason. All we hope for the future existence we receive from nature and revelation, and the latter have been handed down to us for 1,800 years or more by men who believed it, but have no positive proof of miracles themselves.

There seems to me to be enough evidence to warrant taking a good deal on trust – especially as I am unable to contain all the evidences at once – you see I am avoiding saying anything about feelings, they may be right or wrong but they are not to be trusted as far as I can see. If that part of me which wishes to live cautiously (that is in duty to our creator & ourselves) was separated from our feelings, our passions, and our other weaknesses of head, heart, and blood, I can imagine a happy state of existence. [But when] we have to fight with them and the devil, how is it possible to be contented, especially as [an] occasional defeat is certain? You may say 'but victory has been won for us.' True, but we must follow the victor and fight. Still, what is the use of a fight being done as long as enemies last, and envy, love of money, love of power, and sex are enemies which were conquered by our Saviour but which must be fought by us?

I have written enough, for I may think we are at ease or not. I will hope to meet you and Papa in a better world.[8]

It is evident from his other letters that Moss rejected a dogmatic approach to religion and did not interpret the scriptures literally. There was too much that he could not accept; too much that he doubted when The Word appeared to be in conflict with his rationality.

On April 9, 1870, after four years and two months aboard *Simoom*, Moss was appointed to Portland Sick Quarters on the stark and narrow Portland Peninsula across the bay from Weymouth, Dorset. Before reporting for duty he took eight weeks' leave back home, returning to England in June to sit his examinations for promotion to the rank of Surgeon. This proved to be no great obstacle, and he passed early in July. Later he would write a short Blue Book article questioning the value of examination marks.

Portland Sick Quarters in Dorset would now be his home for at least eighteen months.

6: Portland, Dorset

"Service Ashore"

Thomas Hardy, the great English novelist and poet, once called Portland the "Gibraltar of Wessex," an apt name for the almost treeless two-mile mass of rock capped by Portland Castle. This stronghold, towering five hundred feet above the harbour, was built by Henry VIII in 1536 from stone quarried from the peninsula, and Sir Christopher Wren used the same type of brown, rough-textured Portland stone for St. Paul's Cathedral. The surrounding area is also well known to geologists and palaeontologists for the abundance of ancient fossils found in the quarries and high cliffs of shale and limestone.

Modern Portland is a major British naval base, with a huge harbour and a long breakwater, completed in 1872 after twenty-three years of work by convict labourers. The original Portland Sick Quarters of Moss's day was made up of four small officer's wards and two larger men's wards built ten or so years earlier.[1] In addition to looking after patients at the Hospital, the surgeon in charge was responsible for the health of the young seamen (aged between 14 and 16 years) on HMS *Boscawen*, the training ship stationed there at the time. All things considered, Portland was a pleasant posting after four years afloat, and once Edward settled in and made a few friends, he was happy there most of the time.

Moss's letters from Portland strengthen earlier impressions of his character, personality, and his relationship with his mother – a relationship that seems to have been quite open. For example, his oblique reference in September 1869 to the periodic failure to conquer the desire for sex was surprisingly frank for the times, and while his letters to his mother were generally signed in a way that would suggest a very formal relationship, the gently humorous asides that he occasionally tossed into his letters tend to offset the formal impression. Some parts of his letters also appear to have been attempts to reply to her questions about his rather sceptical attitude in matters of religious faith.

On November 15, 1870, his mother asked if he had a close Christian friend or minister at Portland. He replied that he was not going to church and, although he was acquainted with four ministers "all of them more or less good," he was not on intimate terms with any of them and had no intention to be. In another letter describing the last hours and funeral service for a sailor who had died from inflammation of the lungs [pneumonia] he expressed his personal view about the Anglican funeral liturgy.

> The poor fellow died at four on Friday morning. At three he asked me to write a note to his mother and father, and he signed it himself. I read the last of Matthew and the first verse of 8th Romans to him, and sometime afterwards when I came into the ward I found two of his messmates praying for him – one of them was the man I told you about who was so near dying. My late patient was a man of 35 years who had what even sailors called a hard life, yet he died with a quiet expression of calm hope and dignity that I expect would be a very good example to some of those who call themselves [the] 'elect' [of God].
>
> We buried him today in the usual way that we (his mother, reported wife etc.) gave God hearty thanks that he had taken to himself this our brother etc. The sentiment was beautiful, but it was a lie.[2]

Edward Moss unquestionably thought of himself as a Freethinker, leaning in the direction of Unitarianism, which rejects both the concept of the Trinity and the divinity of Christ. His religious views appear to have been similar to those who, during the latter part of the nineteenth century, espoused what was known as the "New Theology" or "Modernism." Many members of the mid-Victorian scientific community were interested in seeking a synthesis that would allow them to combine the results of rational scientific inquiry and biblical criticism into a theological coherence that they could accept intellectually. Geological studies that refuted the biblical creation story were increasingly finding acceptance in the scientific community. Supported by Darwinian theory as well as the "Higher Criticism," they cast serious doubt on the Bible as literal and revealed truth. Edward Moss was clearly in the camp of these scientific and modernist critics of orthodoxy as the following letter, written just after he took charge at Portland, makes evident.

RNH Portland, June 21, 1870
Dear Mother,

You ask me about Dr. Quincey's works. I have only read his autobiography and I am not aware that his books have an authentic atheistic tendency. As for the unrest that is prominent in the minds of people over there, truth won't suffer by the light, though the process of turning a light on a traditional truth is sceptical.

The people who unscripturally defined the three persons of the Deity have themselves to thank for Socinian doctrines, but I think the supra-human character of Christ will come out all the clearer after thoughtful scientific enquiry, so let us prove all things & hold to them which is true. Let us *know* as far as the limited powers God has given us will let us know.

Christianity is a practical as well as a theoretical subject. The theoretical part must be tried and substantiated by our reason and then [it] may come under our experience. Christianity says that if a man submits himself to [God] believing it to be true & does his best to act according to its laws, he will receive super-human power to control his instincts, or that they will be controlled by that power. Well I have not yet found that to be true. If I did, I would have experimental proof of the things my feeble reason leads me to think are true.

I do not put my thoughts into a very intelligible shape I fear, but it is not easy to speak so as to show your thoughts on such subjects to another. Perhaps I would be better if I kept them to myself altogether.

I know nothing about how long I remain here and I don't care a fig one way or another, except that the place gives me an extra £39 a year to send to you, or to hoard up goodness knows for what. I shall receive another increase of pay of £27.7.6 at the end of next month, which will bring me up to £319. I hope I will enjoy it.[3]

Moss's reference to the Socinians gives a clue to his theological orientation. Notorious heretics in the eyes of both Catholics and Protestants, they were named after Faustus Socinus (1539–1604), an Italian philosopher and reformer whose doctrines, particularly the denial of the Trinity, eventually came to be known as Unitarianism. Eighteen months after expressing his own anti-Trinitarianism, Edward revealed to his mother another unconventional view about the claimed infallibility of the scriptures.

Dec. 17/71
Dear Mama,

I have nothing remarkable to write about this Sunday evening. I have not been to Church as the usual evening service at five had to be held at three in consequence of the failure of [the] gas [light]. So I had a quiet tea with the November number of the *Contemporary Review* and was much interested in a paper in it by John Hunt (one of the Christian Evidence Society men) on German theology because it coincided with my views, which latter are not even always capturable by myself.

It seems that the belief in error always carries some punishment with it and he [believes that there will be] some punishments in our country following the belief in the verbal accuracy of our scriptures, or even in the originals, if such are not long lost. It is evident that the scriptures are not all divine, for the language is human, and the more clearly we recognize the human [in them] the more clearly the divine will stand out from it.

I have lately been thinking of the strange statement of First Matthew, the Book of the Generations of Jesus Christ, the Son of David etc. Here the writer proceeds to trace the generations from Abraham & David to Christ, but instead of so doing traces them to Joseph, who according to the same writer has no more to do with Christ's ancestry than I have, but according to a blasphemous human story was the father of Christ. Faulty human custom makes it an ordinary thing to call a woman's child the child of her husband, even when it is known not to be so. The custom is palpably a lying one, and therefore the above gap in the genealogy cannot be stopped up by saying that Joseph was the legal (i.e. customary) father of Christ. I therefore agree with German and other Theologians who say that we have no infallible guide except the "spirit which beareth witness with our spirit."[4]

It is evident that Moss had absorbed quite liberal theological views, and though he might have felt a bit uncomfortable with differing so openly from his mother's more traditional religious beliefs, he was not so constrained that he was unable to frankly express his opinions to her.

Religion, however, was not the usual subject of his letters. More often they were focused on one aspect or another of his day-to-day life. Soon after settling in at Portland, he reported on his finances and off-duty meanderings around the rocky peninsula, the latter perhaps intended more for his brother Richard than for his mother, though with more scientific education than most women of her time, she too would have been interested in his comments. On July 3, 1870, he wrote:

My time has been very much occupied for the last week, for I have to close the quarterly accounts of this establishment, look after several anxious cases, prepare for my promotion examinations etc. I have also paid all my own bills for the 21 days I have been here, the total of my expenditures for that time has been £7.15.4. This also includes some expenses that are exceptional, such as the 10 shillings for water butts, 10s/6d for a book of tickets (at reduced price, taken wholesale) for Weymouth by the steamboat – and a good many other such items, but I think I will find it difficult to spend less than £8 a month. My two servant's monthly money is 10s. My butcher's bill for 21 days was 14/6/1/2, washing 4/4, bread 1/8. My bill for occasional lunch on board any of the ships here 12/. I find I can get first class boots for 18s/6d, and that is an improvement on Portsmouth. After much deliberation I have ordered *Nature* & I thought at first that Richard and I could manage to share it, but I don't see how it could be done, besides it did not look well to see me altogether without a paper here.

You will see that I intend to live as economically as possible, indeed I grudge spending money on the necessities of a position that is a barren honour such as it is, and in the feeding and clothing of a life that does not return adequate thanks for the expense. You can see that with such ideas about spending money on myself, and with total income of £282 (228 pay 39 hospital allowance, 15 interest on money) I can easily dispense with the £40 to you and the girls. Indeed I ought to give you more, but it is there for you to take if you want it. I have written all this with the intention of making your mind easy on the subject as you spoke on it once when I was on my long leave....

I have more to do this quarter [of the year] than I expect to have in the future, for besides the ordinary work of the place I have been obliged to untangle the accounts of my Second-in-Command, whose predecessor hung himself about two months ago here. I am of course supposed to see that his accounts are all right, but it is easier to see that they are right than put them right when they are wrong. The total sum (not including provisions etc. from the ship) spent on this hospital for the quarter is £29.5.11½....

Today as my wont I wandered amidst the rocks. Rocks here are not like other rocks, for half of them are broken off the cliffs by convicts & other quarrymen. You can find places with any kind of rock you like, from miles of square cut stone to fragments of mountains and high straight cliffs. About half way up the island today I found a fossil bone in an unusual position and I intend to take it out carefully when I have time. Everywhere here you are reminded of the ages of the earth long past. To reach the time when the rocks were formed you have to go back, leaving all trace of men & the present animals behind you, through the past cold period when Europe was Arctic and then after more ages of time when the great chalk cliffs were slowly forming at the bottom of the Atlantic as

> large and deep as our own. Before that Atlantic existed, high land rose here and on its (unclear) buried surface you can see the trunks of great trees with their roots upright in the soil, and in some cases their stumps stand 6 feet high and 4 to 5 feet thick. Then before that land, another great sea rolled here, for its mud still holds the shells of gigantic ammonites in some cases three feet across. [rest of letter missing.][5]

Three weeks later, the subject of money and living expenses was once again raised after some introspective comments about his life ashore. The "Blue Books" referred to in the following letter were parliamentary and governmental reports. Moss undoubtedly hoped that the publication of articles in the Navy Blue Book would bring him a small measure of recognition in the scientific as well as the naval and medical communities. After mentioning to his mother his hope for a few days' leave in August, he observed:

> I get along very well here, month follows month in identical style. I always feel the time has [not] gone by fruitfully unless something in the way of an addition to science is made, and alas little has been done in the year just gone. I have written two papers for our Blue Book and a rough text on a sea creature, but no original research (excepting the very troublesome one into the value of examination marks) has been made. There has been too much amusement. I could not tell you how many picnics, dances, musical parties, etc. etc. I have been at, and one can't help but regret the lost time. My present analysing mood is probably caused by the fact that we had a large afternoon party on board HMS *Boscawen* yesterday evening.
>
> I have a swim every day with an officer of artillery called Watson. He was born at County Wicklow, and both his parents were Quakers. He is an old acquaintance of mine, and we brought him to Canada in *Simoom* this day last year. I put £40 to my account at Uncle Woods and the total sum I have sent home within the year is £205.10, which excepting one or two private fees has come from my pay, how I don't know.[6]

Mundane financial matters continued to dominate his letters in early August, but the outbreak of the Franco-Prussian War a month earlier prompted some unusual comments about crime, war, and murder. It was not always easy to follow the Quaker tenets of pacifism or the biblical admonition to "Judge not, that ye be not judged."

Dear Mamma,

One thing or another has caused me to put off writing you for nearly a week. The Director-General has not made the yearly inspection of this Hospital yet. I have been expecting him for the last three days. Before that I was busy writing an article on some blood diseases for the Navy Blue Book, and on Saturday got a most complimentary letter about my 'most interesting and suggestive paper' – which would be most gratifying if I did not suspect that they say the same thing to everybody. I wrote back a strong hint that I would again enlighten them after I had an opportunity of making up the literature on another subject at some large library. I cannot tell just what my expenses for the last month have been. Milk, vegetables, eggs, butter & mustard cost £1.0.2. I received the *Simoom*'s salvage money of £8.15.

The probability of getting into the war is slight but is increasing every day. No one can guess at the end of the present complications. So much for the peace peoples [Quakers] look at the universal sign of peace.

As a rule the crime in a nation does not seem to be increased by war. Ordinary offences decrease, and is it less mean to murder in war than many of the numerous other ways, slow or sudden? There is a comforting way for anyone who hates crime to look at the war – [and] that is to reflect that every man killed would probably have otherwise committed crimes greater in total than the single one of murdering him [in warfare].

Orders have come here to draft all the trained boys and all the seamen that can be spared from the ships here. We have an immense fleet ready, but we want more men, and sailors can't be made in a week. If war breaks out I would like to be where there was most to be done. It is my only chance of progressing, and I think they would very likely send me afloat, and save shore practitioners to do duty here. If we had a big war & a sudden peace there would be such reductions in the Navy that I might perhaps retire, but it is a long way off at present. I will do you a sketch of my Hospital when I have time.[7]

Two weeks later Moss commented again on the war and French defeats in two major battles. His remarks revealed a distinct lack of sympathy for the French and strong support for the Germans, probably reflecting the old British enmity towards France dating from the Napoleonic Wars. They also reflected widespread British opinion that Napoleon III, in an effort to restore his sagging prestige and maintain French dominance of Europe, was both wrongheaded and reckless in starting a war with Prussia. The decisive battle of this brief clash of arms took place at Sedan on the first of September. There, the French were again defeated and Louis Napoleon was ignominiously forced to raise the white flag and surrender along with over eighty thousand of his troops. When the news of his capture

reached Paris, rebellion swept through the streets, forcing the Legislative Assembly to dissolve and once more proclaim France a republic.

Dear Mamma,

Your letter came this morning and assisted me in getting through breakfast. I find I can't eat with any comfort without a letter or book to read. Your sketch of the Hospital is not done yet. I commenced one and spoilt it & had to wait until I could go to Weymouth to get paper. The Hospital consists of six wards, four small ones for officers, well furnished and almost always empty, and two good large wards for the men. Just now I have nine patients, and though the number is small, I find that by the time I have paid proper attention to each case, seen that their medicines are rightly made up, their diet stipulated, and daily records of each of the above particulars written, I have not very much time on my hands.

You asked me if I would like to see any Dublin papers. I have lots of newspapers. [The] Government sends *Good Words*, and *Chambers Journal*. Once a week, the *News of The World*, *Illustrated* [London] *News*, *Punch* and of course I see them first, and I see *The Times* and *The Standard* almost every day on board HMS *Boscawen*, as well as the *Saturday Athenaeum* & my principle difficulty is to get books to read at meal hours and in the long evenings when the lamp is lit and the house is silent.

My case of Typhoid is nearly through the fever and the two broken legs are as well as can be expected. We got a telegram from town on Saturday saying that [French General] McMahon's army were prisoners. The success of the calm German intellect over bragging French [élan] is as it should be, but if I were Germany I would leave France unable to threaten any more. The last of the Latin races has fallen.[8]

But France, though humiliated, was far from prostrated. Wounded national pride, anger over the crushing indemnity of five million francs laid on the nation by the Germans and, above all, bitterness over the loss of Alsace-Lorraine, annexed to Germany under the peace terms, would be potent factors in keeping alive the French desire for *revanche*. In *The Guns of August*, Barbara Tuchman called the memory of Sedan "a stationary dark shadow on the French consciousness" and the thought of "Again" the single most fundamental factor of French policy during the next generation.[9] The seeds of the two Great Wars of the next century were planted at Sedan and nourished in the soil of Alsace-Lorraine.

Like any other mother, Teresa Moss worried about the physical and moral well-being of her son, exposed as he presumably was to the fleshpots that were found in every seaport. Her concerns prompted him to reassure her that naval life was not turning him into a wastrel.

"Your letter," he wrote on October 10, 1871:

> … warns me against being tainted by the people you call my friends here. I can assure you this danger is altogether on this side as there is not a person here that I associate with that is [not] a great deal better than I am myself and certainly more given to see the bright side of things, as I find out when I spend an evening at home, a thing I don't do more than once a week and would not do so then if I could help it.
>
> You will be glad to hear the Sydenham Society biennial book quotes my paper on blood written last year and published in our Blue Book. I enclose an order for some money – take what you want of it or all of it if you like, I don't see any use for it for I have no prospects whatever. I thought I had once, but reflection has shown that they were visionary and I can't have any, which saves thinking. If I could only feel things in the right way. There is something in the amiable spirit that takes no thought for the morrow and leaves the future to itself.
>
> We have had little but storms here since I came back. Three coastguard men were drowned last week and Mrs. Cooksworthy is getting up a concert for the benefit of their widows, thus pleasing everyone and getting them some money. I have my quarterly reports to get done today. They won't take more than three or four hours and then I think I will treat myself to the band that performs on the pier this evening, as I have never done so yet. I must soon expect to be sent out of this, and am rather sorry, for I will never have a better appointment. I suppose I will look back on this as the best time of my life.[10]

Although Edward was usually a sociable enough person, he also appears to have been prone to periodic bouts of melancholy or pessimism. To what extent these were a normal response to specific circumstances in his private or professional life, or simply part of his emotional makeup, is difficult to determine from the limited family correspondence. An example of this is his comment about "having no prospects whatsoever," taken in the context of seeing no use for the money he was sending home. We can only speculate about its meaning, though it seems less likely that it refers to his career than to a possible betrothal. Edward's mother obviously wanted to see him married and, believing that the eighteen-month shore appointment at Portland would provide a good opportunity for him to find a suitable partner, appears to have been urging him on towards marriage in spite of his periodic professions of reluctance.

On November 6, 1870, he wrote:

> I have just got to the end of another Sunday evening. I am generally glad when such evenings are over, and to pass the last half-hour I write to you. Annie's painting came quite safely and is a great ornament to my room. I got a patient last week who was supposed to be dying of inflammation [*sic*] of both lungs. He came with the vacant half-open eyes and jerking tendons of a dying man, and strange to say he has recovered. I gave him stimulants as fast as possible and after a night of low delirium he slept as patients about to die sometimes do, but he woke conscious and after more stimulation he could speak and now he can sit up in bed without help. I had his wife telegraphed & she came from Plymouth, quite a nice little woman, a good example of the wide difference between a sailor's and a soldier's wife. Her attention considerably assisted his recovery. Such a companion would be as poor for me as for Adam, but our customs prevent anyone from marrying me for the 14 months left before they send me to China or some such place, indeed even the 14 months is uncertain.
>
> Nellie asks whether I will be home for Christmas. I know I would not get leave if I asked for it, so I don't mean to ask. It would have been better for me if I had broken off all home connections at once. People in the Navy have no business with such sentiments. We cannot have everything, and it is a great thing not to have anxiety about tomorrow's bread. So long as I am obedient and don't get drunk I will have money enough to feed and clothe myself as long as I live.[11]

Three weeks earlier he had observed that he had not written for a long time because he didn't feel up to it.

> This kind of appointment is not one to make me feel content with everything, especially in the long evenings, but I have lately changed my mode of life completely, and am now as little 'home' as I can manage. One brilliant expedient for procuring amusement has met with complete success. I have given a lot of four o'clock teas and [invited] no one but ladies in the smallest number I could get to come. There are three young married ladies here who bring their unmarried friends over in the most innocent manner, and my only care is to see they don't all come at the same time.…
>
> I want to make my room as comfortable as possible as it is probably the nearest imitation of a home I will have while I am in the navy. I have been here 4 months now so I have only 14 before me, and I intend to 'live while I live' in those fourteen.[12]

This was about the same time that his mother had asked if he had a close Christian or minister friend. Edward observed rather cynically that he had lots of friends, but none whom he respected, finding most of them only an "amusing study." He added that he had little interest in the company of men unless they were "amusing or instructively scientific," and [he] did not seek their company unless they had women with them. In the next breath he concluded that marriage wasn't justified when he could be not be with his partner most of the time. Much the same attitude was evident seven months later when he told his mother that like a good boy, he was eating properly, wearing his mitts, dressing sensibly, and keeping his feet dry.

> In a letter you wrote some time ago you seemed to think that I won't take care of myself well enough. Now you must know that I am very well off. I have every comfort I want except one, a wife, and I know that as a naval officer a wife would be only a curse to me. I have enough to eat & drink & enough to clothe myself, enough society, no anxiety; no children, no debts, and strange as it may appear the only trouble I have is a [family] over in Ireland. If I hadn't that I would have no cares, but as it is I don't like being sent abroad, and abroad I must go some day. If the great national foundling institutions had been thought of and got working before 1843, I would be in a most enviable position, but as it is I am always wanting to see you and the rest of them, and when you die I will feel sorry for you.
>
> I forgot one little bother that must be added to the nuisance of knowing anything about one's relations, and that is rheumatism, which in spite of flannel night-shirts (I never sleep in anything else) occasionally touches me a little. I keep a good fire in my room and when I go out I wear a muffler & thick gloves. I always take care that my boots are dry, and that my slippers are put to the fire before I put them on.
>
> I have a very comfortable hospital bed to sleep on, lots of blankets and the wolf skins over all, and I get hot water put in my bath. When tea time comes I draw the table over to the fire, prop up the daily paper against the [tea] cosy and devour the *Daily News*'s excellent articles on Tunis, and a sausage at the same time. If the wind would leave the South and turn round to the North East it would be much more agreeable.
>
> Some little novelty in the way of news, such as the blowing up of Tunis, would be acceptable, but should be repeated at least twice a week, and one would soon go through all the cities in Europe at that rate, but a few awful murders and the total loss of a big ship or two might help out.
>
> Your very comfortable & Affectionate Son, Edward[13]

Despite these droll reassurances, some of Edward's other letters were more suggestive of resignation than contentment. He was never entirely at home in the Navy in spite of the fact that some aspects of the military life were clearly appealing. The opportunity for travel or adventure in the outposts of empire (join the Navy and see the world) was certainly something he valued. Moreover, as mentioned earlier, he hoped that a naval career would provide some opportunity to pursue medical or scientific research to follow in the footsteps of Richardson, Hooker, and other famous medical men who had begun their careers as naval surgeons. There were other aspects of the naval life that were less palatable. He deplored the inability to enjoy a settled family life, at least for the foreseeable future. Much of the time he must also have been bored while he was on service afloat, for the atmosphere aboard ship was generally lacking in the kind of intellectual stimulation he craved. His medical work was also less varied or interesting than it would have been in private practice and he sometimes felt that his abilities were unappreciated by his superiors, rendering his status as a medical officer in his own words, "a barren honour" at best. Finally, while appreciating that as a doctor he was more his own master than most officers, he was still subject to the petty regulations and routines of a bureaucratic admiralty where nepotism and seniority was apt to take precedence over competence.

However, in 1870/71, Moss's periodic expressions of discontent with his life seems more than anything else to have originated in the belief that he had failed to live up to his potential, particularly as he saw his younger brothers embarking on more promising, lucrative, and potentially satisfying lives and careers. This feeling was very evident when he wrote to his mother on November 6, 1871:

> I suppose you will get this on your 52nd birthday and I wish you many happy returns. I am always very sad on my birthday[s] for they are disagreeable reminders of the past and future. Very few people grow better as they get older. You must look on yourself as unusually fortunate to have both parents alive (and I suppose glad to see you on your birthday) and no dead children gone before their time. We are nearly all men and women now, and we all know that we have been well and lovingly raised. Some people tell us we have done you credit. Perhaps some of us will do you credit. I will not, for I am conscious of having wasted considerable abilities. Willy, with some help from so-called luck, is in flourishing circumstances and is respected for his energy and goodness. Richard is an honour to my family, but he is in 'his own country and amongst his own kindred' and you don't see it. If you knew young men as well as I do you would be proud to be his mother. Every one of the girls is domestic, not one of them is a flirt, which considering it is part of their nature, does you credit. They ought to make good helpmates for anyone (I hope everyone will be of my mind). We have an artist in the family,[14] and Mary might be a musician if she liked. I hope the artist won't forget to love her mother more than her art. Success in

> open sight is a very trying thing to a girl. Grand as success may be it is worth little beside home love.
>
> You ask how I got through Hallow Eve; well I didn't know anything about it. I got out in a storm of rain and [was] drenched with sea going off to HMS *Achilles* on voluntary duty, which rather pleased me, for I felt careless. Mrs. Patrick had a gathering here in the evening and as young men are scarce I was told to be agreeable, which I wasn't. Mrs. Patrick desires me to say it is time you came over and looked after me, but she takes very good care of me (if I wanted any) herself. A good many people here are curious to see what kind of mother I have.[15]

As far as his medical work was concerned, the winter of 1871/72 was most notable for a major outbreak of contagious diseases in the ships at Portland. Scarlatina [scarlet fever], measles, and more ominously smallpox all put in an appearance in January and February. The emergence of the latter disease was not surprising, for the British Isles was being scourged by the worst smallpox epidemic of the century. In '71 and '72 the disease took more than 42,000 lives in England and Wales, and a half million more worldwide – an unimaginable toll of pandemic breadth and proportion. It is also believed that France suffered 200,000 deaths in 1869–70 and Germany about 125,000 in 1871 and 1872. According to *The Times* (February 9, 1871) London alone recorded 755 smallpox deaths, mainly children, during the first five months of the year. Nor was smallpox the only mass killer of children. Government records reveal that over 30,000 children died from scarlet fever and 18,000 more from measles in England and Wales in 1871 and 1872.

At Portland, the old wooden-walled hulks or sailing ships that housed hundreds of young men were certainly potential breeding grounds for contagious diseases in spite of the emphasis on cleanliness. The seamen slept cheek-by-jowl in areas of the ships with less than adequate ventilation and many opportunities to pass germs about. Below decks their hammocks were strung less than 18 inches apart, making it well nigh impossible to avoid some sort of contact between immediate neighbours. Moss knew how quickly transmittable diseases could spread aboard ships and undoubtedly would have been aware of a severe outbreak of smallpox on HMS *Princess Royal* in 1867.[16] At that time, in spite of the fact that the Medical Branch had instituted mandatory inoculation several years earlier, 117 men came down with the disease. When two cases of smallpox were confirmed at Portland in January, Edward sketched out a possible scenario for the steps he would take if he received more cases.

> This is Sunday evening and for a wonder I have been at church in the village. When I came back I read most of the evening service for my patients as the Chaplain did not come today, because it is thought advisable to have as little communication as possible with the hospital as long as we have Smallpox.

Portland, Dorset

> I received a midshipman yesterday from HMS *Inconstant* and today a boy from the *Boscawen* with Smallpox caught in London on leave at Christmas. It is not so improbable that we will have more of it, the more the better for me. I actually found myself building a castle [in the clouds] today. Suppose the Smallpox brought down from London spread in the training ships of the fleet – I would recommend a hulk to be converted into a temporary hospital and moored along side the breakwater, and I would take charge and be very energetic. The shield of science should shelter the people from the dragon's breath – alas we have no sword that can reach his body. Then at last when he had spread his dark wings and vanished in a cloud of strong disinfectants, I would write the Director-General and bounce him into promoting me into a Surgeon with £319.7.6 a year.
>
> I would have to go abroad for a short time and minor Surgeons find it difficult to get employment and I would be obliged to go on half pay for six months or so. Would I mind this? Oh no, no, no.[17]

The simultaneous appearance of three virulently contagious diseases soon stretched the small Portland Sick Quarters to its limit and beyond, creating a situation that turned Edward's dream into reality. It was only a matter of days after he wrote the above letter that more cases of smallpox were identified. The idea of fitting up a temporary hospital ship was immediately sent to the Director-General of Hospitals and Fleets. Whether the hulk suggestion was passed on as a result of Edward's suggestion to his superiors at Portland is not known for sure, but it is evident that the young doctor moved swiftly and energetically to curb the outbreak when permission to fit up a hulk was granted a few weeks later. As a result Edward's dream scenario unfolded much as he had hoped.

"I have got to 5 o'clock of a very busy Sunday," he wrote on February 15.

> I have received additions to my Smallpox, Scarlatina & Measles cases till I can receive no more. And Admiral Wilmot is getting a hulk turned into a hospital ship. All the men in the fleet are at work about it one way or another, and it may be ready tomorrow, but I have to leave this morning for Portsmouth (Totterdale's Hotel will be my address) and everything is in lovely confusion, for my head man has to come with me, and the new people are not 'up to the ropes.' I telegraphed our Director-General yesterday and have written letters without number to get things in order, with partial success.[18]

The smallpox dragon did not spread his wings and flee until August. Although he would return to England from time to time in future years, it would never be with such vigour and deadly breath. And in the Navy, the disease virtually disappeared after the Medical branch introduced compulsory re-vaccination after the 1871 outbreak. Unfortunately, in the wider community there was still a great deal of resistance to compulsory vaccination and the incidence of death by smallpox did not begin to decisively decline until the late 1880s, probably as much from compulsory isolation of patients as from vaccination.[19]

Edward's rapid and efficient response to the smallpox outbreak did, as he hoped, bring him to the attention of the Medical Director-General as a young man with initiative and it was probably responsible for gaining him another shore appointment. However, as 1871 ebbed away, he had no idea of such a possibility and was only aware that it would soon be time for a new posting, one that was almost certain to be afloat rather than ashore. On New Year's Eve he penned a pensive year-end note to his mother. Perhaps the thought of once again spending two or three lonely years at sea, far away from hearth and home was responsible for his year-end melancholy. Or perhaps (as he wrote) it was only the cold plum pudding conjuring up Dickensian images of Christmas Past or the prospect of Christmases yet to come, not to be spent entirely alone to be sure, but nevertheless without the warmth and love to be found in the bosom of family.

> Dear Mama,
>
> I have got into the last hour of 1871. Being of an extremely sentimental nature I have as usual sat up to see the year out, and for so doing 'I suspect myself a fool' although two years short of 30. The hours that have elapsed since that time have not been conducive to contentment, principally I suspect, because of some cold 'plum pudding' I indulged in. The mind of man is the sport of his stomach, and knowing this we can afford to laugh when the organ in question subjects the eternal spirit to a fit of the blues. There has long been a declaration of war between my head and my body, and they invariably seize on a quiet evening like this to pitch into one another. The old *Simoom* came in here on the evening of the 29th with me on board two years ago. Yesterday the 7th Regiment embarked & the 27th disembarked in teems of rain, [and] it was as usual pitiable to see the crowds of slatternly women and whining children trying to carry their little properties on board. Not having any other remarks to make I will wish you a happy New Year.[20]

Edward did not realize it, but in less than a month he would have reason to view the world and his future in an entirely different light.

7: British Columbia

"A Change of Course"

The gloomy outlook that seems to have taken hold of Edward in the late fall of 1871 vanished with astonishing abruptness in early January, when he received notice that he had been appointed to the headquarters of the Pacific Station at Esquimalt, British Columbia. This was a totally unexpected development, for it is clear that he expected to be sent back to service afloat after finishing his term at Portland Sick Quarters. The change in his mood was strikingly visible when he wrote elatedly to his mother on February 20, 1872.

> I have scarcely a moment to spare. I received a pass for a first class ticket for [the] West Indian Mail [packet] sailing on 2nd March, but will apply for leave up to 2nd April. The appointment to Esquimalt is a splendid one for me. I succeed a man who is more than seven (or nine) years my senior in the service. My pay is increased by £108, and you know I will receive an additional increase of £28 at the end of this month, making a total of £363. Everyone is congratulating me. I have received most flattering expressions of regret at my leaving Portland from Captain Vesey Hamilton & Captain Lethbridge.
>
> I like some of the people here very much, and am almost as sorry as they are that I must leave. I intend to call for a day at least to see Willy and wife to be. I must not regret my own case, I have chosen another path.
>
> The Vancouver Island appointment will last me until my promotion (about 2½ years). Am I not fortunate in always being my own master? I hate being ordered.
>
> Hoping to see you very soon my dear mother.[1]

This was a newly energized Edward, happily looking forward to new opportunities and duties; proud to have been awarded an appointment where he alone would be responsible for the operation of the only British naval hospital on the vast Pacific Station. In truth, the Esquimalt Hospital was modest enough as he would soon discover, but nevertheless the appointment was significant. His worthiness and his talents had been recognized after all by the Director-General of Hospitals and Fleets, Dr. Alexander Armstrong, and confirmed later by Armstrong's personal praise on the eve of his departure. The fact that the Esquimalt appointment would ensure at least two or possibly three more years ashore also reopened, very quickly it seems, the question of marriage. In a second note to his mother a day later, he observed that the reopening of the Esquimalt Hospital was:

> … caused by the doubtful attitude of America in the Alabama business – and the San Juan dispute – the island of San Juan is very close to Esquimalt.[2] The Hospital is at Esquimalt for the accommodation of the whole Pacific Fleet.… Mrs. Patrick [his landlady and wife of another naval person who had been at Esquimalt] tells me that nothing can exceed the natural beauty of the place. It will be covered with wild roses when I get out, and is wooded to the water's edge.… Will you get the girls to see if there is anything about Vancouver's Island in the Institute Library? The natural history of the North Pacific will have great interest for me now. I wonder if it is well that I am neither engaged nor married. Portland has not tempted me. I fear a rolling stone must gather no Mrs. Moss.[3]

In spite of the offhand jocularity of his "rolling stone" comment, it appears that marriage was no longer being ruled out as an option, though in view of such a statement it is surprising how quickly it resurfaced. Early in March, when he was granted a short leave, Edward returned home and became engaged to Thomasina Mary Dugdale of St. James Terrace, Dublin.

It is not absolutely clear if Edward and Thomasina's marriage a year later was an arranged union or a love match, though it can be certain that as members of the small Quaker community in and around Dublin they would have at least known each other. Either explanation could have been the case. Arranged marriages were certainly common enough in Victorian times, and it was often expected that romantic love would blossom with a mutually advantageous match, though a prior attraction was obviously preferred. The case for an arranged marriage is somewhat strengthened by the fact that Thomasina's parents were deceased and that she does not appear to have been a woman of means.

Dr. Edward Moss, ca. 1872. Photographer G. Schroeder, Dublin. British Columbia Archives, No. G-07634.

Mrs. Edward Moss, née Thomasina Dugdale, 1873. Photographers Bradley and Rulofson. British Columbia Archives, No. G-07616.

In the surviving Moss correspondence, the first mention of Thomasina Dugdale appears in a letter Edward wrote to his mother on April 2, the day that he left for Vancouver Island. Lacking other evidence, it can be postulated that some fairly intense family discussions took place during his short leave in Ireland. One can visualize his mother making it clear that with the certainty of two or three more years ashore, there was no acceptable reason for delay and ample reason for a man in his late twenties to get on with the business of taking a wife. However, the details of the scenario are less important than the fact that negotiations for an engagement contract were obviously underway very soon after Edward's appointment. When completed several months later, a dowry of £1,000 – no insignificant sum – was guaranteed by some of Thomasina's relatives. As far as the marriage itself was concerned, in spite of the certainty of long separations, a mid-Victorian gentlewoman in her mid-twenties without an independent income would have had to think very seriously before turning down a marriage offer from a naval doctor of the same Quaker faith, apparent good moral character, good family, and decent career prospects. At twenty-six years of age Thomasina was already "getting on" by then current views of womanhood, which greatly favoured younger women during an age when men were utterly dominant and able to "call the shots" in almost every respect.

In any event, by the first of April Edward was back in England finalizing the arrangements for his long journey. Before leaving, he told his mother about a very gratifying interview he had with the Director-General of Hospitals and Fleets.

> I called on the Director-General in town today and he said many complimentary things. He said my [medical] stores work would be troublesome at first, but I would get onto it. My appointment will last three years. He said 'I think after that time an officer has a right to come home.' If I am promoted over there my passage home will be paid. I did not think it would.... If I live by myself out there for three years I will have at least £20 a year for life. If Senie [Thomasina] comes out, it would hardly be till next year and would cost over £200 I suppose.
>
> I haven't time to think at present – Goodbye.[4]

A day later, the diminutive (5'5", 130 lbs.) neatly bearded young doctor left Portsmouth on the mail packet *Tagus*, bound for Colón on the Isthmus of Panama. From Colón he travelled about thirty miles by boat and train across the malarial neck of land separating the Caribbean Sea from the Pacific Ocean, pausing briefly at Panama City before taking the steamer for San Francisco, where he arrived on May 19. He had a few days to wait for a northbound ship and registered at Lick House, one of San Francisco's best hotels, built on a grand scale compared to most English hostelries. However, neither the hotel, the city, nor anything else American appears to have impressed him during his short time there.

Pensively, in his first letter to his mother from America, Edward again expressed his uncertainty about the fairness of asking Senie to become the wife of a naval officer, destined, as she would certainly be, to spend many years raising children alone.

> I will be glad when I get away from the States. I like nothing American. Saturday I sent Richard a paper with my arrival in it. Mine is the only name in the whole lot spelled correctly. So much for the Yankee papers. I suppose by the time you get this Willy [his younger brother] will be married or close to it. I forget the date of the ceremony, for when I heard it I had too many things to think of. He will be very comfortable – I have often been foolish enough to envy him.
>
> Has Senie come back yet? I suppose not, but it seems years since I left, which is a nice prospect for the future. I intend to give up thinking about the future at all, it involves too much bother. When you write always tell me how Senie is looking. I have grave doubt as to whether I have increased her happiness or not for the next three years, or afterwards either, for this is only one of many separations.[5]

Three days later at 5:30 in the afternoon, Edward stood on the deck of the steamship *Prince Arthur* as she pulled away from the dock. The ship then steamed slowly across San Francisco Bay and between the ramparts of the Golden Gate into the broad swells of the Pacific, bound for Victoria. It arrived there four days later at 7:30 on the evening of Sunday, May 26, just after the annual birthday celebrations for Queen Victoria, then entering the thirty-fifth year of her reign.

It was a pity that he had not arrived a few days earlier, for he would certainly have been invited to join the other naval officers who were among the four hundred guests at the grand soirée hosted by Lieutenant-Governor Joseph Trutch on Friday the 24th.[6] As usual, the Navy had played a major role in the various Victoria Day celebrations and sporting activities over the holiday weekend, the highlight being the annual regatta on the Gorge Inlet on Sunday afternoon.

That Sabbath, the morning dawned dull and showery, giving the regatta organizers some cause for concern but, as is often the case on the southern tip of Vancouver Island, the clouds began to break by mid-morning and at half-past ten two naval ships, *Scout* and *Boxer*, steamed into the inner harbour. Loaded with bluecoats and with flags and pennants flying gloriously, they towed an impressive flotilla of small boats crammed full of sailors and civilians being brought around from Esquimalt. Passing the ship-lined wharves and the customs house, the flotilla turned north into the mouth of the Gorge waterway, past water-side Point Ellice House, home of Judge Peter O'Reilly, and on to the starting point for the boat races about a mile or so up the inlet.[7]

At noon, the official start of the main events was thunderingly announced to the whole community with the firing of one of HMS *Scout*'s guns, the boom reverberating over a horde of spectators lining the shore or in small boats to watch the show, bet on the teams, or just cheer on their favourites during the boat races, which were tackled with Olympian fervour.

Elsewhere in the locality, the weekend was marked by family picnics and outings of all sorts. On the Saturday, two hundred people took a boat trip (organized by the Mechanics Institute[8]) to the British Camp on nearby San Juan Island. There they competed in games and danced the day away, some returning in the evening as well lubricated as the naval seamen given leave for the day.

The Province of British Columbia was newly minted when Edward Moss arrived, having joined Canada in January 1871 to create a country that spanned the continent. It was as yet very lightly populated – according to the 1871 census the province was made up of about thirty-six thousand souls – a figure that was apparently arrived at by ignoring the fact that there were also at least an equal number of aboriginal residents. Victoria, the Capital City, had a population of roughly seven thousand. It had come a long way since its inception as a Hudson's Bay Company fort only eighteen years earlier and was now the proud owner of a set of legislative buildings locally called the "birdcages" because of their unusually quaint colonial design.

An equally eccentric newspaper owner who had taken the name Amor de Cosmos (formerly Bill Smith)[9] was Premier of the province, and Joseph Trutch, formerly the Commissioner of Lands and Works, was the Lieutenant-Governor. Esquimalt was "a small straggling collection of houses" some three miles to the west of Victoria, cheek-by-jowl with the naval base at Duntz Head across the inner harbour from the Esquimalt Naval Hospital at Constance Cove.

Edward was to find the Esquimalt appointment very much to his liking from both a professional and a personal point of view. It suited him in almost every way. From the beginning, he threw himself energetically into the job of renovating the run-down hospital buildings and bringing the operation of the facility up to the standards demanded by the Medical Department. The few years he would spend at the hospital would prove to be among the happiest of his life.

8: Esquimalt

"His Own Master ..."

Immediately after arriving at Esquimalt Moss reported to the senior officer at the base, Post-Captain Cator, commander of HMS *Scout*. Cator would be his superior officer until the arrival of the new Commander-in-Chief of the Pacific Station, Rear-Admiral Charles Farrel Hillyar, who was expected to make an appearance later in the year. Edward's initial impressions of Esquimalt were extremely favourable and were colourfully detailed in his first letter home.

> Royal Naval Hospital Esquimalt
> Vancouver's Island, June 10/72
>
> Dear Mother,
>
> Knowing you would have lots to think of & do I did not write you on my arrival on the 28th, and even now I am very uncertain whether you have come back from England when this gets to Ireland. I am safe enough here. No orders have yet come from the senior officer here about reopening the Hospital. They are expected in two days. I, however, have several patients in my charge and have quite enough to do making over all the survey papers of all the medical & other stores in the place. My own quarters consist of half a building of some size. The other half, completely divided from mine, is for sick officers. I have two sitting rooms, and two bedrooms beside an office and small outhouse containing a kitchen and servant's room. I have a kitchen garden that is well stocked and will help keep me in vegetables. The whole house, however, requires extensive repairs except one sitting room and one bedroom. I have a serious notion to

turn one sitting room into a kitchen, but am still undecided till I see how much can be done. Of course the house is wooden, two stories high surrounded by a verandah eight feet wide. I have two wells with 25 feet of water in them, about 200 yds. from the house, but no water in either house or kitchen. All the water for the Hospital has to be carried nearly 200 yds. and I don't see how pipes can be laid as the ground frost of water bursts them.

The climate is now like an English summer, certainly not warmer, and you cannot imagine anything like the beauty of the country, it is just wild, every two or three miles you come on a little wooden farm house with bits of corn land scattered amongst splendid meadows all cut out of the forest. The woods are quite beyond description, grand dark [fir] trees with here and there an oak or maple, sometimes in close groups, sometimes opening out & letting in light, or little glades of tall ferns with the roses cropping up everywhere. There is no exaggeration in saying it is like a garden run wild. Orange and white lilies and a little blue flower called camas are very plentiful, and the ground, where you can get at it, is covered with wild strawberries. Currants grow wild also, but neither of them as large as English cultivated fruit. Every mile or so a great granite mound scored by ancient glaciers rises up amongst the trees, and when you climb up on it you can see smooth lakes and blue forest-clad trees on the one side, and on the other, way beyond the dark branches and straight stems, the rosy pink tops of the snow covered Olympians or Cascade range in Washington Territory. Add to this a calm air filled with strange fragrance and trembling with the song of birds, and I think no one can blame the place for want of anything beautiful.

The one great drawback is the want of servants. No labourer works for under two dollars (8s/4p per day) no mechanic [tradesman] under 5s. The Chinese cook of the Hospital gets 25 dollars a month and five from me, for cooking for about 14 persons – he is the best cook in the colony. I have been advised to get a Chinaman to attend, wash, and cook for me at 25 dollars a month, but I expect to have two extra hospital attendants and I will get one of them to look after me for less than that, leaving the cooking to be done in the Hospital kitchen 50 ft. off by the Hospital.

As for provisions, they are cheaper here than at home – or at least not much dearer. Milk 6½ cents a pint, eggs 37½ cents a dozen, fowl 75 cents each, butter 37½ lb., beef 16 and mutton 20. I get my tea and wine out of board, and both are I think cheaper than at home. There is a Hudson's Bay store quite close by, and I can get anything there from tea or coffee to an axe or blacking brush. As to my duties, they are much the same as at Portland except that I will have many more troublesome returns [reports, accounts] at the end of each quarter.

If I had known anything about the place I would have come out married. They would, I am told, have provided free passage to my wife both out and home. They offered a free first class passage to my predecessor for himself, wife, and about seven children, but he refused it and stayed out here a year or two in private practice, but didn't get on well because he was generally drunk in the day time and would never go out at night. Private practice is not recognized in the Navy, so I was rather surprised when the Senior Officer Captain Cator told me I would have lots of it. I had my first patient Saturday; a neighbouring farmer's boy knocked out a front tooth. They brought the boy to me to take out the loose tooth and I said "I could not take their offered fee for such a trifle," especially as I expect to hire a horse on more moderate terms from this farmer when I want one.

As far as I am concerned the house is already quite good enough, and I think it likely that I will get it done up pretty well, so that in fact only two things remain to be done. First to get Senie out somehow, & then get married somewhere and somehow. As yet I haven't the faintest idea how this can be accomplished. It seems to me out of the question that I could get to New York, though San Francisco is easy enough I think. In a year's time there will be rail from here to New York via Portland and San Francisco, as well as direct.

I forgot the third obstacle, viz. the great difficulty in getting a female servant – half the people here have to go without and be content with a Chinaman, but I wouldn't have that. I am applying for a married [hospital] attendant whose wife could supervise cooking or working. If I got one of course, the obstacle would be less, but at present there isn't a woman in the place.

There can be no question about the appointment being a splendid one for me. Although everything except food is exceedingly dear, I have little doubt that I can make my hospital allowance alone almost cover my living, including a servant at about £50 a year. Much of my food will be got by fishing or shooting. I must get all clothes out from home – a cheap coat here would cost 30 dollars.

By the time you get this Willy will be a married man.[1] What a very young woman you are becoming! I fear we must wait a long time before the next wedding – at any rate it will be a quiet one, that's a comfort. It is late now, my dog is snoring comfortably in the corner and the wood fire has gone out, so I'll be off to bed.

June 15

Very busy with official correspondence. Heard yesterday that I was not unlikely to get £21 a year extra – quite well and comfortable considering. I must be off now.[2]

Esquimalt

Edward adapted quickly to his new home and responsibilities and lost no time in getting down to business. It was obvious to him that some major renovations were needed if he were to successfully carry out his orders. The Engineer's Barracks were in sad condition. They were really not much more than clapboard buildings devoid of any insulation except a layer of tarpaper covered with plastered and wallpapered walls. Moreover, the buildings had received very little attention since they were taken over by the Navy ten years earlier. In 1868, a request for money to carry out needed repairs was turned down. Instead the Admiralty officially closed the hospital a year later, though unofficially the buildings continued to be used from time to time by ship-borne surgeons. With little or no supervision, they had deteriorated even more during the following three years.

The hospital renovations and medical initiatives carried out during his stay at Esquimalt make Edward Moss well deserving of credit for establishing one of the earliest medical institutions on the West Coast of Canada. While the wooden buildings he renovated at Skinner's Cove would last only fifteen more years before being replaced with more permanent brick structures, the naval hospital as an institution on the original site would continue in one reincarnation or another for fifty more years. In 1922 the hospital site was commissioned as HMCS *Naden* and the Old Hospital buildings became the new west coast training school for the Royal Canadian Navy, which had only come into being a dozen years earlier. Around the time of commissioning, the main buildings were renovated to suit their new function and the garden and lawns in front of the old wards became the new parade square.[3]

Over the years the Esquimalt naval base and dockyard has undergone many similar changes and most of the old historic buildings have long since been demolished. However, three of the 1890s hospital buildings on the original site of the hospital, the Officers' Ward and two of the Men's Wards at "Museum Square," remain, one of them remodelled for a barracks and then later divided to create a Protestant and a Roman Catholic chapel. In the 1990s the latter site was again renovated to house the exhibits of the Esquimalt Naval and Military Museum, and the Canadian government recently designated Museum Square and its historic structures a national heritage site. If he were to come back today, Edward Moss would be proud of the heritage he helped to create at the naval base.

During his time at Esquimalt Moss concentrated his efforts on two main tasks. The first was to bring the hospital buildings up to acceptable medical and naval standards, and the second was to provide the best care possible for the patients under his care. In these endeavours he was generally his own boss as far as most decisions were concerned, though the approval of his superiors was usually required for major repairs. His main constraints were funding limitations and a shortage of cheap or efficient labour to carry out the work that needed to be done.

The first thing that he did was to block the easy access his patients enjoyed to the local "grog shops" in the village of Esquimalt. A trail, running from the nearby Hudson's Bay Company storehouse through the hospital grounds and on to the village, was blocked

Front of Doctor Moss's quarters, Royal Naval Hospital, Esquimalt, 1873. British Columbia Archives, No. H-00104.

off. This action reflected his views about health as well as the use of strong spirits at the hospital – a clear breach of naval regulations. Abstemious himself in the use of alcohol, Moss strongly favoured moderation and always counselled strict abstention for patients with illnesses that appeared to arise directly or indirectly from the use or abuse of spirits. Not surprisingly though, some of his healthier patients or those just awaiting passage home still managed to smuggle liquor onto the premises behind his back. Of course this was a cat-and-mouse game that seamen had always been accustomed to playing, and without the ability to supervise the wards day and night, keeping patients away from the demon rum was not always possible in spite of his best efforts.

However, the matter that demanded most of Moss's immediate attention was the state of the latrines. In his first annual report six months later he wrote:

> The pits were so full and offensive as to taint the air all over the grounds, they could not be emptied on account of the enormous payment required by persons who were applied to for the purpose. They could not be buried, and fresh pits dug, as the space behind the ward was already filled with pits so buried, and it therefore became necessary to adopt either a dry-earth system or regular water closets with proper flooding arrangements. The former system was considered inapplicable as it would involve the constant employment of labour, which it would be difficult if not impossible to supply from on board ship, as ships stationed here are always "short-handed" from the great inducements to desertion offered by the high wages obtainable in Oregon sawmills or inland farms. I therefore proposed a water closet system supplied in summer by a sufficiently large well, and in the winter by drainage off the roofs and the rainfall on a large rock surface behind the ward (i.e. to the eastward), and discharging between high and low water mark through a brick drain to the adjacent beach.[4]

Moss's concerns about "tainted air" and stinking outhouses reflected the stress on cleanliness and sanitation that became a feature of military as well as public medicine after the Crimean War, thanks to Florence Nightingale and other nineteenth-century reformers, who had worked for years to improve public health in England. The belief that cleanliness and fresh air were next to godliness had become an article of faith in the British naval hospitals by 1870. At that time the "miasmic" or atmospheric theory of the origins of disease had not yet given way to bacterial theory, and Moss's efforts to improve sanitation and ventilation in the wards were fully in keeping with the practices of the day. Every naval surgeon was also provided with a well-stocked chest of about one hundred medicinals, ranging from laudanum to bicarbonate of soda, though in reality bed rest in a clean and well-ventilated ward, helped along with a well-balanced diet, often proved more efficacious than anything else in returning a patient to health.

Before officially taking responsibility for the hospital Moss surveyed the site to produce a map showing the location of the various buildings. Then he asked Captain Cator to accompany him on a thorough inspection of all the buildings and stores. Moss could see that extensive repairs were going to be necessary, but he wanted to be sure that his superiors in England were made aware of all the existing deficiencies. A number of recommendations based on this inspection were approved by Cator, and a request for $2,500 was submitted to the Admiralty Medical Department on July 18. Moss did not wait for approval before starting work on the buildings and his planned changes to the water and sewage systems. By October he was ready to tackle repairs to the General Wards – painting, plastering, repairing furniture – everything that was most essential. All of the roofs needed to be re-shingled, and according to his Journal the roofing of the last building was finally completed on the day the first winter rains began that year.

The two-storey building that doubled as the Officers' Ward and Medical Officer's Quarters required an extensive overhaul. It had been built on wooden timbers that had rotted away over the years, so Moss had it jacked up and set properly on a new stone foundation. Repairs of various kinds continued on all of the buildings throughout the autumn until the "liberal sum" provided by the Admiralty was exhausted. This still left much of the interior of the Officers' Ward and the Medical Officer's quarters to be plastered, wallpapered, and painted the following year if additional funds were forthcoming. In his year-end annual report (January 1873), Edward expressed concern that the completed work would not meet Admiralty standards, both in terms of the quality of the finished work as well as the final cost:

> Considerable anxiety, and I think some loss, has been incurred by the absence of any specially qualified person to design, superintend, and inspect the work done by persons employed at great expense from Victoria, as neither the Senior Officer nor myself were sufficiently acquainted with Colonial work to do so.[5]

The naval ships on the West Coast at the time were almost always short-handed and Moss soon found that supplying men to work at the hospital was low on the Senior Officer's list of priorities. Under the circumstances he had to make do as best he could and, while Cator could usually be talked into providing some aid, his successor was less cooperative.

In 1872, the Esquimalt Hospital cared for a daily average of about ten patients. Edward and one permanent sickbed steward made up the only regular staff. The steward appeared to have plenty to do in spite of the small numbers of men under treatment, and Moss recorded that his own time that year was "completely occupied in the direct supervision of the wards, administration of medicines, care of depot Stores, and the reception and issue of provisions from the Senior Officer's ship, Dockyard, or from local tradesmen." He soon concluded that more assistance would be needed if the hospital were to be adequately staffed.

Rear of Dr. Moss's quarters and officers' sick bay, Royal Naval Hospital, Esquimalt, 1872. British Columbia Archives, No. A-03091.

At first Moss was able to obtain some men from the ships to act as temporary attendants, but he complained that this was unsatisfactory because no sooner had he trained someone for ward duties, than the man would be ordered back to his ship for sea duty. Fortunately, towards the end of the year he was able to make good use of a party of marines from San Juan Island who were temporarily quartered at the hospital while awaiting passage back to England. This helped considerably, as he was able to use them for various menial jobs such as cleaning the wards, hauling water and provisions, and as orderlies to help with a paralyzed patient. However, this was only a temporary expedient, and in his annual report he lobbied for a permanent nurse or attendant, and a cook, basing his appeal to the Director-General on what he claimed were the special circumstances at Esquimalt:

> An establishment with such a small annual number of sick (daily average 10.3) appears to require fewer than three attendants in addition to a cook permanently appointed, but the peculiar circumstances of the Hospital will account for the necessity [of three] – all the buildings are separate, the patients require constant supervision as the boundary fence is easily crossed and numerous 'grog shops' exist in the vicinity. I believe that one permanently appointed attendant or nurse would do all the duty which has been required from the two men constantly lent from the ships, for they are necessarily acquainted with the work and it is not in their interest to support hospital discipline at the risk of losing popularity with their mess mates. Further, in the event of any epidemic contagion existing in the hospital, returning attendants looking after infected cases to the ships would be a step which the Medical Officer could not but oppose. I am therefore of the opinion that the appointment of at least one permanent nurse would not only be an advantage, but an economy. A marine from HMS *Scout* has been continuously employed as gardener in Hospital grounds. A working party of four men come ashore every Thursday to scrub out the wards, verandahs, and the rooms.[6]

Moss's request was granted and in late May of 1873, a husband and wife team of cook and male nurse arrived from England.

As far as feeding the patients was concerned, most of the basics were requisitioned and supplied from the Senior Officer's ship. Food supplies that would stand the voyage out from England were obtained from the ship's Paymaster, but other necessities such as milk, eggs, butter, extra vegetables, mutton, and beer were bought from local suppliers.

In August Edward wrote that he was worried about the cost of carrying out the repairs and renovations to the Men's Wards, for he was acutely aware that the penny-pinching Admiralty clerks kept a close watch on even the smallest expenditures. It is clear from Moss's first Annual Report, that by the end of 1872 there was still quite a bit of work needed to put the hospital on what he termed "an efficient footing." The money he requested to complete the remaining repairs and alterations was granted in April 1873, but the work did not get underway until November due to various bureaucratic impediments compounded by changes of command on the Station. Although Moss fretted over the delay he could do nothing about it.

> At the request of various Senior Officers, and finally of the Commander-in-Chief, I had furnished several statements of defects. The leading requirements in all being the plastering of one of the Men's Wards, the finishing of the repairs of the Officers' as well as my own quarters, the repair of the boat house, and the construction of ventilators for the general as well as the Officers' Wards. There were numerous other smaller items such as moving [the stoves] to a safe distance from the wooden walls in the Officers Ward, the construction of a path from the kitchen to the wards, the cleaning out of two wells. The painting of all the buildings inside and out was also required, and several rooms needed re-papering.
>
> The repairs were begun in November and were still in progress at the close of the year. It was unfortunate that they had not been undertaken sooner, for snow often prevented the men from being present. Frost damaged the plastering work and occasioned the expenditure of fuel to keep the newly plastered rooms warm, and painting and papering done in winter and wet weather is never worth as much as if done in a warm and dry season.
>
> The Commander-in-Chief added several items to the lists of defects furnished by me. The principle of these was the construction of a bathroom with boiler for heating water – patients have previously bathed in a tin bath in the wards. He also sanctioned the construction of porches to my quarters and the Stewards house, and some arrangement to lessen the sound between my rooms and the Officers' Wards.[7]

A year's experience had also shown Moss that ventilating pipes were needed for the water closets to prevent sewer gas from invading the nearby wards, and he made various efforts, not entirely successful, to rectify the situation. Other matters that called for his attention in 1873 were adequate fire protection, the theft of the hospital's small boat and, of course, liquor control, for, in spite of his efforts, it was not always possible to prevent alcohol from being smuggled into the wards. When blocking off the pathway to the nearest public house did not work, he instructed that any parcels destined for the hospital were to be held until picked up by hospital staff. A window was also put in the Nurse and Cook's Quarters, positioned so that (in theory) the comings and goings of patients and friends could be monitored. At the beginning of the year he was concerned when he was ordered to quarter twenty marines from San Juan Island in the empty Infectious Diseases Ward and the Medical Officer's Kitchen. He feared their presence would lead to a slackening of discipline, damage to his newly repaired buildings and more problems with liquor, but, for the most part, these fears proved groundless. As mentioned earlier, during the six months they were at the hospital, the marines turned out to be very useful as extra help at many tasks and also as guards to help isolate the hospital during an outbreak of scarlet fever and enteric fever (dysentery) in the spring.

Deserters from HMS *Scout* stole the hospital's small boat in April 1873 and rowed it twenty or so miles across the Strait of Juan de Fuca to the American village of Port Angeles on the Olympic Peninsula of Washington State. When the boat was located four months later, the new senior officer at Esquimalt, Captain Day, refused to retrieve it, and although it was worth double the amount requested, refused to pay $35 to the man who had found it. However, Moss felt that a small boat at the hospital was essential and went over Day's head to the new Commander-in-Chief, Rear-Admiral Cochrane, who approved the purchase of a new boat that fall. To avoid a repetition of the theft, Moss had a locked boathouse built down at the cove.

Fire was always a concern at the hospital, and Moss noted in his report that there had been several of them close by since his arrival.[8] In September 1873, one broke out on the grounds caused, he believed, by failure to follow his smoking regulations. Fortunately it burned only about twenty yards of fence, but he knew that if a fire ever broke out during a strong wind, the results would likely have been much different. Although there was a reservoir filled with about a thousand cubic feet of water, as well as a hand-pulled fire engine on site, Moss believed his small staff could not put it into operation in time to save a building if it caught fire. Fortunately, the various structures were somewhat separated from one another, making it likely that help could come from the ships in time to save the rest of the buildings.

When word was received in April that the cook and male nurse were coming, Edward obtained approval to go ahead with renovations to the kitchen area in order to create living quarters for them. The building, like the Officers' Ward, was raised and placed on a stone foundation, then a new floor was installed and the interior was partitioned off to provide a bedroom and a sitting room for the couple. When Mr. Roberts, the male nurse, arrived, he was found to be neither as young nor as active as expected, but his wife turned out to be a very good cook who could prepare "the little niceties expected if an officer happened to be in hospital." Edward's interest in having a good hospital cook went beyond keeping fussy officers happy though – it fitted with his overall concern about a proper diet for his patients.

"I am of the opinion" he wrote in his Journal, "that a varied vegetable diet is often of great importance to men long confined to salt and preserved meat or stored vegetables." During that summer, he was given approval to regularly employ the marine who had been acting as the hospital gardener and, with this full time help, was able to carry out his plan to supply the hospital with half of its provisions at the insignificant expense of a soldier's wages. While the local markets had only been able to supply potatoes, carrots, and onions,

he advised the Director-General that because of the garden he could now provide his patients with the full range of green and root vegetables that could be grown locally.

The "General Remarks" section of Dr. Moss's 1874 Medical and Surgical Journal indicates that the last of the alterations and repairs to the buildings were not completed until late in March of that year. By then, experience had shown that the water closets were not sufficiently trapped, so ventilating pipes had been installed, making the WC's completely acceptable, or so he hoped. Getting work parties from the ships to man the wards and for help with other necessary tasks continued to be a problem, causing him to comment that:

> One of the most unpleasant duties devolving on the Surgeon in charge of the Hospital is the constant going aboard the senior officer's ship to ask for working parties to man the wards or store rooms, or to pump the water supply tank from the wells. Since the departure of HMS *Scout* early in 1873 the regular weekly [work] parties have been suspended. The most that I could accomplish has been the obtaining of a single work party for a few hours. I have several times written letters on the subject, but they proved so irksome that Captain Day, senior officer of HMS *Tenedos*, finally told me that we would have no more written communication about working parties. I believe that it will ultimately be necessary to employ Indians to do this work, and I am of the opinion that their wages of $1.00 per day would be less expensive than the pay and cheque money of men from the ships.[9]

This was Edward Moss's last official observation about the Esquimalt Hospital renovations. During his two and one-half years there, he had taken a run-down collection of ramshackle buildings and turned them into an efficient medical facility. Except for some minor alterations, the Esquimalt Naval Hospital remained for the next fifteen or more years very much as Edward left it in January 1875.

It had been a job well done.

9: Esquimalt Hospital

"Do No Harm"

Perhaps the most fundamental principle of medicine since the time of Hippocrates has been that a physician should at least leave the patient no worse than he or she was before receiving treatment. The admonition "above all, do no harm" is still put forth in one form or another to neophyte doctors even if they no longer have to swear the Hippocratic Oath. Indeed, the warning may even be more appropriate today than it was when Edward Moss was practising medicine, given the almost limitless number and range of drugs, technological procedures, alternative remedies, and treatments that are now available.

Most people take modern miracle drugs and computerized wizardry very much for granted, but the practice of medicine as a "science" is a very recent development, and the rapidity of changes in medical theory and practice shows that much remains unknown or imperfectly understood about the human body and the causes or treatment of many illnesses. That said, we have come a long way since Edward Moss's day. Incredible progress has been made in the treatment and cure of diseases and conditions that savagely – and almost routinely – struck down individuals or ravished whole communities until very recently.

In Moss's time, physicians had few sure remedies for most illnesses even when they knew the cause. This reality was a regular source of frustration to a conscientious practitioner. Edward's letters from Portland Sick Quarters at the time of the 1871 smallpox outbreak, and the more detailed case records of the Esquimalt Hospital Journals illustrate how little could actually be done for patients with serious conditions or diseases. Perhaps it would be stretching the point to suggest that benign neglect was as useful as many of the medical treatments in use a hundred and thirty years ago, but it was not far from the truth.

That is not to say that most physicians were passive in their approach to illness, as the medical journals of Edward Moss and Matthew Coates, the two doctors who served at Esquimalt from 1872 to 1878 clearly illustrate.

The Medical Department issued every surgeon with a book of standard regulations as a guide in the prevention and treatment of diseases. This was based on the vast compendium of medical lore accumulated by the department over many decades,[1] and included guidelines for using the hundred-odd medicines issued with the standard medical kit. Conscientious surgeons (and Moss was one) generally subscribed to *The Lancet* to keep abreast of developments and other pertinent issues related to public health and their profession. It is quite clear that both Moss and Coates were conscientious, competent, and proactive in taking care of their patients. The first concern for both men was to make sure the hospital facilities met departmental standards as far as cleanliness, warmth, adequate ventilation, and sewage disposal were concerned. Once these amenities were assured and when adequate and healthy food was made available both believed that the basic conditions for patient recovery or cure were present.

The number of patients treated at the Esquimalt Naval Hospital between 1872 and 1877 was never very high, averaging only between thirty and forty a year. Usually these were the more serious or chronic cases that could not be treated properly aboard ship, particularly when long-term care was necessary. The hospital was also used as a holding facility for patients awaiting passage to England after being judged medically unfit for service by a local medical board. Not listed in the annual report of patients treated, but also entitled to the services of the Medical Officer, were the families of Paymaster Innes and other dockyard personnel, though only as out-patients.

The venereal diseases – primary and secondary syphilis, gonorrhoea, and symptomatic venereal outbreaks (buboes or ulcerated sores) – unfortunately constituted a significant percentage of the cases treated in 1872. Most of these were San Juan Island marines quartered at the hospital awaiting a ship to take them back to England. Matthew Coates treated fewer venereal disease patients, not because the common seamen or marines had suddenly become more careful or less horny, but simply because the marines were gone and there were fewer naval vessels at Esquimalt during his tenure. He reported that VD accounted for about 16 per cent of his patients.

Coates treated more wounds than Moss, and injuries of various kinds made up the second highest category while both men were at Esquimalt. Almost all were injuries suffered at work, with the exception of one attempted murder and some accidental gunshot wounds. Rheumatism, bronchitis, phisitis [TB], pneumonia, and fevers of one sort or another made up the majority of the other cases, although patients with systemic heart disease, scurvy, epilepsy, alcoholism, shingles, and dysentery were also treated. Fewer than five patient deaths were recorded at the hospital between 1872 and 1877.

Patients were usually admitted after referral by one of the ship-borne surgeons, who provided a case statement listing the symptoms, diagnosis, and treatment up to that time.

Upon admission, the patient underwent a second examination and diagnosis before treatment was prescribed. A change in diet was usually the first course of action. Fresh meat and eggs, as well as vegetables and fruit in season, were usually available on shore to supplement the standard naval rations requisitioned from the Senior Officer's ship. If and when treatment was successful the doctor would send the man back to active duty or, in the case of a chronic or incurable condition, he would request a review board made up of himself and one or two other medical officers from ships in the harbour. The board would then decide if the man should be kept at the hospital, returned to his ship, or invalided back to England with the likelihood of discharge or retirement from the service. A sampling of cases from the Moss and Coates Journals will serve to illustrate some of the treatments and medicines used at the hospital during the 1870s.

Benjamin Holland, a thirty-seven-year-old private in the Royal Marine Light Infantry detachment from San Juan, was admitted on October 1, 1872, with a diagnosis of primary syphilis. His complaint illustrated a common maxim of the times: "One night with Venus, and a lifetime with Mercury." Private Holland did not present a very attractive visage to his new doctor, who described him as:

> A very tall emaciated man covered with syphilitic blotches, thin feeble hair, quavering voice, and tottering gait. He had contracted a sore from a San Juan squaw. It appeared nearly a month after connection and was in existence for fourteen days before admission. He had several times suffered from venereal ulcers before, but no accurate description of the form could be obtained. The present sore was a non-indurating sloughing ulcer through the swollen and dark purple prepuce [of the penis]. It was dressed with nitric acid lotions, and the patient put on a full diet with wine and a mixture of gentian and trichloride of iron administered every fourth hour. No improvement occurred in a fortnight, and new ulcers were forming on the already scarred skin. He had taken considerable quantities of iodide of potassium, and I therefore resolved to try the effect of a mild mercurial course; the bichloride [of mercury] was consequently given in 1/8-grain doses three times a day from October 12th. On November 9th all the ulcers were healing, but the mercurial treatment had produced no other indication of its effect and was omitted. On the 25th November the patient caught a slight cold (the ward being unplastered, every wind passed through the chinks in the woodwork of the walls, making the ward very draughty and involving great waste of coal) and though little (unclear) or other constitutional disorder was present the sputum became copious, rusty, and viscid as it would have been in an advanced case of severe pneumonia. The stethoscope detected limited lobular pneumonia of the right middle lobe.
>
> Hot fomentations [poultices] constituted the only treatment directed against the local disease, as its character was undoubtedly syphilitic. The patient was

> still on full diet. Extra wine was ordered and a custard or pudding given at dinner. The pneumonia lasted but ten days and on its resolution ulcers on the penis and skin again opened, and a periostial puffiness appeared on the upper part of the frontal bone. A large pustule on the right hip scabbed and ulcerated, and a similar scab was formed on the (unclear) but did not suppurate. This cicotization [scarring] had occurred in the skin beneath. Iodide of potassium and sarsaparilla were given with cod-liver oil and his diet made as nutritious as possible. The patient accumulated flabby surface fat, but specific fibrous deposits continued to open: the left nostril of the nose became indurated, swollen, and nodulated, an excavated ulcer partly covered with thick 'lupoid' cicatrix. Local applications were equally useless, but the iodide seemed to produce some improvement. On the 28th of December all the ulcers had taken a healing action, but whether the existing lesions could be cured or not, the patient will be of little use to the service as the cure of the syphilis is hardly to be hoped for.[2]

Edward's comment was accurate, for there was no sure cure for syphilis in his day. The use of mercury, generally in combination with other nostrums, usually lessened the severity of the attack, but the fact is that the visible symptoms of the disease were usually self-limiting – treated or not – giving the appearance of a cure. And if a physician did not take care, the treatment could do more harm than good as mercury is highly toxic and dosage needed to be carefully controlled.

Venereal diseases were certainly viewed as a major social problem during the latter half of the nineteenth century. Between 1864 and 1869 the British Parliament enacted public health legislation intended to combat such diseases.[3] These Acts focused on the high rate of infection in the ranks of the Army and Navy. Moss's successor, Staff Surgeon Coates, observed in his first annual report that he could:

> Only account for the intractable character of this malady [gonorrhoea] by the fact of the port being totally unprotected by any Contagious Diseases Act. The women who are frequented by the seamen are chiefly Indian half-castes & Chinese prostitutes. They ply their trade without any hindrance, and hence the disease rages in its most unmitigated form. The advisability of drawing this to the attention of the local legislature is apparent.[4]

In England, the Contagious Diseases Acts were apparently applied only to the six main military and naval districts. These laws were clearly discriminatory for they could force medical examination and treatment upon female prostitutes but not for their male clients. A twenty-year political campaign led by Josephine Butler and other early feminist reformers eventually brought about the repeal of the Acts in 1886, though they lingered on for many years in some of the colonies and other appendages of empire.[5]

Throughout most of the nineteenth century, there was little real help for people who suffered from many of the most serious medical problems. Heart disease is an obvious example. Thirty-one-year-old Robert Lewis, a seaman from HMS *Scout*, was in hospital awaiting passage home when Moss arrived at Esquimalt in 1872. He had already been diagnosed with cardiac disease (aneurysm of the aorta). After his admittance examination, Edward recorded that:

> His symptoms were at first of a vague character, but shortly after he came under my care indications of aortic aneurism [*sic*] appeared, and accounted for the cardiac distress from which he previously suffered.…
>
> Treatment: On 5th June, being satisfied that the symptoms indicated aneurism I commenced a system of modified diet, excluding fluids as much as possible and reducing solids to the lowest scale compatible with health. The patient was kept in bed in a state of perfect rest; instability was allayed by opium, and the heart's action reduced by veratrin [a poisonous compound used as a local irritant for treatment of neuralgia and rheumatism]. The disease, however, evidently advanced and the patient's general health suffered from the constantly increasing pain.
>
> The case passed from my notice when he was discharged to HMS *Scout* on 27th June for passage on the mail steamer about to leave Victoria for San Francisco, having been ordered home via Panama by the Senior Officer Captain Cator. I learnt indirectly that the case proved fatal in Panama, violent haemoptosis [coughing] preceding dissolution.[6]

Today, given the tremendous advances in the treatment of heart disease, Robert Lewis would almost certainly have survived and very likely would have lived for many years. In the latter part of the nineteenth century, however, it was usually just a question of when the Grim Reaper would make his appearance.

Another case of early onset heart disease was twenty-five-year-old William Tapp, who was received from HMS *Repulse* on May 22, 1875, suffering from symptoms of angina. He was immediately put on a half-diet that included eggs, butter, and one-quarter pint of port wine daily. A clear diagnosis of systemic aortic disease was made two weeks later and belladonna was prescribed. However, Tapp continued to experience troublesome heart palpitations and a pulse rate of 120, so digitalis was administered and a full diet prescribed. Three months later he was invalided home when these treatments failed to produce any significant improvement. It was not an encouraging prognosis.

In the late fall of 1872, Edward Moss admitted a young patient from HMS *Cameleon*, which had been at sea somewhere in the North Pacific for almost three months. Moss wrote in his Journal that towards the end of her voyage the provisions "were not only salt, [salt pork or beef] but deficient in quantity." He diagnosed the eighteen-year-old

First-Class Boy Seaman as being in the early stages of scorbutus [scurvy], a condition that was generally believed to have been vanquished from the Navy for many years. After being put on a full diet with extra vegetables and milk, the symptoms diminished rapidly and three weeks later Moss pronounced the young lad cured and fit for duty.[7]

A second case from *Cameleon* also exhibited symptoms of scurvy, presenting in the form of ulcers around the mouth and on the tongue and lips. Deficient diet was again identified as the culprit. The ulcers were cauterized with nitrate of silver, and with a full diet bolstered by extra vegetables and milk, the patient recovered fully after a month of treatment. Four years later Moss would have cause to recall these cases of scorbutus.

In the Prevalent Diseases section of his Medical Remarks for both 1872 and 1873, Edward noted that chronic rheumatism and paralysis appeared to be very common in the Victoria-Esquimalt area. The former was not unreasonably put down to the "extremely damp and variable nature of the winter." He observed that even in the summer great changes in temperature were unavoidable as the shaded roads through the woods were always cold and damp, and he passed the condition off without further comment. However, his interest was aroused by "the curious prevalence" of paralytic diseases along the whole Pacific Coast, and observed that he was making inquiries among the leading medical men of the colony as well as others in California, to see if they had an explanation for the peculiar phenomenon.[8]

A year later he noted that the symptoms came on suddenly and patients usually recovered, though they were not always completely free of the after-effects of the condition. He prescribed quinine and strychnine for the malady and claimed some degree of success with that regime but noted that as far as the cause was concerned "the utmost diversity of opinion prevails. In this colony it is commonly attributed by medical men and lay persons to sexual excesses with Indian women. In California, it is said to spring from the gold excitement. It appears to me to be connected with malaria. Its victims have a malarious appearance, and have not infrequently suffered from ague [a malarial bout of sweating and fever]."[9]

By the end of 1873, Moss's ministrations to female patients at the dockyard, along with anecdotal evidence from his few private female patients, led him to take note of "uterine disorders," which he claimed were more common in the colony than paralysis or rheumatism. He thought menstrual disorders were "most strangely frequent" and, although he did not accept it as the cause, he referred to "the unproven deterioration of the race," a peculiar, almost Darwinian theory that was beginning to gain a certain amount of credibility in English society at the time. In his Journal a year later he returned once more to the subject of female complaints, noting that about a third of his medical practice at Esquimalt was devoted to the fifty or so family members of the dockyard staff. He again claimed that uterine complaints were the most prevalent and conspicuous group of disorders found among the white female inhabitants of the island. It was his opinion that 40 per cent of all married women in the colony and a large percentage of the unmarried ones were subject to uterine disorders of one type or another. "No one whose medical practice has given him a knowledge of the facts can fail to be impressed with the enormous preponderance of disorders of the female generative system." As examples, he presented three cases of women in their mid-forties who had ceased to menstruate before leaving England, but whose periods had resumed sometime after coming to Esquimalt. Two of them had borne children in their late forties and another at age fifty-two. Moss claimed these were only a few of many such cases he had collected, but the cause of the vaguely described female complaints continued to evade him.

> A similar, but I think less prominent predisposition to uterine irritability extends along the whole coast of the Pacific United States. Many local practitioners attribute it to the harder work entailed on women through the scarcity of domestic servants, but a large number of the cases that I have noted occurred in women, who from their station in life, were in the habit of working quite hard before they came to the colony. I have no theory to put forward myself, but I think that the paralysis so common among the male population is not unlikely to owe its prevalence to lasciviousness caused by a like generative activity.[10]

Perhaps a better and more abundant diet played an important role in what Moss referred to as "the rejuvenation of the uterine systems of immigrants who have ceased to be actively female" for we now know that dietary deficiencies can interfere with hormonal balance and thus affect the menstrual cycle.

During the summer of 1875, some months after Edward Moss had left for England, his successor, Matthew Coates, reported that smallpox was prevalent among the island natives and that it had spread as well to the white and Chinese residents of Victoria. Fortunately Esquimalt was spared its ravages. The Navy's practice of obligatory vaccination of servicemen was undoubtedly a factor in preventing an outbreak in the small community. A supply of smallpox vaccine was always available at the hospital and Coates lost no time in inoculating almost all of the village children. As far as other infectious diseases were concerned, aside from a single case of scarlatina [scarlet fever] at nearby Maplebank, then the rented residence of the Honourable Richard Hare, Commander of HMS *Myrmidon*, there were no other cases of infectious diseases reported in 1875.

As might be expected, there were always a few injuries to be treated every year. In 1875, Matthew Coates experienced a minor epidemic of wounds, fractures, contusions, and concussions. Four of the wounds were the result of careless use of firearms. These injuries occurred aboard HMS *Repulse* when a midshipman who had been out bird-hunting came back aboard with a loaded shotgun. As he came on deck he handed the weapon to his servant. Unaware that there was a cartridge in the chamber, the man pulled the trigger – with the result that four men gathered nearby listening to band music were sprayed with #6 bird shot, one receiving twenty-two shot pellets in the region of his shoulder. Three of

the four seamen were sent ashore to be treated by Dr. Coates. Except for the length of their stay in hospital, the treatment was not too dissimilar to that would be given today, except for the use of antibiotics.

Problems related one way or another to the use and abuse of alcohol were the source of quite a few of the medical problems that brought seamen into the hospital. Moss's Journal records that:

> Mr. Peter Murray aged 33 Engineer was received from HMS *Sparrowhawk* on 28th May and was transferred to my charge suffering from the typical delusions of alcoholic mania with tremulous tongue dry and furred, small rapidly fluttering pulse, and the whole body perspiring and trembling with the effects of terror from the dread of instant death. He had no sleep for 48 hours or more & was with difficulty persuaded to take a little beef tea. Opium was given but produced no repose.
>
> On the morning of May 30 he became violent and it became necessary to apply to the Senior Officer for attendants. A strong purgative draught was given with difficulty and a little beef tea given in the evening. Next day his violence greatly increased and being a powerful man he required all the persuasion and much of the force his four attendants could exert. XL 7 grs. Opium having no effect XXV grs. Of Chloral Hydrate were given at bedtime. He slept three hours and on awaking spoke for the first time rationally. The delusions continued all day (June 1) but he lay in bed with only an occasional attempt to rise. On 2nd June having slept a little without medicine, the delusions became less constant and small quantities of beef tea, milk, eggs etc. were taken with avidity. He was also allowed a glass of beer. June 3 almost entirely free from delusion but exceedingly tremulous, nutrients taken freely. 4th – a gentian and ginger mixture prescribed.
>
> 6th – The last trace of delusion occurred late in the evening. He suffers from Bronchitis contracted while in the violent stages of the disease.… He was kept on liberal diet with extra milk, eggs, etc. but without stimulants. The patient continued in a feeble state all July, slight exertion causing faintness and rapid pulse. The cough however improved, after 17th July it only occurred on rising or going to bed and it was further relieved by iodine inhalations. He was discharged to duty on 5th August having recovered his strength and become a "total abstainer."[11]

Unquestionably the most interesting injury case treated at the hospital during the Moss/Coates period arose from an attempted murder aboard HMS *Repulse* on June 5, 1875, shortly after Edward Moss had returned to England. Coates described this case as "highly interesting," a modest statement that held true for more than just the medical aspects of the case, which took ten legal-size pages of his year-end Journal to describe.

Most people have a natural tendency to believe that during the "good old days," which could mean anything from the end of the nineteenth century to a generation ago, individuals and society were more civilized and moral than they are today. Unfortunately, the facts do not always bear out this assumption. During the mid-Victorian era, even in small communities such as Esquimalt or Victoria, the newspapers regularly recorded a surprising number of robberies, assaults, and murders or attempted murders. Public drunkenness was also commonplace.

What was labelled by the local newspaper as "The Case of the Brutalised Bandsman" originated in a smouldering desire for revenge fuelled by liquor; and both parties – John Bell, the hapless victim of the murderous assault, and Charles Brading, the brutalizing attacker – paid a heavy price for their actions.

On July 14, 1875, the *Victoria Daily Colonist* reported that Brading, a Bandsman on HMS *Repulse*, had been indicted for maliciously assaulting Acting Corporal Bell five weeks earlier "with intent to kill." Testimony at the preliminary hearing in Victoria indicated that on the evening of June 5 a group of marines and seamen were enjoying a smoke and chat on deck when the accused came up to Bell, spoke something to him in a low voice, then drew an iron bar from his coat and lashed out to strike twice on Bell's head before being grabbed and restrained by the men around him. At the trial, Corporal James Fountain testified that, following the assault, Brading had been heard to state "By God, I have done my work, I was unjustly reprimanded."

Midshipman Stuart Garde testified that the previous day, when Bell took the roll call at the morning muster, he had reprimanded a Sergeant of Marines for not responding clearly when his name was called. Moments later, when Bell called out Brading's name, the latter replied in a loud an insolent manner. Garde ordered Bell to put Brading on Report, which he did that evening. Paraded before the Officer of the Watch, Brading was discharged with only a reprimand. Nevertheless, the Bandsman felt he had been treated unjustly and the next day, after drinking rum and ale, he appeared on deck about 7:30 p.m. determined to get his revenge. How much he had actually drunk is unclear, for the Officer of the Watch testified that, when Brading was brought before him only a few minutes after the attack, as far as he could see, the Bandsman was not drunk. However, when the man was questioned he had voluntarily admitted that he meant to kill Bell.

This was the gist of the testimony at the preliminary hearing, and as a result Brading was held in custody for trial. During the hearing, the ship's medical officer, Assistant Surgeon William Hoggin, who had attended to the unconscious Bell, testified as to the severity of the wounds and agreed that the twenty-three-inch-long, almost 4 lb. iron bar entered in evidence as the attack weapon was capable of producing the patient's wounds. The surgeon also stated that he had known the prisoner for two years, that as far as he knew his conduct was good and that shortly after June 5th he had examined Brading and considered him to be sane. Other witnesses claimed to be unaware of any ill will between the parties prior to the incident.

The trial took place on July 19 with the Crown prosecutor, A. R. Robertson, seeking conviction for attempted murder (wounding with intent to kill). In rebuttal Mr. McCreight, the defence attorney (and recently the first premier of the fledgling province), claimed that the offence had been carried out while the accused was under the influence of liquor, and that no sanely sober man would have so openly attempted a murder in front of many witnesses. He argued that, rather than attempted murder, only an aggravated assault had taken place. After deliberating for an hour, the jury found Brading guilty of the lesser charge, and the judge sentenced him to four years of penal servitude. John Bell, was still in hospital and unable to testify in person at the trial. He remained there for three and one-half months before he was declared fit enough to return to duty. When the extent of his injury, recorded with great thoroughness in Coates's medical journal, is considered, it was amazing that Bell survived, let alone that he recovered and was able to return to duty.

To sum up, the day-to-day practice of medicine at the hospital was relatively routine during Moss's tenure. He was certainly not overworked and was left free to run his own show with minimal supervision. This suited him very well indeed, and it helped to make the first few years of Edward and Senie's marriage extremely happy and memorable, as Thomasina recalled wistfully in her 1928 letter to Robie Louis Reid.

Edward's next assignment was to prove much more challenging.

Dr. Moss on the hospital pier, Royal Naval Hospital, Esquimalt, 1873. British Columbia Archives, No. H-00105.

10: Vancouver Island

"The Best of Times"

During the wintry days of December 1872, Edward spent many hours crafting his Annual Report to the Admiralty Medical Department. His medical journal was in two parts; the first was a "General Remarks" section, where he described the hospital and the changes he had made since his arrival, and the second was a comprehensive clinical and nosological report classifying and describing the treatment of each patient cared for during the year. As he worked on the report Edward felt pleased with the work he had accomplished during the six months he had been at Esquimalt. It was true that the hospital upgrade was still incomplete, and he was not prepared to pronounce all the work satisfactory, but given the resources at his disposal, it had been a good start. He hoped that his diligence, along with the modest scientific articles he had authored, would continue to mark him as a young man with potential. This was important, because opportunities for advancement were diminishing. Between 1864 and 1879, the numerical strength of the British Navy dropped from 53,000 to 46,000 men. During the last half of the century, the number of naval surgeons alone decreased by almost one third, mainly during the years Moss was in the service.[1] For this reason thoughts about his future career prospects were probably never far from Edward's mind, given the family responsibilities that would soon come with his marriage. Still, it was the immediate rather than the distant future that preoccupied his thoughts at the beginning of 1873. This was apparent late in January when he wrote a brief but chatty reply to a letter and Christmas parcel sent to him by Thomasina's sister, Marie Malone.

> I have just got your letter, and if I don't answer it at once it has no chance I am so busy. With its New Years enclosure it was really welcome, but I thought till I opened it that it was for Senie. Let me in return wish you as happy a New Year as mine, for you may – for all I know – have as good reason to expect one as

I have. You must know that at present I am 'rejoicing in the work of my hands' for the place is beginning to be in good order and to look very nice. I am afraid I am in everyone's black books at home though for I hardly ever write, except to Senie.... The whole duty of reorganizing the establishment has fallen upon me. Letters and returns occupy me every night, and if it were not for a smart little mare I bought I could not see all my patients in a day. Perhaps you have heard that part of the garrison of San Juan [Island] are quartered at the Hospital. I have made them very useful, planting trees, making roads & a garden, and one of them copies in the day, the work I get done at night. In a month I will be nearly idle, and in April (about the 10th) I hope to cross via Olympia through Oregon to San Fran and New York. I will not stay more than a week in N.Y., as it is necessary to get back here as soon as possible. Please give my love to your sisters and brothers. Wishing for the time when I can call you my affectionate brother-in-law, I remain,

Edward L. Moss[2]

Many telegrams and letters must have gone back and forth between Edward and Senie as they tried to make arrangements for their upcoming nuptials. By the middle of February, the place and date for the marriage had been changed to San Francisco in late March, rather than New York in April. An opportunity had arisen for Senie to travel all the way to the West Coast with a family who were coming to America, so marrying in California rather than New York became an obvious and much preferable option. On March 12 Edward boarded the mail packet for San Francisco to await Thomasina's arrival and complete the wedding details. He stayed once again at Lick House and ten days before the wedding sat down at the writing desk to scrawl a note to his mother.

Seine has made arrangements for a crossing and meeting me here. Her letters telling me so, and a telegram saying she would leave about the 17th, [of February] reached me 10 days ago. It is most fortunate that friends of the people with whom she has been staying should be crossing over, for I had very serious fears that in the absence of HMS *Scout*, the expected arrival of the Admiral and of a stores ship would have prevented me getting leave to go to New York – and besides the irregular way the telegraph is carried on in Victoria might have prevented me from arranging any time. Another thing was that any unforeseen delay might have prolonged my absence and lost me the appointment, for the Director-General [of Hospitals and Fleets] is very particular.

However the good sense and resolution of my darling Senie has disposed of all these difficulties. I am hourly expecting a telegram from her, and on receiving it will make arrangements for our marriage. She will probably reach here on the 26th about 8 p.m., will stay either with her friends or with a lady here, the aunt of a patient of mine in Victoria, who kindly offered the use of a very handsome house here. The [British] Consul is very considerate and has given me all sorts of assistance. I think we will probably be married by Dean Mason at Trinity Church on about 5:30 on the 27th or 28th, and will then take our own quarters in the hotel, the best of the [unclear] like hotels in this town, and leave for home by the 5th of April.

I have lots of money, and received a letter saying that £20 was added to my pay just before I left Victoria on the 12th. My house [there] is already furnished and I think compares favourably with any in the colony. I must go now & look after some of my letters of introduction. At any rate I can't write any more as my sleeve is too tight in my armpit.[3]

San Francisco was well known to British naval officers on the Pacific Station during the latter half of the nineteenth century, so it is not surprising that Edward would have been carrying letters of introduction to people there. Included among them was one to William Kip, an old friend of George Hills, the Anglican Bishop of British Columbia, whom he had met in Victoria. In spite of Edward's worries, everything worked out perfectly. Thomasina arrived on schedule and the marriage took place on the March 28 as planned. That evening Edward jotted off a typically droll note to his mother.

Senie and I were married by the Bishop of California at Trinity Church at 3 p.m. today. I really have nothing more to say just now, except that her housekeeping is not at all the thing. She only found out there was salmon for dinner when we were winding up with the ice [cream]. We leave here for our west home on 5th April, and are quite satisfied with ourselves – excepting in particular the above mentioned. All the boxes are about the place but we haven't opened any.

Senie has greatly improved in looks since she left Ireland.[4]

Under the circumstances, even this brief message was surprising as Edward undoubtedly had more pressing matters on his mind.

By midsummer Edward and Senie were becoming an old married couple and their happiness together was evident in a letter home on the 27th of June. The date was an anniversary of sorts, for it was just three days short of a year since Edward had taken over management of the hospital and just three months since his marriage.

Apparently there was some curiosity among family and friends about why the couple had chosen to be married in the Episcopalian Church rather than at a Quaker meeting house. Edward passed the matter off rather casually though, as he pointed out, in their circumstances it would have been quite impossible anyway because of the rigid marriage prerequisites laid down by the Society of Friends. When they returned to Esquimalt the couple joined St. Paul's Anglican Church at the Esquimalt Dockyard. At first glance this also appears surprising given their Quaker family roots. Moreover, Edward was very much a freethinker and it is difficult to imagine him in the role of an Anglican Church warden – a position to which he was soon co-opted. The two of them also began to teach Sunday School. It seems probable that this new-found church involvement arose in part from a desire to introduce Senie into the Esquimalt and Victoria communities, though there was no Quaker church to attend even if they had wanted to do so. This was not an unusual situation for either Quakers or Unitarians, who often found themselves too few in number to form a church or even a worship group, and therefore had to decide between attending a mainstream Protestant congregation or no church at all.

The irony of their situation was not lost on Edward and he could not resist a comment about it before ending his letter home with a typical Victorian comment about women, who were (so he believed) dominated by emotion rather than reason.

> We got your letter yesterday and will not expect to hear of all the work and excitement of Annie's marriage. I hope it won't be too much for you, especially as you are to be 'forsaken' afterwards. I'm sorry Senie and I are not home to keep you company, not on our account, as we could not be better 'located.' I only hope we may continue to be as well off, as it is a splendid place. Senie likes it as well as I do. This evening at 5 o'clock we started off to a place called Beacon Hill beyond Victoria and had a delightful canter on the broad undulating expanse of soft turf under grand old trees. The smooth sea, the cloudless sky, and the snowy mountains glowing salmon colour in the sunset made a picture we won't easily forget.
>
> We have not forgotten your caution to Mrs. Mullen. Perhaps I should say I have not forgotten it, and we therefore act advisedly. You see there is no other means of taking exercise here, driving is simply bumping. After our ride we came in to strawberry tea and here we are sitting at our round table. Senie is working point lace and looking extremely well. I am getting used to my hunting boots (I have greased them on my feet) ready for a hunt tomorrow. We want some venison for next week's dinners. You must know that our house looks uncommon nice, covered with hops and roses. Some of the latter fine firm fellows as big as a cabbage others nearly black. We have done our very best to eat our garden down, but [it] has beaten us hollow. Things grow like magic. I have just had the hay cut (it costs me nothing) and expect to have lots of feed for my horse all the winter. Indeed, I am thinking of buying a second, for my own has doubled in value though I never feed her. We could easily keep a cow but neither of us can milk and I fear the Chinaman would make a hash of it, though he is uncommonly clever at bottle feeding our kid [goat]. It is pleasant to see this

> place looking well as it is all my doing, garden, hops, roses and all. Everyone wonders at the change.
>
> We had a letter from Maria saying that they all liked Annie's choice. Well as far as I can see it would be a very good thing if a number of similar professors [she married palaeontologist Dr. Ramsay Traquair] were safely united to all our cousins, not to mention the few girls you have left. Senie and I are both pleased to hear that our friends approved of our conduct in that matter of the Bishop – you see we could not possibly have got married in a meeting house, as they require a month's warning. We would have given them a week's. There were a few other objections – and besides we didn't like to.
>
> I have written to Willy several times, so that you need not send me more than a dozen more hints. I will write to you again soon. Being married doesn't conduce to letter writing, more especially when your wife always wants you to come to bed (this in confidence). I, however, greatly object to having to leave my letters etc. unfinished and then sit waiting while she finishes her hair.
>
> We take a class each in the Sunday School and teach what seems to us fit. Neither of us has anything to do with the catechism, or other such formularies [*sic*]. They have got a great church warden in me, and I am also on the committee of the Divescium [?] Society – elected without my knowledge. My line will simply be anti-form and anti-priest, free church, and let the poor in. We have heard of the revival amongst [the Society of] Friends but not of its type. We can't see its fruits so we can't judge it, even if we would. I hope it is not like others, a mere matter of feeling, where the majority of the influenced are women or weak men. It seems to me that many people incur a horrible risk of treating feeling, which may be their own, as the unusual effects of the spirit of God.
>
> It is now late so we both unite in love to you dear mother. When you want it, do not on any account hesitate to draw cash from my account at Uncle Moodie's.[5]

This was the last of Edward's 1873 letters that have come to light, but Thomasina wrote to one of her sisters on December 8th, commenting briefly on the quiet winter life at Esquimalt. By then the weather had turned cold and the ground had been snow-covered for two weeks. It was a newsy letter, full of small details about their daily life. She wrote that Edward was trying (with limited success) to teach her to skate, and the horses (they now had two) were restless from being kept in the stable so long. Edward had rescued one of the three kittens being nurtured by "Pop," their cat (it had fallen in the well). She wanted some recipes for hot cakes and puddings, and finally Papa [Malone] was thanked for sending out copies of *The Friend*, the newspaper of the British Quakers. She also reported that Edward, who was responsible for establishing a Naval Reading Room at Esquimalt, had been elected president of the new organization, and as such was expected to deliver the

Black bear shot by Dr. Moss, Vancouver Island, July 1874. University of British Columbia, Special Collections Archives.

Black-tailed buck in velvet, shot by Dr. Moss, Vancouver Island, July 1874. University of British Columbia, Special Collections Archives.

first lecture to the members. He was beside her at the table working on the draft of a talk titled "Ocean Temperature Effects on Marine Life," which was delivered ten days later to a reported audience of almost one hundred people.[6] Taking the lead in creating the Naval Reading Room was a noteworthy civic effort, marking Edward off in the eyes of the local community as a man of science and letters.

By the end of the year, the young couple were well established. Julia Trutch, wife of the Lieutenant-Governor, had become one of Edward's patients and Trutch's brother-in-law, Judge Peter O'Reilly, was among those who welcomed the couple into Victoria's social circle by regularly including them on the guest list at Point Ellis, their home on the Gorge waterway. In spite of the relatively low social status of a naval surgeon (members of the "civil" as opposed to the "military" branch of the Navy were still somewhat down in the military pecking order), both he and Senie would probably have been welcomed into local society in any case. At the social, recreational, and political levels, naval officers were often sought after to participate in private or public events in the community.

All in all, being included in the social life of the upper class on Vancouver Island was very pleasant experience for the young couple, though the main interests of Edward's life were Senie and his daily work at the hospital. When he found the time, he also indulged in his sporting, artistic, or scientific interests. The opportunity to get away from his duties for a few hours or even a day or two was relished, and with only a handful of patients under care, he managed to do some hunting during the summer and early fall of 1874.

In September he spent three days on a bear hunt in the mountains near Sooke, fifteen miles west of Victoria. Two photographs from his first bear hunt in July depicting a fine buck and a large black bear shot on an earlier hunting trip were sent to Robie Louis Reid by Thomasina in 1928. After the September hunt, a colourful letter describing the adventure was sent to Grandfather Richardson back in Ireland. Eventually it became the subject of an article, "Sport in British Columbia," that Edward managed to get published in a London weekly, *The Graphic* during the summer of 1876.

> 29 Sept/74
> Dear Richard,
>
> We heard [by mail] this morning about Grandpa shooting partridge and I resolved to send him an account of my last performance but came to the conclusion that my writing is not very [legible]. I had better send it to you to read to him – here it is.
>
> My Second Bear Hunt
>
> A week's hard rain early in September looked very like the setting in of an early winter and hunters say we are to have it both early and severe this year, 74,

because all the game is fat about the entrails, berries are unusually numerous, and the duck are coming in already. Monday [the] 14th however turned out fine, and counting on the chance of Indian Summer I made preparations and started on my mare to Sooke at 11 p.m. the next morning. Reached Muir's farm at 4 p.m., left 'Miss Flirt' in a very snug stable, and in order to reach Tugwell's hemlock bark post before dusk lost no time getting on the trail. Skupac – the Indian hunter – carried my little packsack containing 1 lb. biscuit, 1/2 lb. ham, 2 oz. preserved milk & a little tea, chocolate, and sugar, as well as a very small axe, a tin can & cup, and a pencil & paper. He also carried his own rifle and blanket – I had my blanket strapped firmly so as not to interfere with my rifle. A belt carrying ammunition completed my outfit.

The first trace of game we saw was the track of a large panther in a swamp two miles beyond Muir's. He had evidently been after the mallards that were quacking in alarm at our intrusion. We did the six miles in fair time, and 'put up' at Tugwell's, but if I ever go there again I will keep to the bush for the fleas gave me no rest. Never till then did I have any idea what they could do!

I was glad to turn out at daylight to get a cup of coffee and take the trail for the hills. Once through the dark thick of the forest that lies between the sea and the hills there was no more trail, and no one who has not seen the west, can form an idea of the roughness and wildness of the land. My object was to push on as far as we could in daylight and then camp by any water we could find. Passed numerous tracks both of deer and bear but our heavily laden tread gave plenty of notice and we saw no live things.

In the afternoon the sky became overcast, and a few drops of rain warned us to be on the lookout for a dry bed before it came down heavily, and about 3 p.m. we camped in the hollow of a huge fallen tree, so large that I could easily stand upright. We scarcely had pulled fern enough for beds when down came the rain in a steady pour. The middle of our tree lay over a small stream, and we set our fire beside the water, on the rocks swept clear by winter torrents, and under the shelter of the tree. The Indian took the axe, and in a few moments came back with an armful of long broad strips of cedar bark, which he placed overlapping each other & resting against either side of the tree, so as to make a splendid wigwam round our fire, and there we sat till dusk & and then got a slight supper ready and did the best we could to converse, but as Skupac knew no English, and I knew no Chinook,[7] we didn't get on very well [but communicating] by signs and rough pictures, as the Indian could draw diagrams helped us out however.

He told me he had shot eight bears and gave excited descriptions, or rather acts, of the various encounters and by the way of making me more comfortable for the morrow, told me that a bear had killed a friend of his close to where we were camped. We discoursed also about wolves, winter hunting, medicinal plants etc., etc., and finally retired to our hollow tree and slept soundly, but when the fire went out & and it began to get cool below 'Fido' came in and lay down beside me. It was quite dark then and still raining, but when I next woke up the tracery of the hemlocks was standing out against the pale light of morning and though the trees still dripped, the rain was gone. A small fire – so as not to warn the game – heated one cup of tea and off we marched regularly on the war trail. A high mountain rose to our N.W. and we agreed to separate and take opposite sides, he to the east and I to the west and meet on the other side in the forenoon. I would have felt that there was some risk in doing this if I had not had experience that the Indian could follow my track wherever I went. These Sooke mountains are risky to the white man, for they hold so much iron the compass is not to be trusted.

Of course we were wet through in 5 minutes, but as long as one keeps going it makes no matter, indeed the wet was rather an advantage for the leaves did not rustle to the tread of the moccasin. It is no use trying to hunt in boots, for they slip on the fallen trees and prevent you feeling your footing. With moccasins a man can keep his eyes on his game, and creep along silently as a cat. Fido is well accustomed to 'still hunting,' so we worked steadily along with the light growing stronger behind us, passing numerous bear tracks a day old and keeping in their line. Much to my surprise, for the country was good and we made no noise, I saw no game till I had got well round my side of the mountain. Then Fido set. I shot a blue grouse, and thinking he would make a good breakfast, I sat down on some rocks commanding a good view with the 'Winchester repeater' within easy reach and commenced plucking my bird. I was about 1/2 mile NW of the top of the mountain, and could see mile upon mile of rock and forest, stretching ridge beyond ridge away to both North and West. The bird was about half done when I saw a movement in the bushes on a ridge 150 yards on my right. Out trotted a fine large bear, exposing his whole left side. I wasn't long changing the grouse for the rifle, and fired for behind his shoulder. Before the round had time to reach him he started. I bounded off down the rocks into a ravine full of tangled timber that lay between us and the eastward. He was too active to be badly wounded, so active indeed that though several times I saw the dark mass bounding along, I could not cover him with my rifle.

I didn't half like the idea of facing a wounded bear in such a dense thicket, but if I wanted him there was nothing else for it, so I ran down to get into the narrow part of the gully before he did. Fido didn't see the bear and thinking that a deer was in the question was very anxious to be off. When we got well down in the ravine however, and he heard the bear crunching towards us through the fallen trees he changed his mind and fidgeted a few yards ahead. I had a moment or two to get my breath and chose a steady standing place, when Fido howled and backed to my feet, and Bruin followed him with a roar and a rush. The dog seeing me stand, jumped to the right and made a show of attack. The bear at once struck at him and in doing so exposed his right shoulder, and I put the third bullet in close behind the blade. He fell over but staggered to his feet whenever the dog or I came near him. At last he was unable to rise and I gave him the 'coup de Gras' [*sic*] with the hunting knife.

As I stood over him wondering if Skupac would find me I heard a distant shot, and then another, and felt confident he must have heard my four shots, but knew he would not fire merely to answer me. Thinking a few sign posts desirable I went to the highest point nearby and piled three sticks, with the longest pointing down my way, then set to work and skinned as much of him as I could reach, for he was too heavy for me to move. Skupac appeared about 10 a.m. carrying the haunch, skin, and head of a splendid fat buck. So our larder was comfortably stocked, though now that we had the bear we did not want more than a day's provisions, for there was no use hunting anymore as it would give us all we could do to carry the bear's head paws and skin together with our traps [gear] out of the mountains.

When we had finished the skinning the Indian cut the carcass up and hung the pieces on trees in the shade, so that his messengers would get them in good order. He also stowed away the gallbladder, as Chinamen give from 3 to 5 dollars for it to use as medicine. Then we started off for our camp making many a halt beside bushes like magnified brackens with the true wild flavour, and much more palatable than the 'salal.' A few berries of the *Berberis repens* or 'Oregon Grape' quenched our thirst till we got breakfast ready.

Stewed grouse, boiled venison, & a can of chocolate made a respectable meal to which we both did justice, leaving Fido the remains of the deer's head from which I had cut the forehead & horns.

Reading the description it does not seem very hard work packing in a bear's skin and a bit of venison, but the ground was everywhere covered with fallen timber, and was a perfect labyrinth of rocks and ravines. I forgot to say that every one of my shots had gone through the bear, first through his stomach just six inches to right (side view) of his heart. Second through heart, liver, and haunch, and third through the lungs between the heart and spine. Skupac had also seen a bear, but did not get a shot until he was some way off – 'sia' – and missed him, 'pootsepie.' My impression is that he would have been better pleased if I had been unlucky too.

Well, to make a long story short, we were too tired to leave our camp that day, so we fed and slept in preparation for the morrow, and on Friday at daylight started to Tugwell's ranch, reached Muir's that night, was very hospitably

> entertained, and saddling my mare at 10 the next morning got home about 4 p.m., leaving Skupac to bring the trophies round by canoe.[8]

Edward had obviously enjoyed his very successful hunt in spite of the rain and the agonies of fleas at Tugwell's crude cabin. His comments about the Indian guide taking the gallbladder of the bear suggests that this traditional Chinese medicinal remedy must have been in considerable demand in Victoria, for the price of three to five dollars was at least double the daily wage – a not inconsiderable sum at the time.

Moss's occasional exploration and hunting trips were a pleasant break from his daily routine. Although the number of patients in the hospital at any one time was small, various administrative tasks filled much of his time – replies to letters (called 'returns') to write, staff to supervise, food and other supplies to order – and always a plethora of records to maintain and send to the bureaucrats of the Medical Department.

Getting away once in a while to hunt, fish, or sketch may have been important for Edward's well-being, but undoubtedly the most pleasurable event in his and Senie's life during 1874 was the birth, on August 22, of their first child, christened Ada Dugdale Moss. After the birth the bemused father immediately sent a reassuring note to his mother:

> Senie was safely confined at 2:30 p.m. today. She had the best of health all along – was taken ill at one o'clock last night. We sent for nurse, a very nice home trained woman. Things progressed steadily and at six I sent for Dr. Helmcken.[9] The later stages were a little more difficult but not unduly so. [Your] little granddaughter is a fine fat little thing. The first thing that Senie said was 'Oh, I'm so glad it isn't red like most babies.' Everything is going on furiously, I haven't a minute to spare. I have written to Grandpapa and Mrs. Malone.[10]

A week later he wrote in a similar vein to his sister-in-law, Maria Malone.

> Senie and baby are doing very well but I don't mean to let Senie come downstairs for a good while. Plenty of rest is seldom thrown away. Nurse is a nice motherly woman and makes herself useful in the house and the Chinaman [their servant] is perfectly enthusiastic about the affair, he cooks up the nicest little surprises for Senie. We had all the world calling to enquire after the 'family.' Some people brought Senie grapes, greengages, etc. and I am like to be laid up as a consequence. The little lady is a very respectable looking child, fairly plump with a good head of yellow hair – of course you want a close description. Well, she is remarkably like – especially in her chin eyes nose etc. – humanity in general.[11]

As usual, Edward had been unable to resist a droll one-liner to end his brief letter. His earlier reference to the lengthy "lying in" period deemed essential for the mid-Victorian mother illustrates the profound change in medical practice over the years. Today we know it is best for a new mother to be up and around as soon as possible, but Moss's comments reflected the conventional medical wisdom and child-birthing practices of his day and for almost a century thereafter. With Ada's arrival, life for the couple entered a new phase and, as 1874 began to draw towards a close, they began to think about the next summer when they would almost certainly be returning home.

Firm plans were of course impossible to make until Edward received notice of his next appointment, something that would probably not occur until the long leave he would be entitled to after his stint at Esquimalt. One option available to him was to go on the inactive list at half pay for a period of time. Prior to the middle of the nineteenth century, going on half pay was generally considered a form of pension for officers, but by the 1870s it was more commonly used as a means of filling a short gap in an officer's career.

Sometimes the option was used if there were no prospects for an immediate posting thought to be suitable to an officer's rank or experience. At other times it was taken voluntarily for personal reasons of one kind or another. Edward brought up the subject of their return in a letter to his mother in November as he mused about the possibility of Senie sharing a house with his mother and sisters.

Dear Mother,

You ask me to let you know about taking a house to hold you and Richard. All I can say is that I will probably want part of a house for Senie when we come home, for I am almost certain to be ordered into either a temporary home or a foreign appointment. She is not of a very quarrelsome nature, and may even get along well in the same house as her mother-in-law. Perhaps a big house somewhere on the north side [of Dublin] might suit. For my part, I will always be unable to speak with certainty as long as I am in the Navy, which will probably be 9½ more years.

We are likely to get home about September next – possibly earlier. I must then leave Senie and Ada with you and rush to London to report myself, then if I can't get leave I will try for a little half-pay to work up some of the things brought home from here (I mean sea beasts etc.) We will not be in want of cash as we have nearly £500 here and we are adding to the deposit. As I told you many times you may do what you want with the cash.... If I happen to want it afterwards it will be my own fault.

There is one thing quite certain & that is we will never hold a naval appointment as good as this one. Senie is a good deal tied [down] now [with Ada], and if I had thought about it in time it would have been a good plan *for us* to have

> asked one of the girls to come out and make herself useful. If I knew I was going to stay here for another two years (which is out of the question) I would get one of them to come out, the passage is nothing to a lady travelling by herself, lots of people have come out so.
>
> Senie and I went to skate this afternoon but the ice was thawing & so we had to content ourselves by shooting quail. I sent off an elaborate article for the [Navy] Blue Book today – all about non-nitrogenous diet.
>
> This morning a farmer was here asking me to go down to his place 30 miles off as a gang of wolves had killed two heifers. I would like it well enough but can't get away just now. We have deer, teal, grouse, quail & duck from the shooting in our larder. Ada is getting on famously. She is asleep in her cradle on the other side of our open fire. Senie is quite strong and well.[12]

With the onset of winter, there were many such enjoyable evenings in front of the warm hearth of their hospital home. The happy couple had no inkling that a momentous decision would soon be forced upon them as a result of events that had recently taken place in England, and continued to expect that Edward would almost certainly be ordered back to sea for three or four years and that Senie and Ada would stay in Ireland.

If that turned out to be the case, Edward favoured sharing a big house with his mother and his sisters upon their return – a idea that Senie was probably less enthusiastic about. Being the daughter-in-law in a house managed (or ruled) by Edward's strong-willed mother may not have been a situation she would have found particularly appealing.

Only two letters from December 1874 are in the family collection, but both are important. The first, started by Thomasina to her mother-in-law on December 13, began by describing an idyllic scene of Victorian domestic bliss. Edward was pictured at the table sketching, while Ada was fast asleep in her cradle by the fireplace. Senie wrote her mother-in-law that the past three years [since Edward's proposal] had passed "like a dream" and that she expected they probably would be coming home in the spring. The letter was then interrupted and set aside for week while the couple anxiously tried to come to terms with an unexpected and dramatically changed situation.

On or about the 14th of December, Edward was dumbfounded to receive from the Director-General of the Medical Branch the incredible offer of a position with the new Arctic Expedition that had been approved only a month earlier by Prime Minister Disraeli. This would be the first such British polar initiative since the days of Captain Sir Edward Belcher's unsuccessful search for the missing Franklin expedition over twenty years earlier, and the first attempt to reach the Pole since the days of Parry a half-century earlier. In the midst of the excitement and serious soul-searching this offer created, Senie did not finish her letter to Teresa Moss for a week. Two days after the telegram was received, Edward wired back his refusal to volunteer. The day after receiving the offer, Edward attempted to explain his decision to his mother:

I have today taken a very important step. I have declined the best appointment for me in the Navy – an appointment eagerly sought after by half my brother officers – carrying with it double pay & certain promotion, but necessitating complete separation without even correspondence for two years, perhaps more. Yesterday evening I got the following telegram:

"The Director General to Surgeon Moss.
Do you feel disposed to volunteer for the forthcoming Arctic Expedition? If so I will nominate you there will be double pay reply by telegraph."

I need not say neither of us slept much last night. Rapid advancement of every sort and the probability of never having *another* separation were great temptations, but two years or more of uncertainty was more than we could face, though Senie would not give in.

And today I telegraphed:

"Surgeon Moss to Director-General. I regret that I am unable to volunteer. I forward reasons by post~"

Well I think that if we had been at home I would have taken it. I would have gone if it had been an order, but it would be simply unfair to Senie to voluntarily take such a post without consulting any of you or even knowing exactly what I was volunteering for. Well it is done now. I can never expect anything good from the Director-General after declining an offer, which as far as I know, is unprecedented in the service. I expect to be superseded from this place in a few months and am certain to be sent abroad for 3½ years, but then we can [at least] hear how each other is getting on. Please write at once and tell me what you all think for we are distracted with opposite views. I think that it is just possible that a more forcible telegram may come, & if so I will answer yes, go home, and if things are unfavourable get out of it as best I can even if I have to leave the Service. Under any circumstances you can expect to hear from us by mid- summer.[13]

When Thomasina completed her own letter a few days later, she made it clear to Teresa that she disagreed with her husband's decision, observing that the Governor [Lieutenant-Governor Trutch] and "a great many people" believed he should not have rejected the offer. She expressed a fervent hope that the refusal would not adversely affect his future career.[14]

That, however, was not the end of the matter. Either as a result of Edward's follow-up letter to the Director-General, or from information from some other source (perhaps his superior officer at Esquimalt), word got back to England that he would join the expedition if he was ordered to do so. The reaction was swift. On January 13, 1875, the Director-General requested that orders be issued for Moss's return to England, "his services being required for the Arctic Expedition."[15] Three days later the Senior Officer at Esquimalt, Commander Richard Hare, received a simple and unambiguous telegram: "Send Surgeon Moss and family to England forthwith, by order of [Admiral] Lord Gilford."

Evidently his superiors in England believed that Moss had attributes and capabilities that made him a prime candidate for the coming expedition. They wanted him on board for this great national initiative – and Edward wanted very much to be a part of it in spite of his understandable reluctance to leave Senie and Ada.

Two years earlier he had written to his mother that he had "wasted considerable opportunities." Deep in his heart he knew that he could not pass up the once-in-a-lifetime opportunity that was now being offered to him.

11: England

"The Arctic Expedition"

Twelve days after receiving the order to join the Arctic Expedition, Edward and Senie, with five-month-old Ada swaddled in her mother's arms, boarded the steamer to San Francisco, and then travelled by train to New York, where they took a ship to Queenstown, Ireland, arriving there on February 21.

Edward enjoyed several weeks of leave in Dublin before leaving Senie and Ada to report for duty at Portsmouth Dockyard on April 15, 1875, for the commissioning of HMS *Alert*, then being refitted for her polar mission. A Dundee whaler, purchased by the Navy and renamed HMS *Discovery*, was also being prepared for Arctic service. Work on the two ships had been underway for months amidst the "Polar Fever" that had gripped the imagination of the nation since the announcement of the venture. The extent of public and government enthusiasm for the project was astonishing, considering that disinterest or downright disapproval had met earlier proposals for another Arctic Expedition.

Public discussion on the subject had begun in earnest ten years earlier when Rear-Admiral Sherard Osborn and Clements Markham (Honorary Secretary of the Royal Geographic Society), supported by several other "Old Arctics," began to speak out strongly in favour of a new polar attempt.[1] The two men, who had served together on the 1850–51 search for the ill-fated Franklin expedition, pursued their mission with vigour and determination at every opportunity.

In spite of a distinct lack of support from the Admiralty and the government, and in the face of ridicule from *The Times*, Markham and Osborn, supported by other prominent men in the RGS and the Royal Society, persevered with their campaign until the early 1870s, when public attitudes began to change in their favour. For this there were a number of reasons. Among them was the entry of rival countries into the polar game – the Swedes, the Austrians, and most importantly, the Americans. Was mighty Britain, mistress of the world's oceans, prepared to allow others to best her Britannic Majesty in the polar sweepstakes? Surely not!

Benjamin Disraeli, the shrewd and opportunistic leader of the Conservative Party, echoing John Ruskin's earlier summons to the Empire, correctly gauged the changing public mood in a famous speech at the Crystal Palace in the summer of 1872. At that time, he put forth a passionate imperialistic appeal; Britons had to choose between being citizens of a comfortable, insular, and ordinary country or being an empire whose sons commanded the respect of the world. Half-measures in the search for fame and glory were not enough, he declaimed. Were not the Americans already in the Arctic while Britain remained a mere observer on the sidelines of history? Disraeli was, of course, referring to the 1871 American expedition led by Charles Francis Hall.[2] After learning of the amazing survival of nineteen of Hall's people adrift for many months on a polar ice floe following their leader's mysterious death and the later loss of his ship *Polaris*, British interest in the Arctic was suddenly aroused. This was immediately followed by the discovery of the rest of Hall's party, who were safely brought to Dundee, Scotland, in the early fall of 1873. Almost overnight these events captivated the public imagination to an extent that was almost unbelievable.

A year earlier, the highly respected Clements Markham had published a popular book, "*To the Threshold of the Unknown*," setting forth his view that much had changed since Franklin's day. Scurvy was (so he claimed) no longer to be feared, having become so rare that few naval surgeons had even seen or treated it. He argued that given better ships, better equipment, and hand-picked volunteers, another polar expedition could be carried out safely and successfully. However, Markham also suggested that, while the Pole remained the ultimate goal, the major emphasis of the expedition should be scientific, claiming that the potential gains in geographic and other scientific knowledge far outweighed any risks associated with such an enterprise. Disraeli, after returning to office in 1874, quickly pledged support for such an expedition, formally sanctioning the project in November 1874. Thereafter the Admiralty moved with unusual dispatch to make the revived polar dream a reality, for time was of the essence if the expedition was to get to the Pole, or at least as far north as possible, during the short Arctic summer of the coming year.

In December it was decreed that while the main purpose of the expedition would be a polar attempt, there would also be exploration of parts of northern Greenland and Ellesmere Island. Other scientific work would of be carried out as well, but in the public mind this was viewed as much less important than the goal of "attaining the highest Northern latitude and, if possible, to reach the North Pole."[3]

By the time Edward Moss arrived at Portsmouth in April, almost all of the planning and other preparatory work had already been completed. He had been assigned to *Alert* to serve under Fleet Surgeon Thomas Colan and the expedition leader, Captain George Nares, who was both an experienced Arctic officer and respected leader.[4] While there was no real polar fire in Nares' belly as had been the case with Charles Hall, Nares was considered to be the best naval officer to lead the expedition and would have the assistance of a true zealot, Lieutenant Albert Hastings Markham,[5] a distant cousin of Clements Markham, as his second-in-command.

On the medical side, only a year earlier, Dr. Colan had been the recipient of the Wilber Blane Medal, the highest honour that could be given to a British Medical Officer. A third Medical Officer, destined also to receive the Blane Award some years later was William Coppinger, who was posted to *Discovery*, where Coppinger would be junior to Staff Surgeon Belgrave Ninnis. Edward Moss would be travelling to the Arctic in good company and with the main expedition group.

HMS *Alert* was a 1,045-ton, 430-horsepower, copper-clad screw sloop built in 1856. For the polar adventure she was being completely refitted to carry a crew of sixty-two hand-picked officers and men and all their supplies. This was less than half of her usual complement, and therefore she was being manned by men who were deemed capable of carrying out many different tasks if called upon to do so. Because a great deal of extra space was also needed for every sort of equipment and the huge store of provisions needed for two – or possibly even three – years in the High Arctic, the regular armament was removed, and many changes were made to fit out the ship for maximum comfort and utility.

Moss, like the other officers, was given the freedom to plan and furnish his own private quarters but it is unlikely that he was consulted, let alone included, in many other discussions or decisions. If any of his superiors asked for his views on medical matters (such as how to avoid scurvy), it would probably have been more out of courtesy to a colleague than anything else, for Fleet Surgeon Colan bore the main medical responsibilities aboard the *Alert*.

Edward's medical qualifications were really not the main reason he was offered a position on the expedition in the first place, though, of course, he was known to be a competent physician and would not have been chosen if there was any doubt about that. However, the expedition leaders were also looking for physicians with decent qualifications in the field of science as well as medicine, for it was anticipated that naval personnel rather than civilians would do the scientific work.

When Sir Alexander Armstrong, the Director-General of the Medical Department, asked his staff if there were any medical officers due for leave who appeared to fit the bill (that is, having appropriate medical and scientific credentials), Edward's name was the first of the three that were submitted to him. Armstrong was advised that Moss had "the reputation of being a fair naturalist" who was credited with "natural history and scientific accomplishments," having published articles in the Blue Book, *The Lancet*, and the *Proceedings of the Zoological Society of London*.

In fact, according to *The Lancet*, he had been chosen specifically because of his work in the fields of marine botany and zoology.[6] Soon, however, pressure from the scientific community to have "professional" naturalists attached to each of the two ships for the main botanical and zoological work changed the game. Edward must have found this decision, which he was unaware of until after his return to England, very disappointing for it obviously relegated him to a diminished scientific role. Perhaps it was one of the reasons why, when the opportunity presented itself, he volunteered to command one of the sledge crews assigned to support the main polar parties.

Aside from any other qualifications, successful applicants for positions on the expedition were supposed to be between ages twenty-four and thirty, of sound moral character, very good physical and emotional health, temperate habits, and clean service records as suggested by past and recent evaluations. In practice, the age qualification was not strictly adhered to because of the need for experienced officers, and it is also seems evident that family connections and influence helped some young officers gain a berth on the expedition.

It was claimed that there were almost five thousand applications for the 130 or so positions to be filled. If so, it is no wonder Moss felt that he had received an unprecedented offer in December. He had certainly been around long enough to realize that many other medical officers would have gladly volunteered for this great adventure and once-in-a-lifetime opportunity. This must have made his initial decision to reject the request particularly agonizing, torn as he was between family obligations, which he took very seriously, and his own desire to seize the day, for if the expedition was successful, significant honours and promotion might be expected to accrue to the participants during the rest of their career.

In a letter to his mother shortly after his arrival at Portsmouth, Edward set forth his feelings about the expedition very explicitly as he sought to assuage her worries for her first-born.

> Southsea, May 2, 1875
> Dear Mother,
>
> There is no more occasion to be downhearted now than at any time since I left home [in 1864]. Might I not have been ordered to China and dysentery – West Coast and fever, or many another nameless and honourless danger – instead of voluntarily going with the picked men of our nation on a short service full of every interest? I enclose a note of Captain Nares' lecture – his intent was to disabuse the public mind of the idea that we are going on a mere holiday trip, so he puts the worst of it to his audience.
>
> I would not exchange [it] for any other appointment and double the pay, and but for hastening away from Senie, I am impatient to be at work. Everyone on the *Alert* is of one mind. I think we have the prospect of working well together and 'with God's help we will do our best.'
>
> Senie said to me yesterday, 'what would you do if you were just starting on an ordinary commission for four years?' Danger or no danger, I think Senie would want me to do my duty and I believe you would too.[7]

He could not have responded to his mother's concerns in a more eloquent fashion.

In an earlier letter, written from the Arctic Office at Portsmouth, he described the lodgings that he had chosen at Southsea, and told his mother something about his daily routine:

> I have no doubt Senie has given you whatever news I sent her. She will be over here I hope before Saturday. I have seen almost all the lodgings in Southsea and have I think settled on Bramberly House, Shaftesbury Road. I will there have drawing room floor, bedroom, dressing & sitting room with second bedroom upstairs for 35 shillings per week. I wanted to have the first floor but can't get it. The house looks clean, landlady very much so, & she assures me on the risk of immediate departure that there are no [unclear – fleas, rats?] in the house.
>
> At present I get home from the dockyard at about 4.30 every evening but I have to be in at 9 a.m. or soon after. There is a lot of delay about drawing my back pay. I expect to get it however in a day or so. Meantime I have about 17 shillings to go on with. I will go on board the *Duke of Wellington* about it tomorrow. This to me is the most stupid place to get through one's evenings. My books are all packed up. I get tired of walking in the dockyard. I am invited to dine with Dr. Fashen on Thursday evening, but every other evening I must do the best I can. Today I have written to Dr. Trevan and Mrs. Patrick – of course I visit the *Alert* every day and see how my cabin is getting on, it will be as comfortable as possible I think. They do anything we ask for, so our fittings are according to our own designs. Mine will have [clothes] presses arranged along the side next to the ship's side.… My bed place is fixed & made (like the presses) of mahogany. There are four large drawers underneath. I intend to double felt the floor. There will be no bare ironwork in the ship; all is to be covered with leather. The number of people that come to see the ship is perfectly surprising. Pictures of Captain Nares (I enclose one) are selling in the shop windows. Arctic maps are displayed in others etc. A large room in the dockyard has been fitted up to display the Arctic equipment, a tent is pitched with sleeping bags etc. in place. The sledges are models of strength and lightness. I hope Richard will be able to come over. Bye-the-bye, Senie must have to draw your [house] rent to the Provincial bank. She had better draw [money] for herself too.[8]

Throughout the late spring, preparations moved forward on schedule and, as the departure date drew near, public enthusiasm surged towards an apex of national pride. Numerous social events, glowingly reported in the press, honoured the expedition leaders and their crews as the departure date approached. Finally, late in May, Captain Nares received his sailing orders and on the 29th Edward, Prince of Wales, read a "Godspeed, safe journey" telegram from Her Imperial Majesty. Then, in the presence of a throng of dignitaries,

family members, and hundreds of well-wishers, *Alert* and *Discovery* moved slowly away from their jetties.

It was a glorious Britannic sight: an army band playing "Auld Lang Syne" amidst deafening cheers from men in the rigging of nearby ships as well as from the dozens of small craft surrounding the vessels and from the people lining the shore. Pierre Berton, in *The Arctic Grail: The Quest for the North West Passage and the North Pole, 1818–1909*, cites an excessively chauvinistic commentary by a reporter from the *London Telegraph* that undoubtedly captured the essence of the occasion:

> As we lose sight of the good ships and crews to whose dispatch so many hopes, so much sympathy, and such careful preparation have gone, who is not conscious that the mere fact of their departure amidst such testimonies of pride and enthusiasm does England great good? The feelings that were uttered in those ringing, repeated hearty cheers along the Southsea shore and out into the dancing waves, are shared by all over the country and no man needs to know them personally to call them 'friends.' Friends they are to every household.…
>
> The Admiralty could have filled twenty Arctic ships with volunteers … for the island realm is still rich in the old valorous breed, so little is it true that wealth and peace have corrupted English blood.… The Government … has rightly interpreted the desire of the people not to see another flag other than that of England anticipate us in the crowning feat of maritime discovery.… England is not too rich to be bold, too cynical to be pious, too genteel to believe in honour and glory and the sweetness of self devotion. The England that History knows about … was down along the Channel shores on Saturday … watching her mariners set sail to plant the Jack on top of the globe, if manhood and love of duty can find a way thither.[9]

Of manhood and love of duty there was no lack among the men who were aboard the departing ships. The question was whether these qualities would be enough for them to prevail and achieve the great polar prize where others, no less brave and committed, had failed before them.

12: Greenland

"To the Shores of the Polar Sea"

At 4 p.m. on the afternoon of May 29, 1875, *Alert* and *Discovery* steamed slowly out from Portsmouth harbour to begin their journey.[1] They were accompanied by the steam frigate *Valorous*, packed with supplies and coal to "top up" their bunkers when they reached Greenland. All three vessels were loaded to the gunwales, provisioned for an expedition that might last as long as three years.

The expedition's godfather and mentor, Clements Markham, Honorary Secretary of the Royal Geographical Society, was a welcome guest aboard *Alert*. Unable to resist another opportunity to revisit his beloved Arctic, he was prepared to put up with makeshift quarters in a storeroom containing his hammock, Christmas supplies, and precious little else. Markham, very much in his element, was described by one officer as a veritable travelling encyclopedia of the north.

The voyage to Greenland was exceedingly rough, with whaleboats and other gear on the decks of both ships smashed during recurrent gales that tested the mettle of the men and their vessels. As a consequence, it was early July before *Alert* and *Discovery* reached Disko, at about 70° N, roughly halfway up the southwestern shore of Greenland. At the small village of Lievely, the two ships picked up sled dogs (30 for *Alert* and 25 for *Discovery*) along with two experienced Greenland Eskimo dog handlers who had served on earlier expeditions – Nels Petersen, and forty-one-year-old Hans Hendrick – who had served most recently with Charles Francis Hall.[2] Then it was on to Upernavik, where they were to take on coal and bid farewell to Clements Markham and the *Valorous*. A few days earlier, when Edward wrote to his mother, he expressed his pleasure at "the grand panorama" that greeted them as they worked their way along the Greenland coast.

HMS *Alert*, Ritenbank, North Greenland
6th July 75

My Dear Mother,

I have just finished Senie's letter and she will give you the greater part of the news. We got to Disko on the 6th after a very stormy passage but there our ill luck seemed to stop, for we have had nothing but splendid summer weather and good news since. The *Valorous* takes this home, my next will be from Opernivik, then from the Carey islands in Smith's Sound. The Opernivik letter is certain to get home all right but I don't know about the other unless the *Pandora*[3] or a whaler calls there. We are all in perfect health and spirits – we had no sickness, except of course a little seasickness on the way out. We have all of our sheep still alive, and today Captain Markham and I came back with 70 coots (a kind of duck). It is too warm to wear anything but light English clothes; it is in fact the warmest summer that people here recollect. As I write hundreds of icebergs are in sight but the air is mild & pleasant and our all-day long sunlight delightful to those who want to scribble a line to the dear ones they have left at home. Our letter bag is swelling to formidable dimensions, [Lieut.] Pullen[4] alone has written 50 letters. I, on the contrary have written but one, & that is to my wife. I hope she is as well off as I am. She is better in one respect – she will get more letters – but then she has not the daily excitement of seeing such sights as having been passing in a grand panorama before our eyes for the past fortnight. Over and over again I have heard people amongst us say 'well it is worth coming all this way to see that.'

This morning we saw a huge ice-berg (we were close to it in a boat) surge backwards, forwards and back, & then roll over in sparkling sapphire and emerald. We were then on our way to some cliffs where the 'loons'[5] live. Such cliffs I have never seen before, straight up from the water thousands of feet. The conical mountains where the fossils are found (a sketch of it is in the [Royal] Dublin Society with the fossils) is in sight away on the right of the Wygatt.[6] We will probably call there tomorrow but we do not consider our scientific work commences till we get into Smith's Sound. We have not an inch of room to put specimens in, until we eat into our apparently limitless supply of food.

As I don't know where you are living now, I will send this to St. James Mall. If Senie does not telegraph to me when we come back I will have to go to St. James or do a 'Gilbert à Beckett'[7] through the streets of Dublin. You must not criticize this note too severely for I am writing in haste before our bag closes – It has to be closed 12 hours sooner than we expected, and besides I am not very fresh after shooting all day in a good strong sun and pulling my share of

25 miles. We are nearly all writing. [Lieut.] Egerton is blowing some eggs we got today. There are three bottles of Champs and a lot of glasses in front of me, for we are going to wish Mr. Clements Markham a fair voyage home. He leaves us to go to the *Valorous* in about 1/2 hour. He has been a most pleasant and instructive companion to us & we all regret the necessity of his leaving us.

I have just packed up & addressed a sketch of a rare sea beast to Mr. Gwyn Jeffrey who is aboard the *Valorous*. He is a very senior FRS [Fellow of the Royal Society] and I fancy he has not had many chances of doing the scientific work he expected on board, & he will have fewer on the way home for she has to go straight [back] as we have taken all her provisions. Time is up, so good bye Mother, for a short time.

Love to Richard and all the girls.[8]

A more comprehensive letter written to Thomasina four days after leaving Upernavik and taken to England by a southbound whaler later in the season included a vivid description of the sights and daily adventures as *Alert* steamed north through Baffin Bay. By the 26th, they had navigated through the massive "middle pack" and were at the Carey Islands just south of Smith Sound. It had been tricky navigating through the always dangerous and unpredictable pack ice and Captain Nares had to call upon all of his expertise to come through safely and in such a short time. Not that Edward was worried about the middle pack; he was obviously having the time of his life and was earning the respect and confidence of Captain Nares and Commander Albert Hastings Markham during hunting or exploration sorties with them.

HMS *Alert*, July 26,
off Petrovik glacier north of the crimson cliffs
My Darling Wife,

We will probably reach the Carey Islands this evening and, as we will only stay to land a [supply] depot and our letters, I will write a little to you before commencing my day's zoological work. For the last three [days] I have worked away continuously and made a lot of sketches of [sea] beasts – so an hour's conversation with you will be a pleasant rest.

What a lot I have to tell you. The long 24-hour days here have been full of events since we left Opernivik on Thursday night 22nd. We steamed inshore among the islands under splendid towering cliffs but at night a fog came on & on Friday morning we ran on shore very gently. We improved the occasion by going on to the island and shooting some ducks and gathering Eider Duck eggs (loon and duck eggs are delicious – we have them fried & in omelettes at almost every meal). We soon heard a gun to tell us to come back and we found the tide had lifted us safely off. Then we steamed away NW, hourly expecting to see the pack ice of the dreaded Melville Bay. Captain Nares had been studying the subject closely and he came to the conclusion that the Middle pack route ought to be the best at this time of year.

The horror of our ice-quartermasters[9] may be imagined. No whaler would have advised the Middle Pack. Their maxim is to stick to the land ice and keep it on your right. When we said anything to our own ice-masters we always heard 'yel no git into north water this way,' 'wait a bit we will see ice enou to check yea fasir lang' & so on. Well we steamed at last at 11 a.m. on the 24th. The loom of ice spread all along in front of us, and at 12:45 we saw the great Middle Pack all along the horizon. Full speed ahead, we were soon in it, all young ice at first but soon hummocks and heavier floe but well soft & 'rotten.' It was perfectly calm, and no pen or pencil could describe the beauty of the scene. The flat ice varied in tint from the most tender pink to a glowing violet with glorious transparent blues and greens here and there. Sometimes we would charge into a vast united piece and split it into pieces and steam through. The flat unbroken pieces were often unbroken for farther than we could see to the right or the left, and then in the afternoon we got into a grand lane of open water and went three revolutions a minute faster than we went on our trial trip.

The *Discovery* occasionally came within speaking range and every rope and spar was reflected in the mirror-like sea, a sight not easily forgotten. I could hardly leave the deck, it seemed like the sight of some pageant, but at last I got well to work and after an hour or two felt a little dim about the microscope eye. So I went up again and the very first thing I saw was a bear – a fine big fellow 400 yds. off & walking away apparently quietly enough. I gave a shout that brought every eye on him and I had my rifle & help on deck in a twinkling. Captain Markham, [Lieutenant] May[10] and I lowered the dinghy and were after him on the floe in no time. We often stuck our legs through the soft ice but to get in altogether was quite impossible unless we deliberately jumped into open water. On we went, puffing and panting for the ship had turned out another hunting party of eight or more, and they were coming fast behind us while Bruin was going past us just in front. At last after a run of about 700 yards we saw him striding along at a walk but not letting us gain an inch. The edge of the floe was near & he evidently meant to take to the water so nothing for it but a long shot at 300 or 400 yards. We all fired together I don't think we touched him but he dived into the water at once and left us discomfited. May had no sooner fired when he stepped into a hole and went up to his waist. I helped him out and then fired a hopeless shot at Bruin's fast disappearing head, but Captain Nares who had been all along up in the crows nest saw a lane and put the ship in chase. She came crashing through the ice but never got closer than 300 yds.

of Bruin who of course chose the heavier ice, and in spite of a smart fusillade Bruin got off. I forgot to say that Captain Nares & I had a long 400 yds. shot at a walrus before breakfast – of course we missed him.

Well after much charging [at the] ice, and 'hard a port,' 'hard a starboard' work we safely cleared the Middle Pack that has stopped many, and got to Cape York in the shortest time on record i.e. *70 hours* including the time on shore spent in getting bird's eggs & working. So here we are in the north water past the crimson cliffs,[11] which are not crimson now, though a little of the snow shews pink with 'protococeus,' past dozens of grand glaciers and past Cape Dudley Diggs, which might be called the orange cliffs for the towering rocks are bright orange and brick red with patches of sap green and oxide of chromium tinted moss in their hollows. Every gap is filled with some great glacier stream pouring its fleet of bergs into the smooth sea, and far beyond the glacier are great mound like bosses of snow, smooth and sweeping in outline. We are [now] sounding so I must be up for the bottom beasts.

26th. 11:30 p.m.

We are now going into the Carey Islands and will, I expect, hand over our letters to the *Discovery*, which is six miles astern, to be 'cached.' We will at once make our own depot of provisions and go to Lyttleton Island. There are lots of birds on the Carey Islands & one shooting party will be off presently. All day today we have had a strong current from the north against us. The surface temperature of the sea rose to 40 [degrees F] but remained 28.8° on bottom (i.e. at 280 fathoms) or 90 fathoms under the surface. I have just seen one of my pet Clio's attack, capture & eat a poor little Limacina, a thing like this. The Clio is like this. [small sketch]. I had worked out all the anatomy of the latter and wanted to see how he used his huge teeth.

Captain Nares thinks it unlikely that these letters will be taken home. Perhaps they will arrive after we ourselves do, who knows? At present our prospects are most cheering – sea free of ice except opposite discharging glaciers, magnificent calm summer weather, everyone in perfect health & uproarious spirits and in better time than any expedition before us. Getting out of and through the Middle Pack in 34 hours is a great feat and we have been congratulating ourselves on being the first to do it. I am beginning to think we will get to the Pole. We have at present coal enough on board to steam the whole way there and back without setting a single sail. Provisions in plenty, our sheep untouched, the first that ever came here, lots of ducks hanging up in the rigging, barrels of loon's eggs. Feilden[12] and I had two of them today for lunch, cold boiled, and no

plover's egg could equal their flavour. The only bother we have is the litter our decks are in with casks & coal and tins of meat etc., etc., etc.

Colan is writing a parting letter to [Director-General] Sir A. Armstrong. I have not written, as I had no official communication to make. If we get back in 18 months, which I now admit is possible but not probable, I will find it difficult to get more than the promotion I would have got by seniority at the same time. However, I won't trouble much about it or anything else when home is in sight again. However sweet home may be, there is not a man on board who would go if a mail steamer from some unexplored land came alongside and offered a passage to England. We have a grand opportunity, splendid ships and equipment, and a captain that we all have the greatest confidence in. God protect and guard you darling. He will in good time bring us back to you and our little one. Don't be anxious about me and my welfare or comfort, both are better than you think. I feel confident of at least moderate success.

Good bye Darling,

Your affectionate husband, Edward[13]

13: Floeberg Harbour

"Polar Winter"

After leaving the Carey Islands, Captain Nares managed to force his way through the ice-laden Kennedy Channel and into Hall Basin. On August 25 he located a safe winter harbour for Captain Stephenson and the *Discovery* (Discovery Bay), within the much larger Lady Franklin Bay on the northeast shore of Ellesmere Island.

Then, with the sure knowledge that his window of opportunity was closing rapidly, Nares attempted to sail north once more, only to be stopped immediately by pack ice. This forced a return to the Bay where he watched anxiously for any sign of the ice opening up in front of his path. He tried again three days later but was stopped once more, damaging a rudder during the struggle against the pack. After repairs were made the lookout reported signs of an opening in the icefield, and on the August 29 Nares ventured forth once more. This time he was assisted greatly by an autumn gale from the south, which shifted the ice offshore, thereby allowing *Alert* to pass through the narrow and treacherous Robeson Channel and into the Arctic Ocean. Nares then turned west and began searching for a safe winter harbour. He knew that he had been fortunate. On August 30, 1871, – almost four years earlier to the day – Captain Budington[1] had brought the *Polaris* almost as far up Robeson Channel before being trapped in the ice pack. Then, held fast in its icy maw, he watched helplessly as the relentless southern current carried the pack, and his ship, many miles back south and into Hall's Basin before he was finally able to break free of the ice.[2]

Nares had no time to lose in finding a wintering place. On September 2 he reluctantly chose a shallowly indented north-facing bay about six miles east of what is now Canadian Forces Base Alert, the northernmost military listening post and weather station in North America. There, about 150 feet from shore, and behind a barrier of some grounded eighty-foot-high icebergs, he positioned his ship for the winter.[3]

Discovery in Discovery Bay, in winter.

Alert stopped by ice off Cape Prescott on her way north, August 1875.

Floeburg Harbour

Floeberg Harbour (the name was coined by Nares) was far from an ideal wintering site, but there appeared to be no other alternative, particularly as a new Arctic storm swept in from the north. Edward would later write that soon after *Alert* was moored it was feared she would be driven ashore when ice that was being forced south snapped the hawsers holding her fast to the grounded berg that formed her protective barrier. Fortunately the pressure eased when the wind changed and the ship was once more safely moored. Nevertheless it had been a near thing as everyone understood full well, for it would have been a disaster if the ship had been crushed and driven ashore by the ice pack. A week later Commander Markham and Lieutenant Aldrich[4] made an exploratory trip along the coast but soon concluded that to have continued northwest, if it had been possible at all, would have been a serious mistake, for they found no better refuge than Floeberg Harbour.

Captain Nares' skill and experienced seamanship had brought *Alert* farther north than any other ship had ever been, exceeding the record claimed by Budington by at least twenty miles. There, at 82° 27' north of the Equator, at the tip of Ellesmere Island on the marge of the Polar Sea, the determined explorers settled in and prepared for the long months of polar winter that would soon be upon them.

The preparations began immediately. Supplies of all kinds that could survive subzero temperatures were off-loaded and moved ashore, where a fifty-foot-long ice-block and canvas-roofed warehouse (named Markham Hall) was constructed. Three quite large igloos, christened Kew and Greenwich, were also built, apparently by the officers who, presumably, were trying out a new survival technique. The ice-houses were connected by long tunnels so that the scientific teams could easily access their instruments and take regular meteorological and geophysical readings during inclement weather. Though little noted in most descriptions of the Nares Expedition, the weather and climatic observations taken in 1875/76, covering almost a full year, became the main source for weather and climate information for northern Ellesmere Island until the Canadian Alert Bay weather station was established in 1948. This was no small contribution to our knowledge of the Arctic regions.

By late September, *Alert* was firmly frozen into the ice, and well into October preparations for the winter continued apace. More snow warehouses were built for the storage of casks of salt meat, and the sides of the ship were banked high with snow to provide insulation against the bitter cold that would soon be upon them. Exploratory sledge trips to lay out supply depots for the spring parties were also undertaken.

On September 9, Moss and Feilden were detailed to accompany Pelham Aldrich's dogsled party for the first few days of a twenty-four-day scouting journey intended to provide training for the sledge crews while exploring and laying out provision depots along the coast. Nares, rightly considering the need for fresh meat be "of utmost importance," had ordered a three-day hunting party to be mounted, and Edward, who had already earned the reputation of being the ship's most enthusiastic hunter, was a natural choice to go along. Moss and naturalist Feilden took no part in the actual sledging, concentrating instead on scouting and hunting along the sledge route. They left the Aldrich party to return to the ship on September 12 after exploring about twenty miles of coastline without finding any sign of large animals and little in the way of birds. Although it was not realized at the time, the absence of almost any kind of game in the Floeberg Bay area or elsewhere along the northern Ellesmere coast had the potential to be a fatal impediment.

Still, this outing was merely something akin to the first sea-trial of a newly commissioned ship. The real work began after Aldrich's reconnaissance party returned. At that time a second travelling party of three sledges and twenty-five men led by Commander Markham, assisted by Lieutenants Parr, May, and Egerton continued the exploration and depot provisioning along the anticipated route of the spring journeys. They were out from September 23 until the 15th of October, returning just as the long darkness of winter was descending. The northern sun then dropped below the horizon, not to show its life-giving face for another five and one-half months. Just before the return of Markham's party, Edward, always restless and never content when confined for very long, hiked out alone on snowshoes to meet Markham at Dumbbell Bay, about five miles northwest along the coast.

When Edward met the party, he found Lieutenant May and seven of his men suffering from varying degrees of frostbite. Some of them had very severely frozen feet, and when they regained the ship three of them, including May, underwent the amputation of at least one pedicular appendage. May lost a great toe, but more important in the mind of this future admiral was concern that the injury might cost him the opportunity to command a sledge on one of the spring travelling parties. The cases of frostbite were not the result of especially cold weather, for temperatures had only been in the range of +15° F to –22° F at the time. Most of them came about when some of the half-loaded sledges broke through the thin autumn ice that lay beneath the soft snow that fell on almost every day of the trip. Dragging the sledges back onto firm ice with feet and legs soaking wet was bound to result in some frozen extremities.

The Markham party also had difficulties with the dogs. These arose from two main problems. Inexperience in handling them was of course predictable. How could it have been otherwise when no one except the Greenland Eskimo dog-drivers had any previous experience with dogsleds? This problem was compounded by the fact that the ships' crews, ignoring the advice of the drivers, treated the dogs as pets instead of working animals. As a result they became difficult to control, and this certainly contributed to the difficulties of the fall sledging parties. Evidently this situation prevailed on both ships. Staff Surgeon Belgrave Ninnis thought that on *Discovery* the men indulged the dogs far too much, an opinion Edward Moss shared. He observed later that "[Eskimo dogs] are as a rule utterly destitute of the virtues of the species. They are merely wolves who have found slavery convenient" adding that "sometimes when 'Samuel,' or 'William Henry,' would reach the stage of a fat morsel he would disappear, and some nearby relative would look less hungry." Bleak as this may have been, his judgment expressed the bitter realities that could – and sometimes did – face starving and desperate men as well as hungry dogs in the Arctic. In any event, whether from spoiling or from inexperienced handling, the dogs were a disappointment on the fall excursions, even using the Greenland sled drivers. Moss appears to have been ambivalent about the usefulness of the dogs. On the one hand he would write later that "[the dogs'] value to the expedition cannot be overrated," and that "they could pull at a pinch 100 lbs. each for a long day's march." On the other hand he still believed they were unsuited to the job expected of them on the rough, tumbled-up Arctic ice to the north of the *Alert*.

In *Shores of the Polar Sea*, when Edward commented on some of the "unexpected difficulties" the sledge parties faced, he concluded that the "conditions and not the men" were to blame for the expedition's problems. However, he also observed that the heavy eight and twelve-man sledges, "perfect as they were for their own work," were not suited to land-travelling over soft snow; and "as snowshoes had never been used on Arctic Expeditions, we had but two pairs on the ship." Actually there were four different types of sledges used on the Nares expedition. Most were 130-pound eight-man sledges, but there were also at least two twelve-man types weighing some two hundred pounds, as well as a few light dogsleds weighing a mere thirty-five pounds. The man-hauling sledges, made of elm, and shod with metal runners, were designed by Francis Leopold McClintock, based on a Finnish design that had proved effective on the eastern side of Greenland. Unfortunately, the design turned out to be unsuitable for the conditions faced by the men on Nares northern parties. They were well enough suited for travel over flat wind-blown sea ice (their own work, in the words of Edward Moss), but in the soft, deep coastal snow along the edge of Ellesmere Island and the coast of northwestern Greenland they bogged down with disagreeable regularity, as did the lighter dogsleds for that matter. At such times the dogs, sometimes buried up to their muzzles, were unable to move the loaded sleds from a standing start and simply curled up in the snow, refusing to even try, forcing the five-man crew to assist the animals in an effort to get them moving again. Moreover, when travelling offshore, the incredible fields of jagged pack ice, up-thrust into great hummocks and tilted every which way, were even more daunting and had not been anticipated. It had been expected that once the northern parties travelled a short distance away from the land they would find themselves on a relatively smooth windblown and barely snow-covered polar ice pack.

The use of smaller and lighter sledges would undoubtedly have been an improvement, but even the lightest of well-designed sleds would have had serious problems in the broken and hummock-strewn terrain north of the ship, as Robert Peary later discovered when he left Point Moss (named after Edward) to attempt his own drive for the Pole using dogsleds in ice conditions almost identical to those that thwarted the Nares parties.[5]

There were also health problems among the dogs on the fall trips. Lieutenant Aldrich, who left the ship on September 22 with two sleds and fourteen dogs, reported that he had been greatly delayed by his dogs suffering from Piblokto (hysterical fits), a strange canine disease that was endemic among the Greenland dogs at the time. Eight of them were afflicted on the fall trip, some several times. One suffered so badly it had to be shot, and another was simply untied and turned loose because of its crazy and uncontrollable behaviour. By November half the dogs on the ship had either died or been put down, while some others had simply run off.

In *The Arctic Grail*, Pierre Berton, the prolific author of Canadian popular history, suggested that Nares did not take the use of dogsleds seriously, and that the autumn sledging experience convinced him that in the spring the sledges should be man-hauled.[6] However, this judgment ignores the fact that Nares, following the recommendations of the Arctic Committee, had always intended to use the man-hauling method and had never planned to use the light dog sledges for much more than auxiliary or support work. They were in fact used quite successfully for such work during the following spring and summer.

It was too bad, however, that the sledge parties were not equipped with snowshoes, either because the Admiralty failed to recognize their potential value or because the expedition leaders disregarded advice from some earlier explorers. Only two pairs were brought aboard *Alert*. Apparently one of the officers who did so was acting on the advice of Old Arctic Dr. John Rae of the Hudson's Bay Company, who had used snowshoes during the search for John Franklin twenty years earlier. Edward Moss was probably that officer. The other man was Lieutenant Wyatt Rawson.[7] Moss is known to have used his snowshoes frequently during his outings. In *Shores of the Polar Sea*, he wrote of their value in British Columbia and elsewhere in Canada but suggested that no one, however expert, could have used them where the ice was very rugged – meaning on the tumbled up hummocks of the "Paleocrystic Sea."[8] However, their usefulness in other circumstances was certainly recognized by some members of the crew, two of whom built their own makeshift models during the winter.

By November, the daily routine aboard ship had been firmly established along the traditional lines of British naval discipline, modified somewhat to meet the exigencies of protracted darkness, extreme cold, and limited activity. On almost every morning throughout the long dark winter days, the routine began at 6 a.m. Forty-five minutes was allotted to wash up and stow hammocks and other gear and after breakfast the ratings were assigned to various cleaning tasks. At nine they were mustered on deck and assigned their duties for the day. An hour later they were served up with their ration of lime juice and a short prayer. Thus physically and morally strengthened, the men went off for either a regime of active exercise walking the boring rounds of a cleared path on the ice during the darkest days, or to their work assignment ashore or aboard ship. At 1 p.m. the midday meal was served and afterwards work was resumed until 5. Classes in arithmetic, spelling, navigation, or some other useful subject (such as English for the Greenlanders) were taught in the evening, followed by chess or card games before the day ended with "lights out" at ten o'clock below decks, and an hour later for the officers. While the routine may have been at least partially based on the theory that the Devil makes work for idle hands, it was nevertheless intended to maintain physical and mental fitness as well as discipline.

Pierre Berton was critical of the rigid British naval routine during their polar expeditions, but in fairness, the 1875 party never suffered from the bitter divisiveness, insubordination, and deleterious conflict that became a serious (and fatal) impediment to both the Hall and Greely[9] expeditions, to name only two among many polar efforts marred by strife. On the last Hall Expedition, Captain Budington deliberately chose to leave the men free of any form of organized activity during the winter, with the result that many of his crew members gradually lapsed into profound boredom followed by extreme lassitude. Then, for some among them, the boredom and mental isolation brought withdrawal, suspicion, and paranoia. Personal differences that might have just produced grumbling and annoyance under other circumstances morphed into increasingly bitter grievances that ended in quarrels that poisoned the shipboard atmosphere, making united action for the common cause very difficult, if not impossible.[10]

Berton makes the point that official reports of the British polar expeditions deliberately omitted or downplayed any reference to interpersonal strife or other discord. While that was the case on the 1821–22 Parry voyage as well as some others before 1875, evidence to support the proposition remains singularly lacking in the case of the Nares Expedition. In any case, maintaining reasonably normal naval routines and relationships was sound policy if not carried to extremes, particularly when coupled with efforts to provide diversion and entertainment during the long polar winter.

The tedium of those dark months was relieved in a variety of ways. When the moon waxed full it triggered a short period of extra vitality aboard ship, providing an opportunity (weather permitting) to do more than trudge around the monotonous exercise track marked out near the ship. At such times, groups of young tars and officers would take some of the lighter dogsleds to one of the nearby hills, where they revelled like schoolboys as they "tobogganed" joyfully down the slope with a frivolity that sometimes produced humorous incidents and much laughter during dinner. This levity was all the more welcome because the usual after-dinner conversation on the mess deck or in the ward room gradually became muted, or simply tedious, as subjects and personal viewpoints were explored *ad infinitum*. Edward claimed that "Only theology was a proscribed subject of discussion," cleverly observing that "it was wonderful how many subjects became theological before the winter was over."[11]

Filling the voids in the dinner conversation may have been difficult at times, but filling the working hours was not. Along with his fellow officers, part of Moss's daily routine was taken up with scientific observations, for each officer had been assigned specific scientific tasks in one field or another. Edward was responsible for studying various aspects of Arctic sea water (salinity, temperature, specific gravity) and in its solid form, glaciation and the development of floe ice, plus the characteristics of the Arctic atmosphere. A considerable amount of his time was therefore devoted to taking readings, making notes, or assisting Dr. Colan with medical duties. Reading also filled some of the empty hours, for almost every man aboard was literate, and the ship carried an extensive library, including books and journals by earlier Arctic travellers. These were pored over carefully by ratings and officers alike, all of them intent on finding out how their predecessors had fared.

Edward Moss also had his art, and probably a personal journal to record noteworthy events for the book he had in mind. In quiet moments, and when light and weather conditions permitted, he sketched scenes such as "Serving out the Lime Juice" or "The Deck-Morning Inspection and Prayers." Many such sketches were completed in watercolour in the comfort of his cabin and ultimately reproduced in *Shores of the Polar Sea*. For example, at the beginning of March, in a bitterly inclement temperature of –73 degrees Fahrenheit (this recorded on the back of the painting), Moss went out on the ice to sketch a winter scene of *Alert*, finishing it later back in his quarters. Along with most of his other Arctic paintings and sketches, it is now in the Scott Polar Research Institute at Cambridge, UK.

Winter was also a time for various other monotony-breaking activities intended to maintain morale and develop the team spirit. To this end the "temporarily closed" Royal Arctic Theatre was officially re-opened by Captain Nares on November 18, 1875. As a young Mate[12] on one of the ships searching for Franklin between 1852 and 1854, Nares himself had played a woman, Lady Clara, in an amusing play about Charles the Second. The 1875 theatre actually continued a British tradition that went back over fifty years to the first Parry Expedition of 1818. Aldrich on the piano served as the theatre musician and Moss painted the backdrops for the stage – a worthwhile contribution to the productions. Chaplain Henry Pullen was the amateur playwright who wrote or adapted the skits and poetic selections that were the main weekly offerings. Playbills were printed for each of the Thursday evening productions that were presented on a sheltered stage on the deck in front of the heavily clad and felt-booted audience.

Other diversions also helped to keep the Black Dog of depression away during the months of darkness. Guy Fawkes Day (November 5) was celebrated by making a large papier mâché figure and pulling it on a sled to the top of the great sheltering berg nearby. Shortly afterwards a glorious display of fireworks lit up the sky, followed by a resounding explosion as the Great Traitor was blown to eternity. Naturally, Christmas and New Years were also well celebrated with such time-honoured toasts as "The Queen" and "Absent Friends." The festive season brought special treats for the crew members, who were allowed extra rations of food and spirits. Every officer and man also received small gifts sent by the "Ladies of Queenstown" (Ireland) and the men were permitted to raid the stores for whatever extra food or treats they wanted. On Christmas Eve there was dance on the deck, with music courtesy of Lieutenant Aldrich, who reportedly was given no peace that night or the following evening when the festivities continued. During the early afternoon of Christmas Day the officers were invited to receive the compliments of the season in the men's quarters, gaily decorated for the occasion. Throughout the day the cooks were kept busy preparing a special dinner for both officers and men. The menu for the former group, carefully preserved for posterity, suggests that they were very well fed and in high spirits before the holiday evening was over. The men also fared well, but without the extras available from the personal store of essentials and delectables each officer had been allowed to bring with him.

On New Year's Eve the Yule-tide season ended when the ships bell was struck sixteen times at midnight, eight peels to see the old year out, and another eight to usher in the new. This was preceded by whisky punch for the officers and grog for the men. The next day it was back to the usual routine with the knowledge that although months more of winter remained, the sun was now past the winter solstice. And so, in these ways of work and play, the harsh and dark winter months passed with no visible sign of problems. All seemed to be well. When the crew received its usual monthly check-up after New Year's Day, 1876, Dr. Colan was pleased to report that the men seemed in better health than they were a month previously.

Captain Nares and Commander Markham had every reason to expect a successful spring sledging season, though privately, on the basis of what they had seen of the ice conditions the previous fall, both men had concluded that achieving the Pole was not on. Months later, in his official report, Markham wrote that before the sledging season began "none were so rash as to indulge in any extravagant ideas of successfully reaching such a very high [latitude] as 84 or 85 degrees." This statement, however, did not mean that the Northern Party was not going to give it their best effort.

Preparations for the spring expeditions began around the middle of January. Based on the fall experience the tents were enlarged and alterations were made to the eight-man sledges. Aboard *Discovery* similar work was also afoot. In a note to Nares in March, Captain Stephenson complained that "the whole of the clothing arrangements were badly managed before leaving England." Nares had long since come to the conclusion that issuing outer garments made from Duffle (coarse woollen cloth with a thick nap) was a mistake. In January he observed that "all [who] wear hoods speak of their great warmth and it is decidedly the Esqimaux [*sic*] dress.... We cannot do better than copying them, and I wish there were some nearby from whom we could learn." Other comments also make it clear that he had pored over the books of earlier Arctic explorers in the ship's library in an effort to learn what he could from their experiences before the spring sledging season began.

About the middle of February the first signs of impending daylight were visible and by the first of March, when the sun finally arose over the horizon, preparations were almost finished. On the 13th Nares made the decision to send Markham and Parr on the Northern Party, giving Aldrich command of the Western group. In his private journal Aldrich discussed the various assignments, stating that it was originally planned that he should lead the Northern Party "merely to report on the ice as a travelling medium for next year on an enlarged scale," adding that "however, the Commander is anxious to go and of course I will have to give way." The die was thus cast. Just before the spring parties left, the men were given a final medical exam. Once again Colan's monthly medical report was positive, leaving the clear impression that the crew had come through the winter in excellent condition. Regrettably, in the coming months it would become all too apparent that this was an illusion. Unobserved and never anticipated, presenting no visible symptoms to the medical officers at the time, scurvy was surreptitiously at work on the bodies of most of the men on board both ships.

Thus the stage was set for the tragic third act of the polar drama.

14: Markham and Parr

"Daring to Do All ..."

The spring sledging season commenced with as much ceremonial formality as Captain Nares could muster under the circumstances.

Put your mind's eye to the scene: It is almost 11 o'clock on the morning of April 3, 1876. The temperature is 33 degrees below zero Fahrenheit, and the bitterly cold air is almost still, full of shimmering ice crystals sparkling in the sunshine. The breath of the heavily clad men standing in front of eight fully loaded sledges hangs sullenly around them, as if it is reluctant to venture forth from the warmth of their lungs. There are thirty-six officers and men in the parties that are about to leave the safety and comfort of the *Alert*, starkly outlined against a sky whose special blue is familiar only to those who have spent winter in the coldest regions of the earth. The crews are standing easy beside the man-harnesses they would soon be using to haul the sledges drawn up line astern behind them. Each sledge has a flag standard topped with a colourful pennant featuring the Cross of St. George, along with what appears to be a coat of arms, a figure or some other symbolic signifier arising from the imagination of each sledge commander and his crew. Also, on all but one of the flagstaffs is a motto. While each pennant, symbol, and motto is different, all serve the same purpose: to emphasize the will and the determination of the sledge commanders and their crews to succeed in the daunting test of human endurance that is about to commence. "Fortitude vincet," "Faire sans dire," "Nil desperantum" and on one flagstaff a quotation from Shakespeare (MacBeth, Act 1, Scene 7), hand-stitched by Lady McClintock herself. One wonders if this motif has been chosen by her or the man in command of the Northern Party, Albert Hastings Markham, whose sledge it adorns. Somehow it seems oddly incongruous, for it is made up of words from the mouth of the murderous Macbeth, whose role in Shakespeare's timeless drama exemplifies great physical courage fatally marred by moral weakness. Its subtle meaning seems strangely out of joint in the context of the day and the mission.

> I dare to do all that becomes a man,
> Who dares do more is none.

Another banner, fluttering gently on the standard of Edward Moss's sledge *Bulldog* catches the eye. Stitched on it is the phrase "Tene trahe," Latin for "Hold Fast," which had been Lady Franklin's own motto. It fits well with the tenacious British imagery conjured up by the name of the sledge, but it too would prove somewhat ironic in the end. The eye then returns to Commander Markham, standing in front of the crew of his sledge, *Marco Polo*, which carries both the Union Jack on its forward flagstaff and his personal pennant at the rear. Behind him are the crews and sledges of *Challenger*, *Victoria*, and the four support sledges, *Poppie*, *Bulldog*, *Alexandra*, and *Bloodhound*, a smaller four-man dog-sledge. Captain Nares is slowly walking past each group, pausing regularly to give some personal words of encouragement or farewell to both officers and men.

Nearby, the remaining members of the ship's crew stand along the deck watching the ceremony. A few moments after Nares' inspection they listen solemnly to the words of Chaplain Pullen's prayer and to the Church of England doxology "In praise of God, from whom all blessings flow." Then, after a barely perceptible pause, a rousing salute of three cheers rings out to shatter the icy Arctic silence.

The sledgers now step into their harnesses and move slowly away. Most realize, or at least suspect, that achieving the Pole is out of the question, but like their leaders, they are determined to achieve new polar records if it is humanly possible: prepared to do all that becomes a man, and to stand fast in the face of certain tribulation in the weeks ahead. Later it would become very evident that God must not have listened to Chaplain Pullen's prayers, for he bestowed many trials and very few blessings on the departing cohort of brave and dedicated men.[1]

Commander Markham's Northern Division (or Northern Party) was ably assisted by Lieutenant A. A. Chase Parr, commanding HMS (Her Majesty's Sledge) *Victoria*. Each of these two officers was responsible for seven other men, who would be man-hauling roughly 1,400 pounds of gear and food supplies on each of the big sledges – over 230 pounds per man – on a journey that might last for up to two and one-half months. Markham's orders were to proceed to Cape Joseph Henry, some thirty-five miles to the west along the coast, and then to head directly towards the Pole, some five hundred miles distant as the crow flies.

The Western Party, also made up of two sledges, was commanded by Pelham Aldrich (*Challenger*) assisted by Lieutenant George Giffard[2] (*Poppie*). Their orders were to proceed to Cape Joseph Henry and travel westward along the Ellesmere coast to determine if there was land to the northwest. If this was found to be the case, perhaps the Pole might be

Alert at Floeberg Beach, spring 1876.

reached next year over land rather than over the ice pack. The support groups were to accompany Markham and Aldrich as far as the Cape, where they would top up the main parties' provisions and drop off more supplies before returning to the ship for other duties.

An Eastern Party, led by Lieutenant Lewis Beaumont[3] was already on its way from Discovery Bay to *Alert*, where they would rest for a few days before crossing over Robeson Channel to explore the northwest coast of Greenland. In a letter to Nares ten days before Beaumont left *Discovery*, Captain Stephenson noted that his crew members were "all enthusiastic," some claiming that they would be unable to face their friends in England if they didn't go sledging. Stephenson told Nares that he had promised them "a bellyful of it." He also complained about the clothing and equipment that had been provided to him by the Admiralty. Based on his fall exploration experiences, he had been forced to enlarge the tents (Nares had already done his) and modify his sledges as well as some of the clothing that had been issued in England. On both ships, efforts had been made to condition the sledge crews following their relative inactivity over the long winter. During the previous month Nares had also ordered that the sledge crews were to be issued double rations of both food and lime juice every day, though he did not make the second dose mandatory.

In planning and preparing for the spring sledging, Nares did not order any of the parties to carry more than a small quantity of antiscorbutic in their rations, supposedly because of concern over the extra weight and the difficulty of keeping the lime juice from freezing. The juice was laced with 15 per cent rum, a ratio that was not really effective as antifreeze in spite of the fact that the navy rum of those days was 30 per cent over proof – at least double the strength of regular rum today. *Marco Polo* and *Victoria* each carried only two flasks of lime juice, a quantity that only added about ten pounds to the weight of each sled. Yet Markham and Parr both started the trip with a ten-week supply of rum and "spirits of wine." Markham carried 182 pounds of spirits and Parr carried 152 pounds – a total of 334 pounds of alcohol. Also included was a magnum of the best whisky, gifted by the Anglican Dean of Dundee, to be opened at the apex of the journey, hopefully the Pole. The contrast between the quantity of lime juice and the quantity of alcohol carried on the sledges is self-evident. Later, in Markham's official report, he would claim that the alcohol, though not essential for dietary reasons, was necessary to keep up the morale of the sledge crews. Perhaps the brief pleasure of a tot of rum at the end of the day seemed little enough compensation for the heroic exertions expected of the men, but the decision to carry so much alcohol and so little lime juice would have (or so critics later implied) deadly consequences.

In the brilliant sunshine of the Arctic spring, the sledges moved away from the ship. Progress proved to be painfully slow as the heavily laden sledges dragged abysmally in the deep coastal snow. Over the first week on the trail Edward Moss took careful note of any visible or reported health problems, alleviating minor symptoms with various nostrums from his medical kit. When two of the men exhibited unusual signs of fatigue and exhaustion, he recommended that they be returned to the ship, exchanging them for healthier

Lieutenant Beaumont's sledge party about to leave *Discovery,* April 1876. Library and Archives Canada, No. C52572.

men from one of the supporting parties, a decision that almost certainly saved their lives. The first to show extreme fatigue was ice-master James Berrie. Moss believed he detected signs of "some scorbutic taint," and put it down to the man's previous service on Arctic whalers – the recurrence of an earlier bout of scurvy. A few cases of frostbite, snow-blindness, and cold sores were also observed, but Edward dismissed these as "small ills which we could afford to despise."

However, on April 6, Elias Hill, a marine assigned to Aldrich's sled, began to suffer from severe lower stomach pains, and when a second man in the same party, Royal Marines Colour-Sergeant William Wood, became too exhausted and sick to continue, Aldrich was forced to call a halt for the day. Edward left his own crew and retraced his steps in the 41° below zero temperature to provide assistance, only to find both patients sleeping peacefully after Aldrich had dosed them up with medication and a stiff tot of rum. The next day, Berrie was sent back to the ship with *Bloodhound*. Edward would have liked to have sent marine Elias Hill back at the same time, but thought that the extra weight would have been too much of a load for the dogs and the four-man crew, so he kept Hill with his own party.

Two days later he offered to relieve Lieutenant Parr, who was suffering from a severe case of snow-blindness, from the job of scouting a path through the maze of up-thrust ice, which now blocked their progress. As they were now close to the Cape Joseph Henry supply depot, Parr and another snow-blinded man were left at camp for the day while supplies were replenished on the main sledges or taken over to the cache at the Cape. Finally, on April 12, *Bulldog* and *Alexandra* were detailed to assist the northern parties during the morning. Before the beginning of that day's sledging, Edward made one final medical examination of the men who were to carry their flags to the north and to the west. He examined frostbitten feet and looked for any other visible problems before concluding "there was nothing to discourage advance in any of the men of the extended parties." Joseph Good and William Wood now appeared to be well enough to continue, and (so he reported) all the other men were eager to proceed. Hill, the invalid from Aldrich's party, was exchanged for Able Seaman David Mitchell from Moss's crew. At one o'clock that afternoon, *Bulldog* parted from the northern party, and an hour later Edward bid goodbye to Aldrich after helping him to make it over to the coast.

If Moss had any doubts about the health of the men on the Northern and Western parties, or any questions about the possible success or failure of their respective missions, they were left unexpressed in the official report he filed upon his return to the ship. Prior to his departure for the ship Markham had given him a note for Nares. In it he stated that he would be sorry to lose Edward as he had been "of the greatest assistance to me." He also advised Nares that he no longer expected to get farther north than the 84th parallel of latitude.

So, with Edward in the lead, the *Bulldog* crew began to make their way home. *Alexandra*, the other large support sledge, had been turned over to Markham who, in a last-minute change of plans, had decided to take it along with him. As a result, Moss found himself leading both crews to pull the sledge, now loaded high with the extra tents and other gear from *Alexandra*. With two sick men under his care he wanted to reach *Alert* as soon as possible and was anxious to retrace his path before a storm obliterated the road that had been laboriously cut through the hummocks with pick and shovel on the way out. He would later observe that "the brief experience in path-finding among hummocks in a fog had given me quite enough of it." On the first afternoon of the return journey, the party made good progress – five miles – before camping at 7 o'clock. Then it was up at six the next morning and back into the traces by nine. The travelling was easier than on the way out, for now it was warmer and also the snow had hardened over their tracks. With double the hands to do the hauling, they made fifteen miles before stopping for the second night.

Much of the following day was spent trying to locate the smaller of the two ice-boats that had been left at Depot Point the previous September. Nares wanted it back at the ship, but Moss failed to find it, though he did succeed in locating the larger one, now buried beneath two feet of ice. That day, the temperature dropped down again, and it was 26° below zero by late afternoon, when they left to march another six miles before camping for the night. Edward would have preferred to continue onward, but felt that he should not exhaust Hill, who was unable to walk fast enough to keep warm facing a bitter southwest wind. On April 14, Good Friday, the party reached the ship in mid-afternoon after a seven-mile hike. Moss and his men then took a well-earned rest. He was confident that his medical and sledging duties on the mission had been carried out to the best of his ability and knowledge, and more than happy to be done with sledging, at least for the time being. There was no such respite for Markham's crew.

When Moss left the Northern Party at Cape Joseph Henry, they were hauling three sledges instead of the two that had been anticipated in the original plan. The largest and heaviest of these was *Marco Polo*, which took almost the whole crew to pull. On average, each man was pulling between 220 and 240 pounds. It had been expected that the sledge weights would diminish as the food rations were depleted; this did not happen. Any reduction in the food weight was offset by the added weight of accumulated moisture in the tents and sleeping bags, which froze during the night and never had a chance to dry out before being packed on the sleds the following morning. Markham had originally believed that travelling would probably get easier as they moved further out on the pack, where he still thought he might find level windblown ice. This hope failed to materialize, and with every passing day the work became more and more arduous as the crews hacked, shovelled, dragged, and cursed their way through the jumbled pack-ice that stretched from horizon to horizon without apparent end.

The regime was uncompromisingly brutal. Almost every day the men made as many as five journeys, hauling and marching about five miles for each mile of progress towards the Pole. It was haul the first sledge until stopped by a hummock, where four men began to chop and hack their way over the obstacle. The rest of the crew went back to collect the second sledge and haul it forward before returning for the third one. All this in temperatures as low as –45° F. The mercury never climbed above zero during the first three weeks the Northern Party was on the ice. When they stopped for meals it took forever to heat water or cook their food, and the shivering men had to continually stamp their feet and keep moving in order to avoid becoming frostbitten. But the nights were much worse. They had first to remove their frozen outer clothing before cramming their bodies into sleeping bags frozen from moisture accumulation. There they shivered again (it seemed interminably) until their body heat warmed their bags enough for them to fall asleep. Moreover, the sledgers were rapidly losing their strength. With every passing day, they were weakened more and more by the exhausting labour and by the unrecognized scurvy working its evil throughout their bodies.

Stoker John Shirley was the first man to show symptoms of scorbutus. On April 14 he complained of lameness and swelling of the ankles and knees. The following morning found the party in a howling gale with –33 temperatures, so travel was out of the question. God only knows what the wind-chill factor would have been. Inside the tents the thermometer never rose above –22° F. That evening Markham recorded in his personal journal that "extreme wretchedness and abject misery [was] our lot today," confiding that "it was the most wretched and miserable Easter Sunday any of us have ever passed."[4] He complained that he had no feeling in his feet for forty hours, and that sleep was out of the question. After the storm abated, Shirley (who now was unable to walk) was carried on one of the sledges and was joined a couple of days later by George Porter, a marine from Parr's crew whose legs were badly swollen from his knees to his hips.

On May 19 Markham was forced to abandon one of the iceboats in order to reduce the sledge weight. The invalids showed no improvement, which was a troubling sign, and as for the rest of the crew, Markham remarked in his diary that it was "painful and heart-rendering to see the tremendous exertion of our small force attempting to drag our heavy sledges up some high hummocks." In the ten days since Moss left them, the Northern Party had made barely a mile a day. Then, during the next ten days, they trekked almost twice that distance in warmer weather and somewhat improved ice conditions. However, Markham's hopes were dashed as he was once again faced with extremely rugged and tightly packed ice-hummocks similar to those near Cape Henry, some of them over fifty feet high. How long could they continue? That was a question Markham and Parr preferred to avoid. But when the party stopped for the night on May 2, the two officers could no longer deny the "terrible idea"; the idea that they had already surmised but feared to admit to the men; the idea that "Porter's symptoms [loose teeth and sore gums] appear to be scorbutic." Although they believed that several other men also had "a touch" of the dread disease, they decided to keep this knowledge to themselves. The deliberate decision to withhold this information in order to travel a few more miles north was to say the least callous and lacking in appropriate concern for their trusting men, who had suffered, and would continue to suffer more, putting their lives in serious danger by continuing the march. The only logical explanation for Markham's refusal to inform the men and turn back – aside from pure hubris – was his determination to set a "farthest north" record that would stand, like Parry's,[5] for a generation or more. He knew that he had already established a new polar record by thirty or more miles, but this gain over Parry appeared to be pitifully small, almost insignificant, so he continued the march forward. On May 6 he admitted in his diary that "As far as getting to a high latitude goes I might just as well turn back at once." But still he failed to tell the men that they were suffering from scurvy. Instead he began to serve out lime juice instead of grog and continued to creep north in spite of believing that his "little game [was] played out."

After May 8 there were no more entries in Markham's personal record of the Northern Party's tribulations on the outbound journey. A personal notebook covering the return journey presumably exists – Markham would have needed it to write his official report, which is quite detailed. If so it, it would make interesting reading and would cast more light on the young officer's state of mind during the tragic homeward journey.

In his last journal entry, Commander Markham explained the situation as his heroic band of sledgers approached the apogee of their northern trek:

> We have at length arrived at the conclusion, although with a great deal of reluctance, that our sick men are really suffering from scurvy, and that in no mild form. The discoloration of their limbs, their utter prostration and helplessness, their loss of appetite and depression of spirits, with other symptoms appear decidedly scorbutic. Should our surmise be correct, we can scarcely expect to see the afflicted ones improve until they can be supplied with fresh meat and vegetables. We are unwilling for the men to suspect that they are really suffering from this terrible disease, but at the same time are issuing to those attacked a small quantity of the very little lime juice we brought away with us, in lieu of their grog, as being a better blood purifier.[6]

On May 11 one of the tents became a makeshift hospital for the six most seriously ill men, and the remaining members of the party were given a day of rest. The following morning the healthiest among them made one final march. Packing the sextant and sledge banners, they waded through snow up to their waists before stopping just before noon to plant the Union Jack and the banners in the snow at 83° 20' 26" North Latitude. After returning to the camp, Markham presided over a celebration of sorts, though for him it was probably more of a wake to mourn the failure of his polar dream. Good Havana cigars were passed round with more than the usual tot of rum, and the Dean of Dundee's magnum of whisky was put to good use to wash down the pemmican, bacon, and (though each man had hardly more a taste) the Arctic hare Edward Moss had bagged over a month earlier and donated for this very occasion.

The resulting scene had a surreal quality about it. As the whisky and rum flowed into their bodies to warm their hearts and raise their spirits, the men, including the most halt and infirm among them, had a sing-along back and forth between the tents. They toasted "Absent Friends" and "The Union Jack of Good Old England" before belting out "God Save the Queen" with evangelical fervour. Chaplain Pullen's "Grand Palæocrystic Sledging Chorus," put to a well-known tune, served as a toast to themselves:

Here's a health to all true blue
Who man this expedition handy-o
To the officers and the crew,
And may they ever prove
Both in sledging and in love,
That the tars of old Britannia are dandy-o!

After the party and a good sleep they began the gruelling trek homeward.

Meanwhile, back at *Alert*, Nares and his medical officers had been aware for more than a month that scurvy existed on the ship. At first Nares was not overly concerned, as the early cases seemed explainable by unique individual circumstances. However, by the middle of May, nine of the men who had remained on the ship had developed the malady, and unknown to Nares, there were five others on *Discovery*. Some of the sick men were among those who had been out on various support or research parties, and the others were the individuals who had been exchanged from the long-distance parties.

There had also been a death. Neil [Nels] Carl Petersen, the Greenland Dane interpreter and dog driver, died two months after the first attempt to contact Captain Stephenson to inform him of the location of *Alert* and Nares' plans for the spring sledging season. On March 12, Sub-Lieutenant Egerton, Lieutenant Rawson and Petersen had taken a dog-sled south but were forced to return three days later after the sled driver experienced extreme frostbite and other health problems that made it impossible to continue. When they returned to the ship, Dr. Colan was forced to amputate most of the frontal portions of the bones of both of Petersen's feet. Following the operation Petersen seemed to rally for a time, but then began to gradually slip away. Colan recorded his death on May 14 as the result of "sheer exhaustion, probably partly induced by scorbutic taint." Later, to the credit of some sympathetic souls, a fund was established for his widow and family after the expedition returned to England, for unlike the military men who died, there would be no widow's pension, however modest, for Petersen's family in Greenland.

Three weeks earlier, on April 23, Edward Moss had led another support party to lay down more supplies for George Giffard (*Poppie*) of the Western Division, who was only carrying enough food to last until early May, when it was anticipated that Aldrich and Giffard should be back at Cape Joseph Henry. Nares ordered Moss to travel as much as possible by night, which worked very well, given the rapidly increasing hours of daylight.

Bulldog was loaded with 1,448 pounds of provisions – about 207 pounds per man. To reduce weight Edward omitted a number of items that had previously been carried by the sledging parties. The heavy canvas floor cloth for the tent was exchanged for one made of lighter waterproof material, and a heavy coverlet was also left behind. Where possible, dry medicines were substituted for liquids to save the weight of the glass, which often weighed more than the medicine itself. Opium, morphine, and quinine were taken in gelatinized capsules. Before leaving England he had obtained them from Professor Nils Nordenskiöld,[7] the Swedish Arctic explorer who had led a Greenland Expedition in 1870.

The Moss party left at 11:15 on the night of the 23rd and camped at Mushroom Point, eight miles from the ship, at 5:30 the next morning. When they started off, the temperature was –36° F, but as the days passed it moderated again and was above zero when they returned on May 30. When Edward awoke in the late afternoon that day, he was pleased to find it was 40° F inside the tent with little or no condensation, a situation quite different from his previous trip. Three days earlier, he had observed that his whole crew left the ship with a universal prejudice against night-travelling but had been quickly converted to the change, for it allowed them a much better sleep when the sun warmed the tent and also enabled them to dry out their stockings and other gear during the warmth of the day. All things considered, the second trip went very well, with daily sledging distances greatly in excess of those made during the previous journey.

Edward took his snowshoes and used them in places where he had to traverse soft deep snow. During the trip he also carried out some scientific work, examining and recording information about the various strata of a number of the ancient forty-foot-high ice masses, and on the shore near the provision depot, he picked up some samples of brachiopods and other fossils to take back to Feilden.

Three of his men suffered from swollen ankles and legs on the journey but still managed to carry out their duties well enough. In a postscript attached to his report to Captain Nares, Moss wrote that, although it was later realized that the swollen legs and ankles were symptomatic of scurvy, he "did not at the time believe that was the case."[8] In what appears to have been an afterthought, he carefully added that he had no personal experience with the condition, observing that the records of previous expeditions identified similar ailments as arising from the hard physical work in bitter cold rather than from scurvy. Actually he had treated two mild cases of scurvy at Esquimalt, although the symptoms were different from those his men were now experiencing.

The Moss party made it back to the ship on May 30. By that time, far from the ship, all three of the main parties were in desperate straits. Each of them had been forced to turn back – Markham, as we have seen, on May 13, Aldrich on May 31, and Beaumont about the same time. Markham's small supply of lime juice was being rationed out every two days to the invalids, who were now extremely ill. In fact they were so weak that they had to be assisted with every detail of their bowel movements and sometimes they fainted afterwards from the sheer exertion of this necessity.

A week later Markham was forced to abandon his second iceboat, 170 pounds of pemmican, some ammunition, and most of the remaining rum. The load on the largest sledge was thus reduced to about 1,800 pounds, and on the smaller sledges to about 800 pounds each, weights that included the three men who had to be carried. This meant that only five men were available to pull each of the smaller sledges for some distance before returning to help drag the large sledge forward. This was becoming increasingly difficult for the "perfect band of cripples" as the commander referred to them in his official journal, written back at the ship. By the second of June, the band was reduced to a working crew of six men, including the two officers, who were now also forced into the harness. Everyone realized that the situation was rapidly becoming desperate.

On June 4 Markham and Parr walked a short distance across the ice to the nearby View Point provision depot to get a new supply of lime juice. It must have been unbelievably disheartening to arrive there and find that Nares, May, and Feilden had been at the depot only a day earlier but had gone back to the ship. The one bright spot was that Nares reconnoitering party had shot and cached three Arctic hares for them – an extremely welcome addition to the menu.

What thoughts must have troubled the minds of the men and their leaders that night? The ship, at once so near and yet so far for men so utterly decrepit, must have seemed almost beyond reach in their circumstances. Death was staring them in the face unless they got help, and they all knew it. That night and the next day, Markham and Parr pondered their options, finally deciding that Parr should go for help, while Markham would remain with his men and move forward, however slowly, as long as the group was capable of travel. Only Parr's lonely and desperately swift journey to the ship saved the day, though not for the unfortunate Porter, who died at noon on June 8. A day earlier, recognizing that Porter was "very low," Markham did his best to make him comfortable until, as the end drew near, the seaman was seized by a racking cough and convulsions before he slipped into merciful unconsciousness and passed quietly away. His death was not unexpected, but even so the commander and his remaining men were utterly devastated. After digging down through the snow, his lifeless body, swollen terribly from the ghastly effects of the scurvy, was buried in a coffin-shaped grave cut into the ice below several feet of snow. After the corpse was lowered into its resting place, Markham conducted a brief funeral service before placing a makeshift cross upon the grave. During the ceremony many of the men broke down into tears, no doubt in contemplation of their own precarious situation as well as the loss of a well-liked and respected comrade-in-arms. Markham would later write that it had been the saddest duty that he had ever been called upon to perform.

Immediately after the funeral, Parr set out for the ship, and twenty-three hours later, completely exhausted and well-nigh unrecognizable, he stumbled aboard *Alert* about six o'clock in the evening and reported to Nares, who immediately gave orders to fit out two emergency rescue teams. The first, which left before midnight, was made up of Moss, May, and Able Seaman James Self – the latter driving the dogsled *Clements Markham* loaded with medical supplies and food. Edward travelled ahead on snowshoes and was greeted with understandable elation the next morning at half-past ten when he came into view. His later report on the condition of the Northern Party described the scene as he arrived: "Rawlings, Simpson, Ferbrache, and Pearson [were] staggering along in advance. Captain Markham, Radmore, Joliffe, Maskel, Harley, and Lawrence worked the drag-belts pulling Hawkins, Francombe, Shirley, and Pearce. Porter had died the day before. It was difficult to recognize any of the men, their faces so swollen and peeled and their voices so changed."

Moss immediately put everyone on double doses of lime juice, plus egg flip[9] and port wine. Once he was sure that the party was still capable of travelling, they continued on, albeit very slowly. When they made camp later that day, he carefully examined every man, finding everyone but Joliffe, Radmore, and Markham with all the classic symptoms of scurvy. The invalids were given oysters, mutton, and port wine to speed their recovery, and when May arrived they were fed on four on four Brent geese (*Branta bernicla*),[10] fresh hare, and goose hash. Moss knew quite well that fresh meat was one of the best remedies for scurvy. He also gave them one-half grain doses of opium to counter the shock to their system from the sudden ingestion of fresh meat.

A short time later, Captain Nares arrived with two other relief sleds. His official report recorded that early on the morning of June 14, "Owing to the skill and incessant attention of Dr. E. Moss, and with the assistance of Lieutenant May and Able Seaman James Self, who with a praiseworthy disregard for their own rest, were constantly on the move [helping the sick men], Commander Markham and I had the satisfaction of reaching the ship without further loss of life." However, after seeing what had happened to the Markham party, and having been aware for more than a month of the existence of scurvy among the crew of *Alert*, Nares' anxiety about the fate of the other two expedition parties deepened greatly.

As far as the Northern Party is concerned, it is almost impossible to avoid the conclusion that by continuing north for another week after the presence of scurvy was grudgingly acknowledged, and by failing to inform his men even after its existence was established beyond reasonable doubt, Markham had gambled with all of their lives for no good reason beyond personal ambition. He knew even before he left the ship that the Pole itself was almost certainly out of the question but was determined to best Sir William Parry's farthest north mark by some significant margin. The thirty-five-mile advance over Parry, while indeed a new record, was not enough to assuage his disappointment about not meeting his personal expectations and, in his mind, the expectations of a British public hungry for the polar prize. It was certainly not worth the death of George Porter.

The question of what Albert Markham really knew about scurvy and its symptoms, and when he realized that his men were suffering severely from the malady, is critical to determining whether the young Commander was (or was not) derelict in his duty by not turning back sooner than he did.

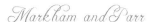

In his official report to Captain Nares, written six weeks after his return to the *Alert*, when it would not be unreasonable to assume that the expedition leaders realized that there would almost certainly be an official inquiry after they returned to England, Markham attempted to justify his decision. He began his report with much deserved praise for his men, "those brave fellows, my companions, who, suffering bodily pain and enduring hardship and privations of no ordinary nature, persevered so cheerfully, willingly, and resolutely, without a murmur – without a complaint – all animated by the same praiseworthy zeal and devotion to the furtherance of the enterprise." Then he carefully laid out his explanation of the "main causes and reasons for our failure, in attempting to carry out the duties that devolved on us."

First there was the difficulty of man-hauling three sledges with only two crews, pulling weights that were expected to decrease as supplies were used up, but in fact increased when some of the men had to be placed on the sledges after they had succumbed to the "terrible ailment" and became too weakened to walk. Then there was the deep spring snow and the difficulty of forcing their way through the chaotic ice barriers that continually blocked their progress, draining the strength of the men even more. He had hoped that they might find an open and flat ice surface as they proceeded northward, but that did not prove to be the case. As a result, he stated unequivocally that: "On one point, however, my opinion is most definitely settled, and that is the utter impracticability of reaching the North Pole over the palæocrystic floes in this locality," which he described as hummocks "resembling diminutive snow mountains … varying from 20 to over 50 feet in height." Even with the lightest of sledges, with all the ship's resources concentrated on a single polar attempt, and with perfectly healthy men, he doubted that the latitude he had achieved could be exceeded by more than sixty miles in the region north of the *Alert*.

The commander then turned directly to the scurvy issue.

> It may be necessary for me to offer some explanation as to why, with so many sick men on the sledges, I did not immediately turn back and endeavour to reach the ship as soon as possible. To this my reply must be that we were for some considerable time unacquainted with the character of the malady with which our party was attacked, and that we naturally concluded that they were suffering only from swollen knees and ankles which we were aware was a frequent occurrence amongst the sledding crews of previous expeditions, and was only what we had been led to expect; but we hoped, with a little rest and judicious treatment, they would soon recover and take their places on the drag ropes. The short distance also that we were from the land was another reason for not turning back, for we felt confident in being able to reach the depot in a few days providing our sick list did not increase at an alarming rate, little dreaming that the entire party would be afflicted and rendered nearly helpless – a case without

> precedent. I may perhaps mention that the men themselves, before the nature of the disease was communicated with them, regarded their ailment as only temporary; and I must say, in justice to themselves, that they shared, equally with their officers, the same eager desire to advance and carry out, to the utmost of their powers, the charge that was entrusted to them.[11]

With this disingenuous disclaimer, Albert Markham sought to avoid any responsibility whatsoever for the death of George Porter or the fact that his own stubborn refusal to turn back had put the lives of his men in the gravest jeopardy. He could hardly have believed that they could have reached land (the Cape Joseph Henry depot) in a few days, given how long (35 days) it had taken the party to get to his northernmost camp. With the virtual inevitability of further deterioration in the health of his men, it should have been predictable that it would take almost as long to return to the cape. In fact, it took three weeks – and even then the ship was at least a week or perhaps even a fortnight away, given the physical condition of the party when it was halted by Porter's death.

15: Aldrich and Beaumont

"Hearts of Oak"

At the time of Porter's death, the situation was not much better for the Western Party. Along the northwestern shore of Ellesmere Island, Lieutenant Aldrich and his men had been going through a similar experience. Six weeks earlier, on April 30th, Aldrich had inspected the leg of Colour-Sergeant William Wood, one of several men who were complaining of severe leg pains.

Wood's limb was badly swollen, with a "very ugly-looking red patch or blotch just above the ankle." The ugly purple blotch was indicative of broken blood vessels under the skin and was classically symptomatic of scurvy, but Aldrich apparently didn't recognize it, even after another man, James Doidge, showed similar symptoms a week later. One by one the rest of Aldrich's men were gradually attacked by the malady while he continued to assume or believe that they were only experiencing ordinary stiffness brought on by the hard work and cold. He claimed later that it was not until the end of May, when sore and tender gums began to show up, that he decided the men were suffering from scurvy. At that time Petty Officer James Doidge put him directly on the spot by posing a question he would have preferred to avoid.[1]

"Is scurvy ever got by sledging, Sir," Doidge asked. Aldrich tried to brush off the question with the reply that Doidge's sore gums were the result of chewing the hardtack without thoroughly soaking it in water to soften the biscuit, but he knew that was untrue. To his credit the Lieutenant decided to turn back immediately, a decision that undoubtedly saved the lives of at least some among his party, for there were one or two who probably would not have made it if they had continued onward. By the time they arrived back at Cape Joseph Henry, six of them were either stumbling along behind the sledge or were being carried upon it, pulled only by Aldrich and Able Seaman Adam Ayles, whose unusually good physical condition would later be a subject of some interest. Even so, they still might not have made it to the ship without loss of life had not Nares, shaken deeply by the condition of the Northern Party, sent out a second rescue team to meet them. And unknown to those back at the ships, the Eastern (Greenland) Party, commanded by Lieutenant Lewis Anthony Beaumont, was in even more serious trouble.

Beaumont's party had arrived at *Alert* on April 16, having taken ten days to travel the seventy-six miles from *Discovery*. Four days later, after a good rest before taking on supplies, they left to cross Robeson Channel, tasked with working their way east along the deeply indented coast of north-western Greenland. The Eastern Party would turn out to be the longest in duration of the main exploration parties.

It would also prove to be the most deadly of the three.

The Party left *Alert* with two eight-man sledges, supported by two other five-man dogsled teams, one of which was commanded by Dr. Richard Coppinger. After crossing Robeson Channel, they made their way along the rugged and deeply indented coast, coping with brutal marches over many mountainous and glaciated headlands barring their path. The party often faced extremely deep snow when they crossed the many inlets where the prevailing west winds did not scour the ice to make sledge travel relatively easy. Beaumont recorded that the spring snow was crusted, but not enough to bear a man's weight, and beneath the crust it had the consistency of wet sugar. After breaking through it "each leg sank to about three inches above the knee, and the effort of lifting them from their tight-fitting holes soon began to tell on the men." Sometimes, almost unbelievably, the men distributed their weight by dragging the sledges crawling on their hands and knees to avoid breaking through the crust, halting every fifty or so yards. In this mode, performing as if they were sled dogs, they would sometimes make better progress than they could when pulling from an upright position! This was an ordeal that soon had a personal cost.

Able Seaman James Hand, was the first man to develop serious problems. He complained of sore legs during the first week of May, about the same time as some of the men in the other travelling parties. Beaumont wrote in his journal on May 8 that: "I examined Hand's legs after breakfast; the marks are getting bigger, and from his description of the pain I am afraid it is scurvy." Lieutenant Rawson, the young officer commanding the support sledge disagreed with the diagnosis, asserting that before they left *Alert* they had been warned to expect stiff and sore legs. Able Seaman Charles Paul was also in bad shape, but as Hand seemed to be the sickest of the two men, Beaumont decided that he should be sent back to Polaris Bay on Rawson's sledge. However, for Hand it was already too late. His condition continued to deteriorate on the return trip and he died only a few hours after Rawson arrived at the Polaris Bay Depot.

In the meantime, according to Beaumont, when he asked the rest of his crew if they thought they had scurvy, they all declared that they were fit and anxious to continue. Nevertheless, whether they acknowledged it or not, the dreadful malignancy was working its will on their bodies. Pride is a very powerful force in determining people's behaviour, and no one wanted to "let down the side." Quitting seemed scarcely a choice: not for the men, and certainly not for their leaders. But pride aside, Beaumont knew, just as Markham and Aldrich had known. On May 19 he wrote in his journal that William Jenkins had told him that he had scurvy, and that meant that Able Seaman Peter Craig, who also had discoloured legs, was similarly afflicted. In his official report Beaumont would later state that he "did not encourage the inspection of legs, and tried to make [the men] think as little of the stiffness as possible, for I knew the unpleasant truth would be forced upon us."[2] One would have thought that by then he would have felt justified in turning back, but like Markham he continued to push ahead in spite of the fact that there was virtually nothing to be gained by doing so, particularly given the snail's pace of their progress. Ten days later, he observed that Craig's legs were very bad, and that the crippled seaman was desperately dispirited and believed he would never get well. Paul was also terribly sick, and every day the rest of the men were getting obviously weaker. Beaumont would later write that "it seemed too cruel to turn back after such hard work." Yet was it not even more cruel to continue on past the point of safe return?

When the party finally did turn back, the trip to Polaris Bay unfolded much like Markham's fatal journey. With each passing hour of each passing day, the condition of the sledgers worsened. Paul had to be placed on the sledge on June 3, and a second man ten days later. By that time, the situation was becoming almost unbearable. Two more sledgers were now barely able to walk and often had to crawl along behind the sledges, resting every twenty yards or so before continuing. On the 12th, Beaumont wrote "Dobring and Jones are at the end of their endurance. If they go down, it will leave only Gray and myself to take the men the 42 remaining miles to Polaris Bay." By then it took the crippled party almost four hours to cook breakfast, break camp, and carry out the other preparations for the daily ordeal. The next two weeks proved to be even more brutal, if that were possible. Fortunately, on June 25, when they were on the brink of complete exhaustion about thirty miles from Polaris Bay, Dr. Coppinger, Lieutenant Rawson, and Hans Hendrick arrived with a dogsled. Coppinger immediately started the men on lemon juice and ministered to them as best he could, though his medical resources were too limited to do very much. Three days later, it was decided to take the sickest men, Paul and Jenkins, to the Polaris camp on the dogsled and leave the rest of the party to follow as best they could. Unfortunately, for Able Seaman Paul, aid had arrived too late, and he died on the late afternoon of June 29. Beaumont and the rest of the party finally staggered into Polaris Bay two days later. Two of his remaining men were now desperately ill, and three others were very sorely afflicted.

On July 3, Able Seaman Paul was buried with full honours, flags set at half-mast on the tents, and a volley of three shots fired over his shallow grave. A month later, Beaumont found a suitable piece of stone and carved upon it a simple inscription to mark Hand's place. The remaining members of the party were still not well enough to travel across Robeson Channel, so the party remained at Polaris Bay for the next six weeks. They recovered very slowly in spite of the ministrations of Dr. Coppinger, fresh game meat (mainly seal and birds) courtesy of Hans, and heavy doses of lemon juice from two thirty-two-gallon kegs left by the Hall Party in 1872. Their two less fortunate shipmates were buried about one hundred yards away from the grave of Charles Hall. Ironically, Captain Stephenson, accompanied by the naturalist Henry Chichester Hart, had made a trip from *Discovery* to Polaris Bay just a month earlier to raise the American flag and place a brass tablet on Hall's grave.[3] It had been made up in England to replace the makeshift wooden headboard planted at the grave at the time of Hall's death. On the plaque was etched the following inscription:

SACRED TO THE MEMORY OF
CAPTAIN C. F. HALL
OF THE U.S. SHIP POLARIS
WHO SACRIFICED HIS LIFE IN THE ADVANCEMENT OF SCIENCE
ON NOV. 8TH 1871
THIS TABLET HAS BEEN ERECTED BY THE BRITISH POLAR EXPEDITION OF 1875, WHO, FOLLOWING IN HIS FOOTSTEPS, HAVE PROFITED FROM HIS EXPERIENCE

Charles Paul and James Hand made no less a sacrifice, and the achievements of the 1875/76 expedition in which they played their part, and for whose ends their lives were expended, exceeded by far those of Hall during his fatal polar attempt five years earlier. In the fields of astronomy, botany, geology, and most importantly in the field of physical geography and mapping, the contributions of the Nares Expedition were immensely valuable. And from a Canadian perspective, through this initiative, it established a solid British claim to the High Arctic of North America, a claim upon which Canadian sovereignty in the polar region would ultimately be grounded.[4]

At Polaris Bay, the summer dragged on in moody weather with warm and sunny days interrupted frequently by periods of cold, rain, and fog. However, by the end of July three of Beaumont's men were declared well enough to travel, and they successfully crossed the channel ice to reach *Discovery*, where they brought an anxious Captain Stephenson word of the Eastern Party's fate. About the same time, Nares managed, with some difficulty, to break out of the icepack at Floeberg Bay, and hugging the coast to make use of such open water as could be found, he steamed back towards his consort. Since Aldrich's return, he had realized that the extent of the scurvy outbreak meant that a second winter in the north was beyond contemplation, and that his only hope was to try and make it south into open water before the icepack began to form again after the brief Arctic summer. It would not be easy; he knew that. Two-thirds of his men were to some degree incapacitated: only twenty members of the crew were free of the dread disease, at least as far as the doctors could tell. As it turned out, even staying close to shore, it was touch and go at times, and *Alert* was "nipped" by the ice twice before finally making it back to Discovery Harbour on August 13.

ALERT NIPPED NEAR CAPE BEECHEY, ROBESON CHANNEL, AUGUST 1876.

Two days later Dr. Coppinger and the rest of the Beaumont Party arrived after undergoing a perilous trip across the ice. They had almost suffered the same fate as Captain Budington and his group of Polaris survivors when the unstable pack ice, in the grip of the swift-flowing Arctic current, swept them south past their destination, forcing a trek back north across the ice to Discovery Harbour. Their arrival had been anticipated, and when the pack opened up three days later, the two ships steamed south without further delay. Passage south through Kane Basin and Kennedy Channel proved to be difficult, and for a while it seemed like they might be caught fast in the ice for another winter, which could have been disastrous. However, on September 9 the ships managed to reach open water.

One month later, on the 27th of October 1876, after an unpleasantly stormy and difficult homeward passage, *Alert* steamed into the harbour at Valencia, on the southern tip of Ireland.

From Valencia, Captain Nares immediately telegraphed the Admiralty:

> ALL WELL. POLE IMPRACTICABLE. NO LAND TO NORTHWARD. OTHERWISE VOYAGE SUCCESSFUL. HIGHEST LATITUDE 83° 20'. ALERT PROCEEDS TO QUEENSTOWN. DISCOVERY EXPECTED HOURLY.[5]

Nares' telegram, although quite understandable from his point of view, was less than frank. All was not really well, except in the broadest and most generous interpretation of the phrase. All was only well in the sense that the two ships had made it home safely. The four deaths and the astonishingly severe outbreak of scurvy aboard both ships could not be so easily dismissed, and Nares knew full well that serious questions would soon be asked by the press and by his superiors at the Admiralty.

A local *Times* correspondent reported the deaths the next day. By then Nares, Moss, and Feilden were on the train to Killarney, where they stayed overnight before travelling on to Dublin. At the Dublin train station an enterprising "special correspondent" of the *Irish Times* (he was actually a cabby) drove Feilden and Nares to the Kingstown (now Dún Laoghaire) harbour, where they were to take the ferry to England. On the way he did his level best to pry information from them. Nares was polite but uncommunicative, stating that he could not talk about anything before presenting his report to the Admiralty. According to the correspondent, Feilden was more inclined to open up until Captain Nares leaned over and whispered something to him, presumably telling him to shut up, for the conversation immediately came to a rather abrupt halt. Edward was not with them; he stayed behind in Dublin for a brief but joyous family reunion before proceeding on to Portsmouth.

Back at Valencia, the *Irish Times* managed to get some very expansive interviews with unnamed sources who provided some long and detailed stories about the expedition. Not everyone spoke off the record. Chaplain Charles Hodgson, who was less reticent than most, gave out a rambling description of various events, even though his first-hand knowledge was confined pretty much to life aboard ship. He told about the "ice theatre" that took ten days for the whole crew to build from ice-blocks, with a roof made of sails covered with snow, and he tut-tutted that during the "dark period" the crew was issued with double rations of grog every day. Later, back in England, the muzzle was put on both crews by someone, either Nares or the Admiralty.[6] This failed to deter the irrepressible Chaplain, who ignored the restriction, apparently preferring the commandments of the ultimate spiritual authority to those of the mortals who ruled the temporal sphere.

When George Nares arrived in London, he immediately reported to the Admiralty. *The Times*, which had already extended its congratulations, downplaying the deaths, which were described as "no more than the ordinary casualties of a long voyage on an expedition fraught with numerous and uncertain perils." As for not reaching the Pole, it didn't really matter anyway according to the paper, which claimed that there was really was no more reason to go the Pole than to the Moon, and that anyway the expedition had firmly established that reaching the Pole was impracticable.

This judgment marked the beginning of what would soon become an acrimonious public debate about the planning and conduct of the expedition.

16: London

"Feet of Clay?"

In spite of their failure to reach the Pole, the initial public reaction after the return of the expedition was extremely positive. On October 30, *The Times* published a long commentary on the condition of the Beaumont Party upon its return to Polaris Bay, and by inference, that of the Markham and Aldrich groups:

> However vivid the description may be, it is difficult for a stranger to the surrounding circumstances and scenery to realize the condition and appearance of those prostrated men separated by distances, their sufferings were unknown to each other or to headquarters on board their respective ships; and yet one and all displayed the same courageous pluck, and, in spite of their general collapse, remained faithful to their duty, resolutely struggling onwards, determined to hold onto each other until the last, their ardour in no way checked as the difficulties of the journey increased, and their manful determination increasing as greater sacrifices were demanded.

When *Alert* and *Discovery* entered Portsmouth harbour five days later, they were also welcomed enthusiastically. At both Gosport and Portsmouth the gun batteries fired salutes, and at least a half-dozen bands, hundreds of family members, spectators, and sailors on deck or in the rigging of nearby vessels cheered them home. It was a triumphant and heartwarming return.

Plans for various celebrations to honour the officers and men were soon launched enthusiastically. Two banquets for the full ships' complements were organized, one under the auspices of the Mayor of Portsmouth, and the second hosted by the Lord Mayor of London. Each of these banquets fêted the men on one occasion and the officers on another.

The latter were also entertained at the Royal Naval College at Greenwich, and at the end of November a dinner was given for them at HMS *Excellent*, the Gunnery School at Portsmouth (in naval parlance a "stone frigate"). In all, the crews were honoured at no less than nine different affairs.

At the Gunnery School banquet a discussion arose about the wisdom or value of using alcohol on the sledging parties.[1] One of the expedition officers pointed out that a comparative check of the sledgers showed that the abstainers had surpassed the drinkers in the total number of days they were away from the ship. Chief Petty Officer Adam Ayles, the lone sledger who was still able to man the traces with Aldrich at the end of the Western Party's harrowing homeward journey, was cited as an example of the benefits of total abstinence. He had taken part in the travelling parties for a total of 110 days without succumbing to scurvy. Aldrich (newly promoted to Commander) stated that although he was not a teetotaller, he was "almost one," commenting that he had diluted his daily tot of rum more than the others in his party, who generally took a double tot. It was also claimed that the doctors were against giving rum during the midday halt for lunch and Dr. Colan, who was present at the dinner, was quoted as being in favour of total abstinence for sledge parties, a position he had taken before the expedition left England in May 1875. At that time Colan reviewed the expedition's diet, clothing, and sanitary regime for *The Lancet*, stating that rum, although forty over-proof, became as thick as treacle in severe weather and "was then nothing better than cold poison." The alcohol issue would continue to arouse considerable interest in the coming months.

The Lord Mayor's banquet at Portsmouth took place the next day. Three hundred people attended and received Captain Nares with "rapturous and long continued applause"[2] when he rose up to reply to the Lord Mayor's toast. In response (one imagines) to the comments made at the HMS *Excellent* dinner the previous day, as well as those in the press, he defended the daily issue of rum, claiming that the usual amount given aboard ship was reduced by one-third on the expedition, and then it was only given when the men were travelling. By this time (how quickly the armchair critics emerged) he was on the defensive. Questions were being raised about several aspects of the expedition, particularly those related to the scurvy epidemic and the heavy sledge weights the men had to pull. Nares had already denied an allegation that the men had been dragging impossible loads. This, according to some critics, had seriously weakened them to the point where they became more vulnerable to scurvy. However, for the moment, the controversy was still limited (at least publicly) to pot-shots back and forth in the press; it did not affect plans to confer distinction on the leaders and men of the expedition. The day after the Portsmouth banquet, Nares and Stephenson were received by the Queen at Windsor, and Captain Nares returned from his audience as Sir George Nares, Knight Commander of the Bath, while Stephenson received the lesser, though still prestigious, CB (Companion of the Bath).

The grandest banquets were those hosted by the Lord Mayor at the Mansion House in London during the first week in December.[3] The banquet for the men began with a dinner at 5:30 p.m. – a less fashionable time than for their officers – but one that allowed the men to return to Portsmouth on the night train. That evening each of them sported full dress uniforms, with the colourfully garbed Marines standing out in conspicuous glory among the more sedate navy blue of the matelots. On behalf of his mates, Colour-Sergeant William Wood moved the vote of thanks with impressive panache. In a final expression of public appreciation, every man present was presented with a pipe and one ounce of the finest tobacco, regardless of whether or not they were smokers. *The Times*, with a remark that spoke volumes about Victorian upper and middle class perceptions of those beneath them in the social order, made a point of stating that the men were on their best behaviour, conducting themselves well. One might well ask why it should have been otherwise; were they not all among the finest representatives of the breed, the "picked men of our nation," in the words of Edward Moss?

A few days later, on December 12, the Royal Geographical Society, replete with Old Arctics and other great men of science, rank, and distinction, gathered at St. James Hall to hear first-hand about the expedition they had so confidently, so determinedly, championed. This was even a grander occasion. Albert Hastings Markham's sledge *Marco Polo* was displayed on the stage, and his uncle, Clements Markham, gave the guest speakers an effusive welcome. The honour of presenting the main talk went of course to Sir George, who wisely focussed on the scientific and geographic benefits of the expedition, pointing out that much had been learned about the ice conditions, ocean currents, and ice-movements in the High Arctic. During his presentation Nares referred to Edward Moss as "an excellent microscopist and an officer of varied scientific attainments." Although Sir George could not entirely avoid the questions that were emerging in some sections of the press, he dwelled skilfully and at length on the ice conditions that had made the journeys so difficult, passing over the more controversial matters as best he could. Regarding the merits and shortcomings of the sledges, he observed that "if the whole journey had been made on soft snow, we should, perhaps adopt the Hudson's Bay plan of flat sledges with light weight, but as the soft snow is never continuous, and heavy pressed-up ice is the usual foe, we must, like the Eskimos keep to the Russian [style] sledges as [being] the most appropriate for general work." He did, however, recommend that any future expeditions should be equipped with snowshoes.

Stephenson then delivered a shorter paper titled "Arctic Winter Experiences," mainly dealing with life aboard *Discovery*. He was followed by Albert Markham, who spoke fairly briefly about sledge travelling, referring to April 3rd, when the departure of the sledges from the *Alert*, as "a brave sight on that cold, fine morning." Markham presented a description of daily life on the Northern Party with a talk that was essentially a verbal summary of his official report. Finally, the queen's surrogate, Edward, Prince of Wales, closed the evening by moving a vote of thanks to the gallant expedition officers. It had been another grand and impressive evening. However, in spite of these laudatory banquets, a troublesome dark cloud was looming over the expedition and its leaders.

One of the first public thunderclaps had already been heard when *The Lancet* launched a lightning bolt on November 18. This influential medical journal observed that it was "inconceivable that the medical officers should not have recommended the issue of lime juice" and suggested a week later that the failure to insist it should be carried by the spring sledging parties was a grave error on the part of Commander Markham. Such criticism went to the heart of the question, provoking other strikes and reverberations.

James Edmunds, Medical Officer of Health for the elegant St. James district in London had already weighed in with a letter to *The Times* on November 2. Edmunds did not understand why the expedition had been stricken so savagely by scurvy, as he believed that there were lots of musk oxen and birds available where the two ships wintered. Therefore they should have had plenty of fresh meat, in his view the best antiscorbutic remedy. He also criticized the use of alcohol instead of tea on the sledging parties and called for an official inquiry into the whole business. The British Medical Association's journal, *The Sanitary Record*, published comments of a similar nature, and by the end of the month it was hot on the trail.[4] Losing some men might be expected on any expedition of this kind, but as the full extent of the scurvy outbreak became widely known, demands at high admiralty and government levels also emerged. Yet, to put it bluntly, some of the statements and letters in the regular press were prematurely judgmental; particularly those of Edmunds, who failed to realize that Nares had taken *Alert* beyond the latitude where any game might be found during the winter months. Even eighty miles south, where *Discovery* wintered, game was anything but plentiful; it was certainly insufficient to provide enough fresh meat to have prevented the scourge.

During the first week of December, *The Times* observed that public interest in the scurvy issue was not diminishing; "indeed it is increasing." Commenting on "current conflicting views about how to prevent scurvy," the editor called the facts about the disease "few and simple: the direct result of the absence in the system of certain matters which are supplied by fresh vegetable juices, and as far as we know can be supplied by no other source." He didn't think that the lack of fresh meat was the problem, pointing out that over five thousand cases of scurvy had occurred during the Crimean War at times when fresh vegetables were unavailable. Finally, the magisterial editor hinted obliquely at possible dereliction of duty, by whom he did not reveal, although by inference it was almost certainly Nares.[5]

The battle lines were drawn rapidly as opinion leaders weighed in on one side or the other, pitting a number of Old Arctics, RGS members, and the expedition leaders against vocal critics inside and outside of Parliament. The magazine *Navy*, an effusively staunch supporter of planting the Union Jack at the Pole when the expedition left England eighteen months earlier, now turned viciously on both the Admiralty and Sir George Nares. Berton claims its response was typical, quoting it as stating that "the nation has reason to blush at the manner in which the very best of the opportunities of reaching the North Pole has been frittered away, and at the ridiculous figure that the First Lord of the Admiralty must cut in the eyes of foreign nations."[6] The publication flatly pronounced the expedition an abysmal failure, calling for both a public inquiry and a court martial for Captain Nares. It made the damning allegation that Nares had shown "an absence of zeal and determination" by abandoning the object of the expedition – making it to the Pole. This was a biased and premature judgment, but it certainly illustrates the passion that characterized the differing views about the expedition during the public debate over the next eight months. It was also a grossly unfair denunciation of the leader of the expedition.

Nares may not have been infected with the "Polar virus" like Hall or Peary, but he was not a quitter, and if his judgment and leadership may be called into question on a number of grounds, lack of zeal or determination is not among them. Nor was it ever seriously suggested as an issue elsewhere in the press or during the inquiry into the planning and conduct of the expedition. It would have been madness to have willingly remained at Floeberg Harbour for a second season.

Clements Markham,[7] Admiral Sir George Richards,[8] and Dr. John Rae[9] were all among the notable "Old Arctics" who entered into the debate. Markham, writing of his 1850–51 journeys in search of Franklin, claimed that, although one-quarter of an ounce of lime juice was issued daily aboard ship, none had been carried on the sledge trips. He also denied that the absence of fresh vegetables was the sole cause of scurvy, pointing out that the Eskimo diet contained practically no vegetable food. Dr. John Rae, on the other hand, sensibly observed that not much was really known about the food habits of the Eskimos, suggesting that perhaps they ate mosses to obtain the nutrients needed to prevent scurvy. He subscribed to the theory that the condition arose from lack of vegetables or lack of sufficient quantities of fresh meat, noting that in 1834 seventeen of his own men had come down with scurvy at Charlton Island on James Bay, far south of Nares' winter quarters. Rae reported curing his men with buds from the vetch plant (wild pea) and dried-up cranberries he found during the spring, but even so, two of his thirty men had died.

The Times, in a long editorial review in early December, discussed the experiences of a number of previous Arctic journeys. The paper acquitted Nares of misrepresenting the facts (as one correspondent had alleged) but at the same time suggested that the daily allowance ordered by Nares was simply insufficient. It was also difficult to believe, wrote the editor, that when the medical officers were consulted in England or on the trip, they could have failed to stress the importance of carrying lime juice on the travelling parties. Nevertheless, Nares' explanation that the only reason more juice was not taken on the travelling parties was to keep down the weight was accepted at face value.[10] And so the public discussion went. Round and round; back and forth up until Christmas, generally with a good deal of heat but with little real enlightenment. In the meantime, the Admiralty had been quietly seeking answers to its own questions since Nares' official report had been received. Within a fortnight of the expedition's return, in response to a query from the Commander-in-Chief at Portsmouth, the Secretary of the Admiralty, the Hon. Algernon F. Egerton MP, indicated that he had no opinion about the scurvy and was awaiting the observations of

Fleet-Surgeon Colan. Actually, within a week of arriving at Portsmouth, Egerton had requested a report on the scurvy outbreak from Inspector-General Armstrong,[11] and shortly after it was received the government took the first steps toward setting up a Committee to investigate the leadership and conduct of the expedition, particularly with respect to the scurvy outbreak. Admiral Sir James Hope, GCB, was appointed to chair the inquiry, and Vice-Admiral E. A. Inglefield,[12] CB (Old Arctic, and Fellow of the Royal Society), James Donnet,[13] MD, Inspector-General of Hospitals and Fleets (another Old Arctic), along with Thomas R. Fraser, MD, made up the investigating committee. The latter two medical men were tasked with researching a paper that would report on prevailing medical opinions about scurvy – diagnosis, causes, treatment, and so forth.

The hearings took place between early January and the end of February 1877. For the next six months, *The Lancet* regularly reported or editorialized on the most cogent details of the proceedings and the official report.

Captain Nares and several other officers, including all four physicians as well as a number of men from the sledging parties, made up the bulk of the forty-seven witnesses called to testify. Several prominent Arctic explorers and civilian medical and scientific men were also included. The instructions called for the Committee to inquire into and report on three main areas of concern: (1) the root cause of the massive outbreak of scurvy; (2) the adequacy of the provisions and diet; and (3) the propriety of Nares' orders to omit lime juice from the provisions of the sledging parties.[14]

Nares was the first to testify, spending three days in front of the committee. He was followed by Stephenson[15] and the officers who had commanded the sledging parties. The main parameters of the review were quickly established: shipboard and sledging diet – the issues around fresh, salt, and preserved (canned) meat, as well as fresh vegetables. The efficacy of lime juice as an antiscorbutic, sledge weights, air quality aboard the ships, rum versus tea, and whether or not lime juice should have been carried by the travelling parties. Strangely, none of the officers commanding the three forward parties – Markham,[16] Aldrich,[17] or Beaumont[18] – were ever seriously questioned about why they failed to recognize the early symptoms of scurvy or why they continued onward for so long that they imperilled the lives of their increasingly disabled men. One would have thought that the committee would have wanted answers to such questions even if it might have stretched the limits of their mandate, but perhaps, because of their obvious devotion to duty and heroic efforts, there was some reluctance to quiz the party leaders about such matters.

The turn of the medical officers began a week later, with the testimony of Dr. Colan.[19] On the subject of air quality aboard *Alert*, he recalled that Moss periodically tested both the air and the water aboard ship (the latter obtained from frozen or thawed pools atop a nearby berg) and declared both to be satisfactory. Once more, diet and the efficacy of lime juice were probed, and Colan responded to questions on current theories about antiscorbutics, particularly the idea that one or more of the acids in lime juice (citric, malic, or tartaric) was the key ingredient that helped to prevent scurvy. However, this was almost an aside. Colan was very specifically targeted over his unsuccessful meeting with Captain Nares regarding the necessity of carrying sufficient antiscorbutic to issue a daily dose to the men on the main travelling parties. He testified that he had neither been consulted when Nares ordered the ration of lime juice doubled for prospective sledgers in March, nor asked by Nares or the sledge commanders for his opinion about taking juice on the sledging parties. However, when he heard via the grapevine that juice would *not* be carried, he resolved to speak to the Captain, stating that he "deemed it right and prudent, if not incumbent on me" to do so. He testified that Nares had rejected his appeal on the grounds that juice could not be sent "unless other things deemed essential were left out." Although Colan believed that he could have done nothing more, some of his inquisitors thought otherwise; apparently believing he should have pressed his case more firmly with Nares.

Colan admitted to his interrogators that his own written medical instructions to the sledge commanders contained no direct mention of scurvy, though in fact he had warned Markham about some of the symptoms to watch for, swollen and discoloured legs, for example, and, if it could be found, advised the use of scurvy grass as a remedy. He also testified he told Markham that if scurvy did occur he should give his men as much dried onion and potato as possible to counteract the condition. Though he was not queried about it, Colan actually had brought up the subject of scurvy during a lecture on food in February. Aldrich, in referring to this lecture in his personal journal, described lime juice as "our greatest preservative – and remedy – if we get [scurvy], our 'sheet anchor' where fresh meat and vegetables are not available." One committee member asked Colan if the expedition was supplied with spruce beer, a bitter antiscorbutic brew sometimes used by natives and Hudson's Bay men in northern Canada. The answer was negative, which was hardly surprising, for both ships were hundreds of miles north of the tree line, and more palatable antiscorbutics were already available aboard ship.

Edward Moss was next to be called.[20] He was questioned in considerable detail, perhaps because, unlike Colan, he had been involved in sledging in addition to his medical and scientific duties. Following a brief description of the various sledging trips he had taken, Moss was asked for his opinion on the shipboard and sledging diets. His answers did not differ significantly from that of the other officers. In general, perhaps because he had been through the *Bulldog* Inquiry in 1866 and was wise enough to avoid volunteering unasked-for information, or because he was reluctant to criticize or contradict his superiors, his testimony was given with apparent caution.

On the issue of air purity, ventilation, and water quality, Moss was probed thoroughly, presumably because Colan had indicated that he was responsible for testing of air and water quality, and because – unlike his counterpart on *Discovery* – Colan had not furnished the results of the tests in his official report. The air quality below deck on *Alert* during the winter, though naturally less pure than the outside atmosphere, was still satisfactory, in his opinion – a reasonable compromise between the need for adequate ventilation and the need to keep the temperature and living conditions aboard ship reasonably comfortable.

As for the food, Moss pronounced both the quality and the quantity satisfactory, though unavoidably lacking in sufficient quantities of fresh meat or vegetables. This lack was the main reason for the scurvy outbreak in his view. When asked if he had examined the lime juice to determine its quality, he answered in the affirmative and suggested that he had thought it might be interesting to test the quality of the juice aboard ship and then again after returning to England, presumably to see if there was deterioration over time. It was acknowledged that such a comparison had not yet been made. In the absence of fresh meat or fresh vegetables, he was sure that lime juice was the most effective antiscorbutic, and while it would be possible to make it available at greater levels of concentration, research would be needed to establish if it would be more efficacious in that form.

And so the questioning went. How aware was he of scurvy reports on previous expeditions? (He was aware of them.); what did he know about the Eskimo diet? (He thought they often survived on seal or other meat alone.); did he or any of the men on his sledge trips suffer from scurvy? (No, though there was some stiffness of joints.); was it necessary to carry and use rum on the trips? (No, but a small quantity was not harmful.); would citric acid alone be a substitute for lime juice? (No, he seemed to recall that experiments had not shown that this approach had any merit.).

Had he ever heard of scurvy at Greenland? (Yes.); on his local explorations or sledge trips did he ever find scurvy-grass, sorrel, or cranberries? (No.); had he ever seen symptoms of scurvy among the Indians at Esquimalt? (Possibly, as on occasion he had observed swollen limbs and scaly skin.); was there any attempt to grow cress or mustard aboard ship during the winter? (Yes, but with little success.); were the "temperance men" more, or less, susceptible to attack by scurvy? (He had no opinion; there were too few of them to make a deduction.); tea? (Good.); tobacco? ("Absolutely injurious."); beer as an antiscorbutic? (No opinion.).

Finally, he was asked again to express his opinion about the reasons for the scurvy outbreak. His response was unequivocal: the outbreak had occurred "because the men had been exposed to conditions known to favour scurvy: that is, being without fresh meat or fresh vegetables, and on the sledges trips, also without lime juice." When asked, he agreed that it would be beneficial to include a doctor on sledge parties. Perhaps, he observed, if a doctor had been along, the symptoms of scurvy would have been recognized sooner and the outbreak would have been less virulent, though a doctor could not have done very much with the limited medical supplies carried on the travelling parties. He thought that regular daily issue of lime juice for the sledgers might have delayed the outbreak but doubted that it would have been able to avert the onset of the condition in the long run.

Moss's testimony may be described as careful and straightforward. He forthrightly answered all the questions but seldom volunteered anything. Asked if there had been any discussion about scurvy aboard *Alert*, he observed that "anything tending to the suggestion of scurvy was very much discountenanced in our [the officers] mess." Queried about whether or not he had ever seen scurvy before, he acknowledged that he had once seen it in a mild form – clearly a reference to the cases that he had treated at Esquimalt a few years earlier. Finally, and presumably because it was known that he had used snowshoes on the expedition, he was asked for his opinion of their value, replying that he had found them useful, recommending that on any future expeditions the Western American type, with pointed tips, should be used. Moss was followed by Staff Surgeon Belgrave Ninnis, the Senior Medical Officer on *Discovery*, whose testimony differed little from that of Colan or Moss.

A crucial witness as the inquiry proceeded was Sir Alexander Armstrong, whose testimony, as the Medical Director-General of the Navy and a recognized authority on scurvy, carried a great deal of weight.[21] He had already submitted his May 1875 memorandum to Nares, in which he had made a whole series of recommendations or instructions (he claimed they had the force of orders) relating to the diet and health of the men, both aboard ship and while travelling. Armstrong's purpose in drawing up the memorandum to Nares was spelled out very clearly in the document:

> The great object in view is to maintain the men in the same health and vigour as when they were entered [into Arctic service].... This can only be done by the use of a liberal diet, both in animal food and vegetables. I consider the former should consist of 2 lbs. of meat daily with a proportionate amount of vegetables and antiscorbutics ... if acted on I would anticipate little or no impairment of the physical powers; but on the contrary with a scale of diet smaller than this I consider the debility of a scorbutic character must ensue, and that at an early period if the men are exposed to hard work and intense cold.[22]

Armstrong also advised that fresh meat should alternate with salt meat each day with an appropriate quantity of vegetables. Cabbage was judged the best choice but "Edward's Preserved Potatoes" should form the bulk of the vegetable food. An issue of lime juice every day was urged very strongly, and cocoa and tea recommended as being "infinitely preferable" to spirits.

The key point, however, was recommendation #11. It stated that "the use of lime juice while travelling should be enforced in the same manner as already recommended for the men aboard ship." This directive was the one that Nares was alleged to have ignored when he failed to order the sledge commanders to carry sufficient lime juice to meet the suggested criteria. Almost all of Armstrong's other recommendations were in fact followed as closely as possible on the expedition. Under questioning, the officers, and more importantly the men who testified, made it clear that the overall diet, though rather boring, was satisfactory or superior to the usual shipboard fare – with the extremely important exception of insufficient quantities of fresh meat and fresh vegetables – and Nares was unable to do much about either of these deficiencies.

Dr. Armstrong was a man with presence and very strong opinions. He responded to his interrogators in a very direct and definite fashion, though at times his replies revealed a certain degree of edginess. One might have thought that he, rather than Nares, was under siege, and in no small measure that was true. His medical advice, the judgment of his medical officers, and by inference the competence of the Medical Branch was being challenged. Armstrong did not take kindly to such notions.

The Director-General made it very clear that he did not accept the miasmic theory that bad air, extended absence of sunlight, or dampness below decks had brought on the scurvy. He felt that sledge weights were excessive and that the men had "struggled like heroes in the attempted performance of an impossible duty." Under the circumstances, the task of reaching the Pole was simply impossible. "I believe," he stated, "that had the ice from the *Alert* to the Pole been as smooth as a bowling green, they could not have reached it with this equipment."[23] Moreover the parties should not have been expected to travel more than forty-five days. As far as carrying an adequate supply of lime juice on the sledges, he had never considered that it was a real problem, believing it would have been better to have slightly limited the potential number of days away in order to carry sufficient juice. Markham had already acknowledged that this would have reduced the number of daily rations by only three days and Armstrong thought such a reduction would have been "most sensible." He was not asked and did not volunteer an opinion about cutting down the stock of spirits as a way to make room for more lime juice.

Towards the end of his testimony, Armstrong was questioned very carefully by Admiral Hope, who recapitulated key testimony about some of the most severe cases of scurvy and pressed the Director-General on the issue of whether or not his May 1875 letter to Nares was just a series of recommendations, or whether it carried the weight of an order. This line of questioning suggests that Hope may have been trying to show that the medical officers themselves did not treat Armstrong's directive as an order. Hope also asked if it was not the "imperative duty" of the medical officers to have urged on their superior officers, in the strongest possible way, the necessity of sending lime juice with the sledge parties. Armstrong replied that he believed Colan had done his duty, and that Nares should not have made his decision to limit the supply of juice without consulting his senior medical officer. When Hope tried to get him to admit that Colan should have put his recommendation to Captain Nares in writing, Armstrong bristled, replying that Colan had no obligation to do so, and that it was a question "upon which officers like Dr. Colan might take a different position."[24] The blame was thus put squarely on Nares for disregarding his Medical Officer's recommendation.

Dr. Donnet came back into the matter by asking (again) if there was any use giving the sledge officers information about recognizing scurvy when they had no real means of treating it. Armstrong did not accept that argument, maintaining that it was the duty of the sledge commanders to return to the ship if scorbutic symptoms appeared. He did, however, think that clear instructions would have enabled them to detect the scurvy earlier. A copy of his book "*Naval Hygiene and Scurvy*" had been provided for the expedition with the idea that the officers would all read it and make themselves acquainted with the symptoms of the disease. Finally, Dr. Fraser asked if it was incumbent on a medical officer, when he gave a recommendation that was disregarded, to record his written opinion. Armstrong thought not, unless the doctor felt for some reason that it was best to do so. There the matter rested until a week later, when Captain Nares was recalled to give what amounted to a rebuttal.[25]

Sir George denied the inference that there was a lack of communication between himself and Colan, claiming that "never for a moment," based on his knowledge of the experience of earlier expeditions, had he thought there would be an outbreak of scurvy during the first year in the Arctic. He denied the claim that the men had insufficient exercise over the winter or that he had not taken proper care or acted prudently in a number of other matters. Regarding Armstrong's statement that the Pole was impossible, he observed that the crews had never been ordered to journey to the Pole: "No commander, with the view of the northern ice before him that I had, would have issued such an order." As for Armstrong's book, he didn't know that there was a copy on the ship, "if so it must have been mislaid," so he never had the opportunity to read it. He continued to claim that previous expeditions had not identified scurvy on their travelling parties but had simply labelled them under the broad category of "debility." Finally, he had expected that his sledging parties would be able to proceed safely without carrying more than medicinal quantities of lime juice, but now he believed that there was more scurvy on previous expeditions than he realized. Clearly, this comment suggested that he would have done things differently had he known more about the symptoms and causes of the condition. But on the question of Armstrong's memorandum he refused to back down, continuing to insist that it was only a series of suggestions rather than an order. That said, he stated that he was still prepared to accept full responsibility for the decisions he had made.

After Nares' second appearance, the Committee quickly wrapped up the investigation and proceeded to prepare its preliminary report, which was released unofficially on March 8. *The Times* reported some of their conclusions, the main one being that Nares had insufficient reason to deviate from the instructions sent to him by Director-General Armstrong. This judgment failed to put an end to the controversy, as some prominent naval persons rallied to defend Sir George. One of the most vocal was the irascible Vice-Admiral Sir George Richards,[26] former Chief Hydrographer of the Navy, Fellow of the Royal Society, close friend of Nares, and legendary Old Arctic sledger. In the May 2 issue of *The Times*, Richards launched an all-out attack on both Armstrong and the medical profession. He condemned the Committee report as "ungenerous" and "vindictive," singling out as well "that portion of the Press representing the medical profession" – clearly a reference to *The Lancet* and *The Sanitary Review*. Medical Director Armstrong was then lashed with the charge that his recommendations to Nares were simply a means of evading his own responsibility. "Official authority," wrote Richards, "says I know what will prevent

you all from getting scurvy; I have never tried it myself, and I know it is impossible [that] you can [try it]; but I shall tell you to do so, and if you do not, and get scurvy, I have no responsibility." Richards stated that the naval service in general would never accept the censure of Sir George Nares, claiming that there was "not one officer living who would not have followed the same course as Nares regarding diet." In Richard's view, lime juice was unnecessary and impossible to administer frozen, and as far as the tea versus rum business was concerned, "Time should not be wasted [during sledging] in boiling tea and melting lime juice to prove our own sense of [the] moral or material impropriety of drinking the usual allowance of spirits." However, Richards' missive was really something of a last-ditch effort to defend the beleaguered Nares. After the release of the final report in June, public interest in the whole matter began to wane, though it certainly continued privately in naval and medical circles.

Along with censuring Nares, the report presented several reasons for the outbreak of scurvy. The "predisposing causes" were listed as the lack of lime juice on the spring parties, absence of sunlight for 142 days over winter, confinement in a comparatively tainted atmosphere, exposure to extreme temperatures, and (especially on *Alert*) the lack of fresh meat. It was declared that all these were aggravated by the brutal work in severe cold and the inability at times to get adequate food or sleep. The quantity and quality of the food and medical supplies was deemed "in every way adequate" and superior to any previous Arctic expedition.

On June 5, 1877, Nares received the official judgment of the Lords of the Admiralty in a letter from Admiralty Secretary Hall, who reported that these notables had accepted the conclusions of the Committee of Inquiry. Hall made allowance for the difficulties Nares had faced in determining the best way to provision the sledges but expressed regret that he had "failed to attach sufficient weight to the recommendations of the Director-General." Nares replied a day later, asking for a competent tribunal to allow him to clear his name, with the opportunity to call his own witnesses and have the advice of Counsel because of "the injury [he] had suffered." His request was ignored.

The overall conclusions about the root causes of scurvy were a curious mixture of then current medical, scientific, and conventional wisdom. They were essentially based on the Donnet/Fraser paper on scurvy, where the prevailing views were laid out after consultation with almost a dozen pre-eminent medical authorities, including Sir Alexander Armstrong. A Mr. Busk was the main scientist who had been consulted and his conclusions were intuitively on the right track when he described scurvy as "a disease of defective rather than deficient nutrition … a species of starvation due to the want of a particular element, the nature of which … we are entirely ignorant, but according to most authorities is afforded by vegetable juices."[27]

It would be over fifty years before vitamin C (ascorbic acid) was discovered and identified as the critical element that was required for the prevention of scorbutus. In 1877 neither the Government nor the Navy showed any interest in following up on a suggestion made by one MP during debate over the scurvy issue. He asked if the government intended to initiate scientific studies into the cause of scurvy so that when (or if) another polar expedition was launched there would be no repetition of the 1876 deaths. The Administration's reply was in the negative, only suggesting that this could be done prior to any future venture. Yet many years later, when Robert Scott went to the Antarctic, medical knowledge of the root cause of scurvy had scarcely improved. In Antarctica on August 18, 1911, the Scott Expedition doctor, E. L. Atkinson, gave the men a lecture on the causes, symptoms, and remedies for scurvy. He reviewed its history and the remedies that had long been in used in the Navy. When it came to discussing the cause, Atkinson could do no better (and some might say worse) than medical men of the previous generation, listing tainted food and "acid intoxification of the blood" along with the usual culprits of bad air, cold, and over-exertion. Fresh vegetables were considered the best curative, lime juice only if used regularly, and doubt was expressed about the value of fresh meat, except perhaps in Arctic conditions.[28] This description seems astonishingly inadequate for that late date, but it illustrates the confusion and ignorance that continued to exist in the medical profession long after the Nares episode.

In his article "Scurvy During Some British Arctic Expeditions, 1875–1917" (Polar Record, 1955), Dr. Richard Kendall analyzed the diet and estimated the vitamin C content of the daily rations issued to the men on each of the two ships, using the original supply and dietary information submitted to the Scurvy Inquiry. Once the ships were in their winter quarters, and when they had used up their supplies of fresh vegetables, the cooks were dependent on canned or dried carrots, peas, potatoes, and "compressed" vegetables. Given the canning methods of the day, the canned food probably contained little vitamin C, and the vegetables were generally re-cooked before serving, thereby losing most of the small amount of vitamin C that remained. He concluded that the daily ration of preserved and salt meat aboard ship was satisfactory in terms of quantity, amounting to roughly two pounds a day on each vessel, with salt pork and salt beef being alternated almost equally with preserved (canned) meat and suet in daily meals. Contrary to Pierre Berton's claim,[29] the men never had to endure a steady diet of salt meat. The lack of fresh meat and fresh vegetables was of course the stickler. The men on *Discovery*, because game was more plentiful in their location, averaged about six ounces per day of fresh meat while those on *Alert* averaged less than an ounce. However, Kendall believed that because more bottled fruit was served aboard *Alert*, the quantity of vitamin C the men received, including their daily ration of lime juice, was about equal on both ships, varying within an estimated range of 3.2 to 5.5 milligrams daily. The real problem was that the quantity of juice issued, and therefore the quantity of vitamin C, was insufficient to maintain their health over a long period of time. At least four times the given dosage would have been necessary. Kendall came to the following, undoubtedly correct, conclusion about the outbreak of scurvy on the Nares Expedition:

> More game, a winter diet richer in fruit and vegetables, and fresh lemon juice instead of preserved lime juice would all have raised the level of vitamin C to a safer level, but it is probable that, in addition, a supply of game would have been necessary during the long sledge journeys to avoid the disease altogether. In the circumstances, the length of the expedition's journeys is quite remarkable.[30]

This conclusion does not differ significantly from that of Edward Moss, who believed that even if greater quantities of lime juice had been carried and administered on the sledging parties, the scurvy outbreak would only have been deferred, but not prevented.

The 1875–76 expedition was the last great British north polar attempt until the British Trans-Arctic Expedition (1968–69). After more failed attempts by others over the next generation, it was an American, Robert Peary, who in 1909 would lay claim to the Polar prize. However, today it is widely believed that neither Peary, nor his challenger Dr. Frederick Cook,[31] who also claimed the honour, ever stood at the apex of the world, though Peary came closer than any man until more recent times. As for the British, it was the South, rather than the North, Pole that next caught the imagination of the public. It was also Clements Markham who once again promoted the South Pole odyssey, and the tragic death of Robert Scott and others members of his party demonstrated once more how unforgiving the polar regions could be when mistakes are made.

As for Edward Moss, the Nares Expedition, like the *Bulldog* episode in 1865, was characterized by considerable ambivalence. He had accepted with great enthusiasm the opportunity to join in the grand adventure, and in December 1874 had written his mother that he thought that the expedition offered "the opportunity for rapid advancement of every sort" and the probability of shore appointments, and therefore no more family separations, for the rest of his career. It did not take long for him to realize that these were likely to be vain hopes.

However, his career ambitions were only part of the story. The idea of taking part in such an important expedition went to the very depth of Edward Moss's soul. The zeal, which he brought to all his duties while in the Arctic, attested to by the fulsome compliments of his peers as well as his superiors, demonstrates his commitment to every aim of the expedition. Thankfully no hint of impropriety, incompetence, or lack of zeal was ever laid at Edward Moss's door. He was proud, and had every reason to proud, of the contributions that he had made during his eighteen months along the shore of the polar sea. His mother, and his grandfathers, who had danced round the room at his parents' wedding holding hands and singing "from my youth I have kept it [my name] unsullied by blame, and it still from a spot shall be free," would have been pleased with the credit he had brought to himself and his family.

Until the spring of 1876, Edward's medical duties aboard *Alert* appear to have been fairly minimal, assisting Colan with patients when necessary, taking shipboard air and water samples, or perhaps offering advice about medical matters. Although he had no direct responsibility for decisions that were made about the use of lime juice on the sledge parties, one can surmise what his view would have been on this matter. When he was in a position to make his own medical decisions, as he was during the first twelve days of the spring sledging, he was very conscientious and quite cautious. Also, Near Cape Joseph Henry, as the northern and western parties were about to go forward on their own, he did not hesitate to suggest the replacement of James Berrie and Elias Hill with healthier men, a decision that undoubtedly saved their lives. His finest efforts were the swift snowshoe journey to aid the Markham party and his around-the-clock care for the sick on the return trek and aboard ship during the long recovery period. Once again, as during the *Bulldog* affair, he had shown his mettle.

Yet Edward also had reason to be somewhat disappointed about his role in the scientific aspects of the Arctic experience. He had been chosen for the appointment, in the main, because of his reputed credentials as a naturalist and zoologist. Then, even before he made it home from Esquimalt, pressures were allegedly brought to bear by the Royal Society to use a "professional," Feilden, for the main zoological and botanical work, with the result that he had to accept a lesser scientific role. As things turned out, this left him in a situation where he could also volunteer to command one of the sledges, an assignment that in many ways was much more to his liking, for it promised adventure and action, things he always craved. Still, he returned from the Arctic hankering for recognition and respect from the intellectual and scientific community, and this he tried to garner by writing and illustrating a book and producing several short papers on aspects of his scientific work in the Arctic. The latter were published over the next couple of years in the proceedings of the Royal Society, the Linnean Society, the Royal Dublin Society, and the Royal Irish Academy. The *Irish Times* reported that he read a paper, "The Recent Arctic Expedition" and exhibited his clothing, specimens, and some other articles at the RDS on January 13, 1877, and in March he was awarded an honorary membership in the institution "for his eminence as a naturalist" and because of his "important donation," presumably an artefact brought back from the North.

Also on the positive side of the ledger was the recognition at the several banquets honouring the expedition participants, though unfortunately, the pleasure derived from them quickly faded as a result of the controversy and negativity that emerged over the next few months. By the time *Shores of the Polar Sea* was completed and published in the spring of 1878, the public had lost interest in the expedition, and it is unlikely that either Edward or his publisher ever made any money from his informative and beautifully illustrated work.

Shortly after their return, Edward, along with the other medical officers, were awarded the Arctic Medal (First Class) and, with the exception of Dr. Colan, an immediate promotion. The failure to promote Colan suggested to some observers that he was being punished or that judgment was being reserved about his conduct. Although this was officially denied, it seems likely that it was the case. On March 2 the question of Colan's absence from the promotion list was raised in Parliament, and the administration response was that, because positions at the next higher rank were limited, there were no immediate vacancies. However, his promotion was granted just one day after the question was posed, which does suggest that it might have been withheld until he was officially cleared of neglect of duty for not lodging a formal complaint with the Captain over the question of carrying lime juice on the sledging parties. Moreover, the Navy List for the period does indicate that other appointments to the rank of Fleet Surgeon were made during the time his promotion was being withheld.

As for the expedition, important questions remained unanswered after the Scurvy Inquiry, particularly regarding the judgment and conduct of the officers who commanded the main sledging parties. They remain unanswered to this day, for remarkably few private diaries, letters, or reminiscences have surfaced over the years to throw more light on the subject. More likely than not, some are bundled together gathering dust in a family attic or amidst family correspondence in a local archive, their possible importance as yet unrecognized and unrevealed.

17: Kingstown, Ireland

"Brief Interlude"

In February, after the inquiry was over, Edward returned to Ireland where he spent most of the next eighteen months with Senie and the children. His service record indicates that for much of that period he was either on leave or on half-pay. During the first six months, he was borne on the books of HMS *Iron Duke*, stationed at Kingstown (now Dún Laoghaire) just south of Dublin, and for the next year on the roster of HMS *Topaze*.

At that time both vessels were classified as "Static Ships," functioning at Kingstown as local coastguard headquarters. In the Navy List, Edward is recorded as junior to the fleet surgeon on board, but most likely he was simply being borne on the ship's books for pay purposes. However, very little is really known about his activities during this interlude back in Ireland, and it is possible that he may have filled in for the Fleet Surgeon from time to time.

Ada, who was only nine months old and barely walking when Edward had left for the Arctic, must now have been a vocal and active two-year-old. She would hardly have remembered her father, for an eighteen-month separation is a long time in the life of such a small child. Thirteen months after Edward's return, there was a new addition to the family when she was joined by a little sister, Beatrice Mary, born at Dublin on December 29, 1877.

Between the double pay he had received for the Arctic service and his half-pay, he was in good shape financially, and the long break from sea duty allowed him to complete the manuscript and illustrations for *Shores of the Polar Sea*. He chose the Belfast firm of Marcus Ward & Co., a well-known and respected publisher noted for high quality printing and chromolithography, to do the book. As a result, *Shores* emerged as a genuine work of art and Edward must have been extremely happy with the result. It was a large 20" x 15" tabletop book bound with an exquisitely embossed blue and gold leather cover, and featured sixteen superb colour reproductions of Edward's best Arctic watercolours, as well as many fine pen and ink sketches. When it was reviewed in the *Illustrated London News* in July 1878, it was rightly touted as a "handsome portfolio."

> Dr. Moss has written a very entertaining and sufficient commentary, narrative, and description, to accompany these striking views of Arctic scenery and pictures of the various positions of the ships, sledges etc., and the crews of the detached parties of the men, which form a vivid representation of all of the outward aspects most worthy to be remembered in their experience of the wonderful region. It would make a good Christmas gift.[1]

This was a reasonable judgment. The narrative was generally understated and matter-of-fact, although when Edward's heart, eye, and mind coalesced imaginatively, he created evocative and perceptive descriptions of the scenes and events that accompanied his artistry. In the preface he stated that the book was intended to be only "a sketch book with text included merely to comment and describe the pictures," but this was a deceptively modest description, for the narrative did – and was intended to do – considerably more than that. What it did *not* do, however, was to provide enlightenment about any of the controversial aspects of the expedition, for right from the beginning he deemed the scurvy issue "improper to discuss here." The work was a straightforward and interesting chronicle, but it failed to capture the real depth of the human drama and tragedy experienced during the long marches of the travelling parties. Nor does the reader get any real sense of the character and personalities of the men who so valiantly served or died on the polar ice and the bleak Greenland shore. While the dogged determination and hardship of the sledge crews is apparent both visually and textually, most of the leading characters in the drama remain little more than names to the reader, and Edward Moss himself does not emerge personally, except in a decidedly oblique fashion. The work was in no sense intended to be autobiographical, and unless the reader had known the author personally or through his letters and official reports, it would be difficult to recognize where he had written himself into the narrative. This literary approach, however, was very much in keeping with the times for books of a similar genre and should not be overemphasized.

Edward's approach to his subject was undoubtedly influenced by the fact that both Nares and Markham were also writing books about the expedition. As a junior officer and ancillary player, he was hardly in a position to contradict what he knew to be their version of events even if he were so inclined – which he was not. He was not lacking in *esprit de corps*, the characteristic devotion and pride in the group that often creates an almost unbreakable bond between those who have shared great tribulations or desperate adventures. If he harboured any criticisms about the leadership or conduct of the expedition, they were kept within his naval family. As a result, the narrative was intentionally cautious and non-judgmental. The disclaimer in his preface established the parameters: the work was deliberately crafted to ensure that he would not appear to impinge on Nares and Markham's territory. He had not written the book to justify anything or to criticize the actions of others but only, as he put it, "to inform" by providing the necessary context for his paintings and sketches.

Unfortunately, *Shores of the Polar Sea* never lived up to Edward's hopes, either in terms of commercial success or personal acclaim. Becoming a published author undoubtedly gave him a great deal of satisfaction, but the work failed to compensate the time, effort, or money that he (and Marcus Ward) had put into it. A year after it was published, he wrote that he did not believe the publisher had made expenses on the project. Today, the rarely found copies of his book are highly prized and extremely expensive.

Shores was not Edward's only literary or artistic effort. While he was still in the Arctic, an article, *Sport in British Columbia*, based on the story of his second bear hunt on Vancouver Island, appeared in *The Graphic* (London) in June of 1876. He spiced up the adventure with eight small sketches illustrating the hunt, one of them depicting him being charged by the wounded bear. Apparently he also sent some other sketches to *The Graphic* from Greenland, for they were published in a special Arctic supplement of the paper in September 1875. At the academic level he also authored some modest articles after his return from the North.[2] "On Specimens of *Osteocela Septentrionalis*" (whatever these sea creatures were) was presented at the Museum of Natural History in Edinburgh within weeks of his return, and other scientific papers were published by the Linnean Society, the Royal Dublin Society, the Royal Society, and the Royal Irish Academy between 1876 and 1878. Edward continued to seek recognition and respect as a true man of science like his brother Richard or his brother-in-law, paleontologist Dr. Ramsay Traquair, and these modest papers were small steps toward that goal.

In seven or eight years he would be eligible to leave the Navy with a modest pension. At that time he would still be young enough to begin a new professional life, either in the field of science or in private medical practice. Alternatively, he might even remain in the Navy if he was promoted to a well-paid sinecure that would allow him to remain ashore and follow his personal bliss at the same time. However, the latter scenario seemed unlikely unless Britain were drawn into a major European war, which was always a possibility. The number of medical officers in the Navy had been declining for years, and it was not until the mid-1880s that their numbers began to gradually increase with the growth of British naval strength during the latter years of the century.

But this was a future Edward could not have foretold in 1877. He only knew that before long there would be a new posting, most likely for service afloat in the Eastern Mediterranean, where a powerful British fleet was positioned near the Dardanelles, keeping watch over a worrisome situation involving the Turks, the Russians, and the other Slavic peoples of the Balkans. In spite of a declared truce and much diplomatic manoeuvring, England might still be dragged into this morass and open conflict with Tsarist Russia. It was the possibility of such a war that ultimately took Edward to Beshika Bay, Turkey, where a major portion of the British Mediterranean Fleet lay at anchor. There he was destined to meet the most widely known and controversial archaeologist of the day, Heinrich Schliemann, who was conducting excavations at Hisarlik, close to Beshika Bay.

Schliemann claimed Hisarlik, some twelve miles from the Bay, was the site of ancient Troy. Moss, like most educated men of his day, was very familiar with the classics, including Homer's *Iliad*, the timeless epic of the siege of Troy. Schliemann had been very much in the public eye for several years, and during the spring and early summer of 1877 he spent several months in London, overseeing the publication of his latest book about his excavations at Mycenae, in Greece. Reports of his discoveries at Hisarlik and at Mycenae had already appeared from time to time in *The Times*, and in London the Great Man had been lionized as he made the rounds of the most prestigious learned societies delivering lectures about his theories and discoveries. Given Edward's scientific predilections, it would have been be very surprising indeed if he had not followed the newspaper reports about Schliemann's triumphant progress. It would be equally surprising if he did not intend to visit Hisarlik after he arrived at Beshika Bay and decide for himself if Hisarlik was, as Schliemann claimed it to be, Homer's Troy.

18: Beshika Bay, Turkey

"Letters from Troy"

Trouble in the Balkans was anything but new. The war drums rolled with distressing regularity in this hotbed of religious differences and nationalist aspirations, so it was really no surprise when the centuries-old "Eastern Question" re-emerged in the mid-1870s. The Ottoman Turks and the Russians had been at each others throats in the Balkans in almost every generation since the sixteenth century without resolving the myriad issues and grievances between the two powers, or within the Balkan provinces under Turkish rule. The depth of the ancient grievances within the region, and between the two empires, was great; it seemed as if nothing was ever forgotten, nothing ever forgiven. The most recent 1990s outbreak of bloodshed and "ethnic cleansing" in the Balkans merely demonstrates once more the apparently intractable nature of the problems (with new ones added from time to time) in the "the tinderbox of Europe" as the Balkans was commonly referred to before the First World War.

In 1875, rebellion against Turkish rule broke out in Herzegovina and Bosnia and then spread like a virus to the Bulgarians who, hungering mightily to get out from under the yoke of their Ottoman masters, also rose in revolt, only to be ruthlessly massacred by the thousands for their temerity. When a wave of revulsion and anger against this slaughter of their Slavic brethren swept across Serbia and Montenegro, they too joined the rebel cause. Unfortunately the Serb armies failed to prevail, and by late 1876 Turkish forces were on the doorstep of Belgrade, the Serbian capital. At that point Russia issued an ultimatum demanding that the Turks accept a temporary truce, and this was followed (at the instigation of the British) by a conference of the "Great Powers"[1] of Europe. However, two months of discussions failed to produce a settlement. The Ottoman Sultan refused to agree to anything that would impinge on Turkish independence or sovereignty over his subject peoples, Christian or Moslem. At a second conference, the "Powers" approved a modest agreement that would have at least protected the Christians who were under Turkish rule, but this too was spurned by the Sultan. At that point, Tsar Alexander II, caught up in the drumbeat of patriotic pan-Slavic fervour, declared war on Turkey.

The details of the 1876–78 Russo-Turkish War need not be gone into here. It is enough to observe that the British government had absolutely no intention of allowing the Russians to take control of the Dardanelles, thereby threatening the Suez trade route to India. Disraeli warned the Tsar that if his armies entered Constantinople there would be war. To make this absolutely clear, the Mediterranean Fleet was strengthened and on July 3, 1877, a powerful naval flotilla arrived at Beshika Bay, close to the western entrance to the Dardanelles, tasked with ensuring control of the Sea of Marmora and guaranteeing that Constantinople did not fall into Russian hands. It was to Beshika Bay, for service aboard the small battleship HMS *Research*, that Edward Moss was ordered in the early fall of 1878. Before he left for the Mediterranean, Edward moved Senie and the girls back to Southsea, and then in October left to join *Research*.

By that time the British had long since secured the Dardanelles. Admiral Hornby had steamed past the Turkish gun batteries protecting the Dardenelles and entered the Sea of Marmora many months earlier.[2] The Russians, believing that the British were serious, stopped short of trying to take Constantinople. During the truce that followed, they forced the Turks to sign the Treaty of San Stefano, which revised the map of the Balkans along lines that greatly favoured Russia, but satisfied none of the other European powers. Public opinion in England was particularly incensed over this turn of events. One result was the coining of a new phrase "jingoism" which would ever after describe a bellicose, blustering, posture towards another country. Its origin was a popular London music-hall ditty containing the following lines of verse:

> We don't want to fight, yet by jingo! if we do,
> We've got the ships, we've got the men,
> And we've got the money too.

But bluster aside, the aging Disraeli (now Lord Beaconsfield) had no stomach for another war with Russia. He joined with the dual monarchy of Austria-Hungary to convene the Congress of Berlin, where Bismarck,[3] Chancellor of Prussia, acted as mediator. Ultimately these deliberations produced a new agreement (the Treaty of Berlin) that rearranged the map of the Balkans in ways beneficial to both Austria-Hungary and Britain while reducing the power and influence of both the Russians and the Turks in the Balkans. During all this complicated bargaining, the fleet remained in a state of readiness only a dozen or so miles from Hisarlik.

When Moss arrived at Beshika Bay he found there only a rough settlement of sorts catering to the needs or wants of the men aboard the ships. It was a singularly unappealing place. An 1878 sketch in the *Illustrated London News* portrays some primitive sheds sheltering horses for rent to the naval officers (Edward among them) who wanted to do some hunting or local exploration to break the monotony of ship-board life in such a boring place. The opportunity to visit Schliemann's dig provided a distraction, and around the time Edward arrived a number of officers rode out to Hisarlik, where Henry Schliemann[4] was excavating at the site he believed to be ancient Troy.

Ten years earlier, on his first trip to Turkey, Schliemann had met Frank Calvert, a local landowner and part-time archaeologist, who had conducted some preliminary excavations at Hisarlik in 1865 in the belief that it was Homer's Troy. However, Calvert lacked the financial resources to carry out extensive excavations and was unable to extract even the most miserly funding from the British Museum for such a project. Enter Schliemann, self-made millionaire and largely self-educated archaeologist; a man with a consuming passion and deep enough pockets to take on the task. He would later claim that he, not Calvert, had first put forth the idea that Hisarlik was ancient Troy and that Calvert had merely confirmed his view, a claim that does not stand up to scrutiny. However, with Calvert's help Schliemann obtained the necessary government permit to excavate at Hisarlik (Calvert owned part of the land at the site) and during the 1873–74 dig Schliemann was rewarded with the discovery of a trove he claimed to be "Priam's Treasure." That may or may not have been the case. David A. Trail, author of *Schliemann of Troy: Treasure and Deceit*, questions the legitimacy of some of Schliemann's discoveries at Hisarlik and also at Mycenae, in Greece. Moreover, at least a year before Edward Moss arrived at Hisarlik, a noted British journalist and artist who visited the site published a very critical article about Schliemann and his claims in *Fraser's Magazine*, a highly respected British periodical. A second article attacking Schliemann's credibility appeared in the same magazine in February of 1878.

Given his intellectual interests, Edward would have followed the ongoing saga of Schliemann's theories, claims, and discoveries over the years. He certainly would have discussed them with his brother Richard, Registrar of the Royal Dublin Society, and his brother-in-law, paleontologist Dr. Ramsay Traquair, Curator of the Natural History Museum in Edinburgh, as well as with other friends or acquaintances in the scientific community. He would also have been aware that Schliemann had been lionized in London's scientific and social circles in the spring and early summer of 1877, while he was there supervising the production of his new book, *Mycenae*. Schliemann had already published *Troy and its Remains* (1874), the story of his first dig at Hisarlik, and Edward would also have been familiar with that work, if only through reviews or articles. It would have been completely in character for him to take advantage of the opportunity to empirically test Schliemann's claims (as well as those of his critics) by visiting Hisarlik himself.

Because of his own death before Schliemann published *Ilios* (in which he credited Edward for his help), we cannot know for sure what Moss's final conclusions about Schliemann might have been. However, three of his letters in the fall of 1878 provide clear evidence of his views after meeting and spending some time with the famous archaeologist. These letters contain observations that are candidly critical of Schliemann. Two of them, published by David A. Trail and the writer in "Letters from Troy" (*Archaeology*, January/February 2002), are very revealing. Trail, a leading authority on Schliemann's life and work, concluded that "besides giving us useful information about Schliemann's 1878 excavations, [they] help us to view Schliemann from the perspective of a discriminating contemporary and throw interesting sidelights on his enigmatic character."[5] The first letter was sent by Moss to his mother on November 11, followed by a second, very similar letter, to Thomasina the next day, and a third to his sister-in-law Maria a month later.

Schliemann had returned to Hisarlik at the end of September 1878 and was soon hard at work with a crew of over a hundred men, plus ten armed guards to provide protection against local brigands and to keep a close eye on the workmen, who might pocket valuable finds if they were not closely watched. It was not long before the dig was being visited by curious or bored naval officers looking for some respite from the shipboard routine. On October 21 seven of them (according to Schliemann they were from HMS *Monarch*) were reportedly present when a large number of gold earrings, necklaces, and bracelets were discovered. Perhaps Edward first visited the site with this group, for it took place just about the time he joined HMS *Research*. Schliemann later claimed that Moss was either a "frequent visitor" in October and November or "came daily to visit my works" during that time. It is very unlikely that the latter statement was true though, for Moss's medical duties would certainly have prevented him from making daily visits. In any case, Edward's first letter suggests that he had already been to the site several times.

> My Dear Mother,
>
> I got your letter of 30th October yesterday – on my return from a curious adventure. About eight miles from here Dr. Schliemann, the discoverer of the Mycenae treasures has been digging into the mounds of Hissarjic [*sic*] and thinks he has found old Troy. I have been out several times, and he certainly has found the remains of a prehistoric town destroyed by fire in the very spot that Troy ought to be, but there is nothing splendid in the ruins except the occasional gold things that turn up. The so-called 'Treasure Chest of Priam' held a great lot of gold, silver & bronze, but he has found nothing else so grand. There is no cut stone and the things he calls Trojan houses are of large burnt brick, plastered in a primitive way.
>
> Well on the morning of the 9th I thought I would ride out and see what progress had been made in five days, so I went ashore and got a horse called Balbec and started off. There are no roads here, but the way was easy crossing a marsh near here. It lay through a wood of Valencia Oak, then past a castle and a ruined mosque, then through a broad swamp with tall grass and reeds high overhead and a very old causeway of stone about a foot under water. Then the mound of Ilium or Hissarjic [*sic*] was in sight across a broad plain divided by the river Scammander or Meandre (origin of the word meander). Getting clear

of the marsh I found a thunderstorm coming on from the west, and putting the spurs to Balbec I pressed on and crossed the ford of the Scammander just up to the horse's knees and reached Troy a few minutes before the rain came down.

Schliemann's huts are the only houses there & the doctor put me up very comfortably. I spent the time during the rain in making a sketch of a gold pin he had found. About 4.30 the rain cleared off but did not leave [me] time to go back to the ship before dark so I stayed, and Schliemann gave me a feather bed to sleep on, as well as a dinner consisting of some kind of fearfully sour macaroni soup and some eggs and sour cabbage chopped fine. We also had some country wine like a rough claret. The Turkish official in charge of Schliemann's 'finds' joined us. Before retiring I had a walk to the top of one of the mounds and surveyed the old walls in glorious moonlight, then turned in.

Schliemann was off before daybreak for his usual sea bath in the Dardanelles, just an hour's ride off. I got up and made a sketch and then being very anxious to get on board [ship] before the usual Sunday [Church] Parade, I got out my horse and packed my bag of Trojan bones (one of the Turkish labourers wanted to know if we eat them in the ships) and bits of pottery. Altogether I had my little valise pretty full, and my coat pockets quite so.

Schliemann observed me putting on my right gaiter and spur before the left, and said that he never did that, said that 'many years ago [I] was a poor grocer but a wise man told me never to omit putting on the left stocking first, and I have been successful ever since.' This ridiculous superstition sounds queer from a man who believes that no historic Christ ever existed, but it is quite consistent with Schliemann. He has not the slightest idea of what scientific evidence is – any old wall is Priam's palace – any old gold Helen's treasure etc., etc. Anyhow I did put on the right gaiter first in spite of his remonstrance, and I went off as fast as my horse could carry me. Schliemann had entrusted me with a telegram to the editor of *The Times*.

When I got to the Scammander I could hardly believe my eyes. The rivulet of yesterday was a yellow foaming torrent with its edges only marked by the tops of the willows on either side. What was to be done? There was no bridge. Captain Wilson would think me very remiss in not being present for my weekly report at Parade, Schliemann's telegram would be late and being absent without leave would be a bad example for my junior medical officer, whom I [already] had to speak to on the subject.

So I determined to swim it on horseback. I easily found the ford where the opposite bank was shelving and would allow me to land. The shelving part was about 50 yds. long and I had remarked [noticed] that a big willow tree grew where the sheltering bank ended and the steep bank began. Making due allowance for the current, which was easily done by watching the bits of trees & logs

> it swept down, I plunged in. The first step took Balbec [up] to the middle of the saddle. My valise and sketchbook were on my shoulders. I loosened them and held them in front of me. In a minute we were afloat, the horse striking out first rate. I kept my eyes on the bank which seemed to fly by uncommon quick. We were well midstream when the landing place seemed just right for us. Presently the horse touched ground not a yard inside the big willow, gave a stagger or two, and was swept on his broadside, sousing me & my bag & sweeping me clear out of the saddle. Finding I could swim with the bag and my pockets full of bones & crockery easier than I thought, I held on pushing the bag before me and soon was in out of the current and landed waist deep amidst the willows.
>
> Then I began to think of the horse. He was swimming right down stream trying every now and then to land on my side but the bank was too steep and each time he touched the sweep of the yellow current threw him on his side, but at last he made for the opposite shore and got out in about the only spot he could have found for miles.
>
> There I was, feeling uncommon heavy & with the horse on the other side of the river. I first thought of stripping and & swimming [over to get him] but on consideration came to the conclusion that I had better not try again. For 1/4 hour there was not a soul in site but then I saw a flock of sheep and shouted and the shepherd came up and by saying Baksheesh – Schliemann – Hissarjik – I got him to understand that he was to take the horse to Schliemann. Meantime I had been wringing my clothes, but I was not particular, as I had the flooded causeway through the marsh before me [to traverse]. I got back to within a couple of miles of Beshika Bay and then met one of our midshipmen, Peel (grandson of Sir Robert) on horseback. The Captain had sent him to search for tidings of me. They were all very glad to get me on board again, and today I got a letter from Schliemann (sent by a bridge which after all existed about 12 miles down) congratulating me on what he calls my 'miraculous escape.' I sent his telegram all right. The river will probably be down again in a few days but I won't swim it again. The sketches are rather washy but I will be able to touch them up. I enclose for Richard a small parcel requiring tender handling. He will explain.[6]

In his letter to Thomasina the next day, Edward once again covered the basic ground of his story, adding a few more details about his adventure while downplaying somewhat his "miraculous escape" from drowning in the Scammander. Just before the rainstorm came on he had made a sketch of one of the gold pins Schliemann had discovered recently – one he had described to Thomasina in a previous letter. Some time later he had a goldsmith at Malta make a copy of it as a gift for her. He also mentioned that when the three men sat down to dinner in Schliemann's tent the Turkish officer in charge of the finds "took a great interest in the Eskimo [meaning himself] and wanted to hear all I could tell." Afterwards, when the discussion turned to the political situation, Schliemann effusively praised the "noble policy followed by England that all the world admires." The archaeologist (who had something of a fixation on owls) also quizzed Moss (the naturalist) constantly about them, stating "ever since I have been married I like owls because my [second] wife [who was Greek] is like an owl – all the women of Attica are like owls."

The two men also had a discussion about religious matters, leading Edward to tell Senie that "he is a queer man – an utter pagan – believing that no such person as Christ ever lived and that the history of him is only the crystallization of old longings for human perfection." According to David Trail, the Moss letters provide the first really clear confirmation that Schliemann, the son of a Lutheran pastor, was no longer a believer.[7]

In the third of the Beshika Bay letters, written to Thomasina's sister Maria early in December, Edward returned once again to the subject of Schliemann's archaeological abilities and methods. Towards the end of November, Schliemann closed his excavation site for the winter and returned to London. With the excavation site closed, Edward began to spend his free time hunting and exploring the local countryside. During these outings he spent some time with Frank Calvert, whose opinions of Schliemann and his methods pretty well matched his own. Moss's December letter to his sister-in-law ranged widely over a variety of subjects from the ancient history of the region to his opinions about the local washerwomen who were making a few shillings from doing washing for the officers aboard the ships anchored at Beshika Bay.

> For some time I have been threatening to write to you instead of Senie for her letters come very irregularly and you might be a better correspondent, but though I love you very much I have not cast her off altogether (a little note to her goes by this mail). Till Friday night I had a great mind to write to someone and ask what had become of her ladyship for I got no letters for four or five mails, but then lo and behold they came in a lump – such little practical jokes can be expected when Turks have anything to do about anything. Every Turk ought to have a Scandinavian to push him along. I believe our letters home were also delayed, and if so I don't know what the wives did for cash.
>
> This would be a bad place for anyone who could not live without society. There is but one English family within reach. A man called Calvert has a farm about 8 miles off and lives there with his mother (widow of Frederick Calvert the late American Consul) and nieces. The girls are very nice – our bachelors wonder how such girls are brought up in such a wilderness. They often ride to the hounds. This is a good place for sport – lots of woodcock, snipe, etc. and I am told lots of [wild] pigs in the hills. I mean to have a go at the pig before long.
>
> When you land here you have to run [the boat] up the dry sand out of the way of the wave coming in after you, then you see low hills all covered with bushes

knee deep and that is all. Here there are a lot of wretched huts called a village – one is Greek and that is awfully dirty, the next is Turk and that is dirtier still. The land is very rich. They scrape it in places with a stick fastened to a pair of bullocks and it gives splendid wheat. You can ride almost anywhere; there are no hedges except here and there near the villages where they have enclosures for the grapes. The grapes are not trained and grow anyhow on the ground. A few days ago three of us bought the full of our three shooting bags of raisins for one shilling. The Calverts are very anxious to get someone to come out and settle the country. There is a large farm of 2,000 acres going for £15,00. The Valencia Oak alone on it would nearly pay for its purchase. Just at present the Scammander is so full that we are cut off from the Calverts and from Hissalik [*sic*]. You know Schliemann has been digging Troy out of Hissalik, perhaps you saw his mention of his friend [Edward] in *The Times* of 27 inst.

He is a very uncritical old man and is altogether too sceptical in some things and overwhelmingly credulous about others. I would not trust even his most secure conclusions. Nevertheless, I think he has dug into something as old as Troy out of Hissalik. Standing among the calcimined walls and huge jars of pottery one could not but feel the extreme trivialness of individual life. Oh that these walls could speak. Enclosed in one jar we found a great lot of others – one of them held the bones of an unborn baby. Not far from it were spinning distaffs with the thread still wound on them, and in the same house two heavy gold bracelets and a pile of necklaces & ear-rings. City after city had been built on these remains, and generations of Syrians and Greeks and Turks had lived over them. Lyamichus, one of Alexander's generals built a temple on top of the mound but it is near the surface and a mere thing of yesterday compared to the old burnt walls below, but Schliemann came like a vandal and grubbed the whole lot so no better man can hope to tell which is which afterwards. Hissalik is certainly the site of old Troy. In very ancient times it was not questioned, but in the last fifty years other places have been put down as possible if not preferable sites. The fact is the whole country is full of ruins and tombs of every age and race. All the successive waves of human overflow have pushed westward past here and checked for a moment at the Hellespont. Within a quarter of a mile of Calvert's house there are acres of grapes. The ploughshare comes on a big old earthen jar – inside you find a skeleton within an urn. Some of the urns are very old. Sometimes they find bracelets – often little corkscrews of gold and silver that were twisted around braids of hair. The history of the land is known for more than 2,000 years but now no one knows who these [people] were – "there lies Elam and all his company slain by the sword," but enough about bones....

There is splendid tobacco grown here, all our people have become quite connoisseurs. I almost regret that I am not a smoker when I see the cigarettes come from the islands that are here. Everyone gets a touch of ague [a malarial fever] in the summer, and you can't image anything as bad as the washing. When my garments came off last week I looked at them with despair, many parts of them still hung together, but they were varnished with some kind of brown paste and rubbed with a rusty iron. This was the work of some dirty harpies with long platted hair and dragged trousers. These excuses for washerwomen have been got together by an enterprising Greek. In consideration of my utter despondency when viewing the handiwork of his maidens he only charged us 2s a dozen. I felt it was cheap – in fact dirt-cheap. Some of our people send their things down to Malta to get washed. They come back clean but worn out in the most mysterious way. I wish it were proper to take a nice laundress for a servant, but there are no 'Mrs. Grundy's' aboard a Man of War.

I am reading Lecky's *History of European Morals*, a tough book but interesting. He sticks up for Quakers – says (vol. 2, p. 12) that they are like the early Christians of the first two centuries etc. Some people would think the book very free thinking – perhaps worse – but the perfectly clear way he traces the renovation or rather the redemption of society to a 'sample record of three short years of [Christ's] active life' is very striking, and more so in such a writer. After all, this is the main evidence we have nowadays – and it is stronger than ever. Some people might say that such a life was not necessarily miraculous, but I would like to know what they would call miraculous and divine if not. Now, having treated you to a little bit of everything and wound up with theology, I

Remain yours affectionately,
Edward L. Moss[8]

In spite of Moss's trenchant criticism of Schliemann, he had not been averse to helping the archaeologist with the business of the letters to *The Times*, and he continued to assist him various ways during the next year or so. In July 1879 when HMS *Research* arrived back in England for a refit, Edward wrote to Schliemann from the Chatham Dockyard before returning to Southsea on leave.

Dear Dr. Schliemann,

Have you any objection to my showing some of the bones at the British Association?

My ship only arrived at Chatham Dockyard two days ago and I have not therefore had time to identify all the fragments. I presume however that [Dr.]

Virchow[9] has identified all that he saw for you. I write you from Chatham but the above is my permanent address. A goldsmith in Strada Reale, Malta, made me an excellent reproduction of the gold pin, which greatly delighted my wife. I saw the design destroyed so that he cannot make any more than the pin you so kindly allowed me to copy.[10]

Moss's last known letter to Schliemann was written from his Southsea home in early November, just before he left again for service afloat aboard HMS *Atalanta*, a training ship for young seamen. By then he had identified most of the bones and the shells of the various molluscs he had brought from Troy and was reporting back on his conclusions:

The bones from your excavation at Hissarlik have no doubt been looked over by naturalists much more capable than I am, but cannot leave England without sending you a note about those you allowed me to collect from the 'burnt layer' with my own hands, and which, bye-the-bye, so nearly brought me to grief in the Scammander.[11]

Moss went on to list the various species, closing with the remark that he had seen no human bones other than those of a child of about six months, found in an earthen pot. Schliemann replied about two weeks later, but Edward would never have the opportunity of reading his letter.

Dear Dr. Moss,

I have very great pleasure in receiving your very kind and highly interesting letter of the 5th inst. which comes just in time for my next work on Troy, and all the valuable communications in it shall be put to your credit. Also the other communication as to the water flasks intended to be represented as slung on the spears of the Mycenaen warriors is highly interesting and shall appear to your credit in my new edition of *Mycenae*, which I intend to bring out in 1881, because for the present I have all the hands full with the Trojan work. I only beg you will kindly call it to my remembrance at the beginning of 1881. In thanking you cordially for your kind remarks, I remain,

Yours very truly,
Heinrich Schliemann[12]

Edward Moss may have questioned Schliemann's competence as an archaeologist, but the discoverer of Troy seemed to have thought well of his friend's abilities. After the night they spent together at the dig both men appear to have entered into a symbiotic relationship where each stood to gain something from their mutual acquaintance. Edward was willing and able to offer help in the form of his scientific knowledge and training, and probably that of his palaeontologist brother-in-law and other scientist acquaintances. In return for the advice and judgment of a scientifically trained observer and analyst with a broad knowledge base he was promised or anticipated being given recognition in *Ilios*, Schliemann's second book about the excavation of Homer's Troy. Although Edward was dead by the time *Ilios* was published, Schliemann kept his word and did accord him credit for his contributions as he promised, referring to him as "my dear, my honoured, my learned, my deeply mourned friend, Dr. Edward Moss of Arctic celebrity."[13]

It is unlikely, however, that the relationship was really *that* close even if there was much about Schliemann that Edward Moss would have admired in spite of his criticisms. Schliemann's tenacity in pursuing his goals – his determination to "stand fast" and overcome all obstacles to prove that Hisarlik was Troy – that aspect of his character would have been respected. But above all Moss would have enjoyed the opportunity to engage in intellectual discourse with a remarkable man who was already a legend in his own time. He would also have been happy, as he was on the Arctic Expedition, to make a modest contribution to science. Like Schliemann, he was a man in search of honour and respect in the scientific community. He too had his dreams. They may have been more modest than those of Schliemann, but they encompassed more than his career as a naval surgeon had thus far been able to provide. He hoped that publication of his own book (one can imagine him presenting a copy to Schliemann) would be a major step in the direction of gaining the kind of recognition in the scientific and intellectual community that he craved. Instead, his life was destined to be cut short before he had the opportunity to achieve that goal.

But that tragic fate was in a future he could not know. On December 15, his birthday, Edward wrote to his mother from Piraeus, Greece, where *Research* had anchored a day earlier.

> My Dear Mother,
>
> I am thirty-five today, it seems a terrible number of years to count as gone from a little life, but if your son is growing old what must you be? After all, it is just the houses we live in that are growing old; the "I" is as young as ever. It doesn't feel any the worse however often the world may twist around the sun, and for all we know we may feel just as young at the next procession of the equinox. We came here this morning after a rough passage from Beshika. We were ordered down here without the least warning and left on the 13th. I regret [leaving] the wild hills of Beshika and the woodcock and the snipe. I also regret having ordered a fresh stock of ammunition from Malta. The Acropolis is in sight … [remainder of letter missing].[14]

Beshika Bay, Turkey

Apparently *Research* remained at Piraeus, the chief port of Athens, over the winter, for in late February Edward entertained Schliemann and his wife at a party and dance aboard ship, organized by the Captain's wife. Although he must have enjoyed hosting the Schliemanns, Moss was really not at all pleased with being asked to chip in to help pay for the soirée:

> The only guests I entertain are Dr. and Mrs. Schliemann and I expect my share will come to 30 shillings. If I had not a dislike of breaking the peace I would have 'cut up rough' for I consider I am paying for the amusement of others.…
>
> The whole affair has annoyed me.… I don't mean to take part in it. It is a case of you play, I pay. On Monday last I had coffee after dinner and between the coffee and feeling sore about the dance I could not sleep, so yesterday I tried to compose myself enough to go out on a lovely hill near here & make a sketch of Athens. I sketched away from 2 to 5:30 and made one of my best efforts. It didn't make me sleep however.…
>
> I have not written to Marcus Ward[15] because I felt it would be asking for money in doing so. I doubt if they have made their expenses. Bye-the-bye, Roe told me he saw a copy of a book of beautiful chromos at the Royal Military Hospital at Hedley. He had no idea it was mine. Marcus Ward knows that the Royal Dublin Society will always find me and I expect they close their year on the 31st of March.… You talk about my having pocketed your handkerchiefs, but just now when I wanted one for the great afternoon dance I could not find anything except a huge old coarse thing that I use as a duster for my chemicals. I won't be able to supply you with even one for any purpose whatsoever when I get home. The people are arriving now, if I want to blow my nose or anything I will have to come to my cabin and use my chemical duster. I have another marked FFQ but it is too large to go in any pocket. We can use the pair as sheets when I get home. If you lie close to me they will be big enough.
>
> Willy writes to me saying that I may spend £10 on Greek pottery for him but I believe £2 will buy a very decent cup, the commoner a thing is the more likely it is to be genuine. Miss Schliedel has bought me two pots for 4 francs. She is experienced in such negotiations. Do you remember me describing a queer place in the Acropolis where we found some bronze and some pottery? I have a dozen or so little bits of pottery, one has a woman's head crudely painted on it. It turns out that the very spot is described in Woodsworths' *Greece*. The fragments are earlier than the Parthenon and date from the time of the destruction of the older temple by Pepasurns, so we must preserve them as curios in this house of the future that is to be decorated with Greek pots. Where is the house to be I wonder? … [rest of letter missing].[16]

But there was not to be a home of their own in Edward and Senie's future. The Grecian Fates, ever capricious, had been playing games with two forty-odd-year-old frigates, HMS *Eurydice* and HMS *Atalanta*, and in doing so they would deliver Edward Moss and over six hundred other mortals to Poseidon, the unpredictable and often angry god who held dominion over the seas.

19: HMS Atalanta

"The Perils of the Sea"

Atalanta has been described as a sister-ship of HMS *Eurydice*, though cousin would be a more accurate characterization. She was built at Pembroke Dockyard in 1844, a year after *Eurydice*, a sixth-rate frigate of similar tonnage but shorter by ten feet, two feet wider in the beam, and two feet deeper in the hull. *Atalanta* was originally named *Juno* after the wife of Jupiter, giver of victory, and chief god of ancient Rome.

As *Juno*, she seems to have had an unremarkable career during the years she was on active service – actually only eight of the first seventeen years of her life. By 1877, when the story of her reincarnation as HMS *Atalanta* begins, the thirty-four-year-old vessel was in very reduced circumstances. For the past fifteen years she had been in service as a police hulk (essentially a floating police station and jail) at Portsmouth. That ignominious role would certainly have been her final assignment before being condemned and broken up, had not the Admiralty decided that another sailing ship was needed for the training of young seamen.[1]

There is a common misconception that *Juno* was refitted as a replacement for the training ship HMS *Eurydice*, which foundered off the Isle of Wight in March 1878. However, it is quite clear from Admiralty documents that the decision to refit *Juno* for active service was actually made a year earlier, in March 1877.[2] After a series of tests to find out if she was sound enough to warrant a major refit, the old brig was stripped down, repaired, and rebuilt where necessary from stem to stern. After being commissioned on September 17, 1878, Captain Francis Stirling took her on a three-week shakedown cruise, prompting some more modifications and repairs before sailing for the West Indies with a full complement of Ordinary Seamen trainees on board. When Stirling returned the following March, it was evident that he was not satisfied with the handling and condition of the ship, for he immediately presented his superiors with a very substantial list of defects, necessary repairs and suggested modifications. According to his report, *Atalanta* strained at the masts, was unusually leaky, and was unstable at high angles of heel, rolling over ominously in moderately heavy seas before lurching back very sharply. He considered the ship to be "overmasted" (in landlubber terms "top heavy") and requested lighter lower masts, more ballast, and the removal of her guns to decrease the weight up top. His superiors failed to accept the recommendation to install lighter lower masts, but most of the other repairs and suggested changes were approved and carried out as requested.[3] Edward Moss joined the ship on September 29, and on November 7, following a three-week shakedown cruise, the ship left on her second winter training cruise to the West Indies.

Stirling's orders called for *Atalanta* to return home around the first of April 1880. However, unforeseen circumstances led him to cut the cruise short and sail for England on January 31, 1880, rather than March 2 as originally planned. Given fair winds he expected the trip home would take little more than a month, but even if the early spring weather proved to be unusually foul, the trip was unlikely to take more than sixty days. Tragically, it was not to be.

On April 13, two and one-half months later, *The Times* took note of the fact that *Atalanta* had not been heard of since she had left Bermuda. It was not the first time that the vessel had been reported missing or possibly lost. Indeed, there had been rumours of her loss when she took an unusually long time to go from England to Tenerife, Canary Islands, her first port of call. In the days of sail, when ships were utterly dependent on the great wind systems of the Earth for propulsion, delays from violent storms, unfavourable winds, or misfortune of one kind or another often meant that reports of overdue ships were commonplace. However, in April, when *Atalanta* was officially reported to be overdue, it was inevitable that the loss of *Eurydice* two years earlier would be recalled, or that rumours of all sorts about the ship would be granted credibility in the public mind. For this reason it is worthwhile to examine the circumstances behind the demise of the vessel that many referred to as *Atalanta*'s "sister ship."

On the afternoon of March 24th, 1878, HMS *Eurydice*, refitted only a year earlier as a training ship for ordinary seamen, was running up the English Channel after an eighteen-day passage from the West Indies, where she had been sailing since November of the previous year. There was a tangible air of excitement among the ship's complement of nearly three hundred boys and ordinary seamen. Within the next few hours they would be docking at Portsmouth, and they were looking forward to taking leave. Also on board the ship were about three-score army officers and some men who were being invalided home from the Americas. They too were expectantly awaiting the familiar sight of family and home.

About 3:30 p.m. the ship was observed under plain sail in a quiet breeze, bearing for Spithead near the entrance to Portsmouth harbour. At that time the barometer began to fall precipitously and an eerie stillness descended on the ship as a large black cloud was observed approaching from the west. The wind then began to freshen, shifting eastward,

Training ship H.M.S. *Atalanta*, 1880. Illustrated London News.

H M S Atalanta

and at 3:45 the captain, anticipating the weather change, ordered men aloft to reduce sail. Five minutes later the ship shuddered and heeled hard over almost onto her beam-ends, as she was brutally struck by a gale-force squall accompanied by blinding snow. The strength of the onslaught was so powerful that even with six steady men at the wheel the ship could not be held on course, and when she heeled over, tons of water poured through her open upper main-deck ports and into the decks below. Then *Eurydice* hesitantly righted herself for a mere matter of moments before going back over once again to go down from the bow so swiftly that only two men survived to tell what had happened.[4]

Three hundred and seventeen people perished with the *Eurydice*. This tragedy was shocking even for an age when marine disasters with great loss of life were commonplace. The fact that so many of those who died were young men, most in their late teens or early twenties, made the disaster even more troubling. However, the foundering of *Eurydice* seemed explainable: the result of an unusual combination of local weather and human error. The official inquiry into the loss of the ship concluded that the class of sailing frigates to which she belonged, designed by Admiral Wm. Elliot, were quite safe for use as training vessels and that the ship design had little, if anything, to do with the disaster. *Eurydice* did not sink because it was badly designed or unsound in any way, but because Captain Hare had not ordered the closing of the upper main-deck ports before the deadly squall struck the ship. Nevertheless, it was not the open ports that remained in the public consciousness after the inquiry, only the powerful image of *Eurydice* suddenly going down by the bow in an unexpectedly brutal squall. Now, two years later, many people were wondering if *Atalanta* had suffered a similar fate.

On November 11, 1879, six months before *Atalanta* was reported overdue, Edward Moss wrote the first of a series of letters home. It is clear from this letter that he was despondent about being back in service afloat. His state of mind was not improved by being wretchedly seasick in the heavy swell (the aftermath of an Atlantic gale) that was pitching the ship about day after day. In earlier years, when he was aboard *Simoom* traversing back and forth across the North Atlantic, or on *Alert* during the passages to and from Greenland, he had suffered through his share of storms, though he usually took these episodes in his stride with hardly more than a casual remark about a "rough passage." But this time it was different. It was the first time he had served on a full sailing ship. All of his other ships had been either powered entirely by steam or, like *Simoom*, *Alert*, and *Research*, by sail and steam in combination, and such ships were generally able to handle heavy weather better than wind-driven ships. He was not enjoying the experience.

> I think a kind of diary is the best form my letters can take. Each will begin where the other left off and the end of a cruise will leave you with a little volume.

You saw us sail out on Friday [the] 7th. Well for two days we slid along just as we did past Southsea beach. I think you and Ada recognised my waving. I watched you afterwards till you met Mrs. Stirling when she stopped at Southsea castle.

On Sunday we ran out of the Channel and I gave up hope of putting into Plymouth or any other place where I could post the receipt which Currie Petra & [unclear] had sent me to sign for 'Polar Ice.' On Monday it blew fresh and the ship [was] knocked about, perhaps we had the swell from the storm foretold from America, last night was one of those miserable nights that seem to last a lifetime. The bulkheads at my head & feet creaked & screamed. My mattress slipped off the iron bed frame etc., etc. The port leaked and I stuck my sponge in to keep the water off [my] bed. I could not read because the candle smoked so that I couldn't breathe, and all the while there was that wretched feeling of giddiness that I always have, no nausea, but uncertain if every motion is real or not, whether it is my giddiness or the ships heave. Today the sea is quieter but I cannot fix myself to do anything. I want to write the descriptions of the [chromolithograph] plates for Marcus Ward but my ideas whirl about.

Sunday 16th. Nov.

There is no change. There has been nothing but heavy swell and roll, roll, roll, pitch, pitch. We are in [the] latitude of Lisbon and 300 miles off shore. I read Fol's work on the [Appendicularia] yesterday & [the] day before. He has done all that can be done with them. I fear I may give up all idea of adding to what he has done, so I might as well not be at sea. The work Fol has done could not have been done on board ship. The constant motion, darkness, & seasickness is too much of a handicap.

It is slowly dawning on me that I must be content to do nothing and drag out my weary five years in this kind of thing. I would rather be in prison, but then I wouldn't get £365 – it will be £380 in a few days. Unfortunately I get nothing for the £380 except my food and the most wretched kind of life. Captain Stirling tells me it is possible this ship may join the Flying Squadron next year, or [I] may be transferred to man a ship of the Squadron. Blackett [the Senior Lieutenant] knows Vancouver [Island] well, he was there in the *Zealous*. How would you like to go back there for the last two years service and stay out there afterwards? I often think as I am tumbling about at night that it might be better than idleness in England.

We have not had a gale of wind yet. I look forward to a gale with horror. I well remember thinking in the *Simoom* that no recompense on earth would make up for the misery of one gale, and we shall have 4 or 5 before we get

> home again. Perhaps if I had been more pushing I might have got something on shore somewhere instead of this. Willy told me he would get Cross's (the Home Secretary) & the First Lord's interest. Still, even this is better than 4 years abroad. Perhaps I may be forced into doing something definite in the way of refusing to serve or go abroad. It wouldn't take much to make me desperate. The noble £380 a year for which I have sold myself must be risked however.
>
> Monday 24th.
>
> We are somewhere about 100 miles (1/4 inch on your globe) to the NW of the Canary Islands and it has blown a gale ever since I last wrote. The ship behaves extremely well, is as dry on deck as possible, but is terribly lively. This morning at 3:30 she jerked a man off the main topgallant yard. He was a recently joined Able Seaman named Hugh McClure. The lifebuoy was let go but didn't light. A boat was lowered at great risk and was soon lost to sight in the sea & darkness for 3/4 hour but saw nothing of him or the life buoy.
>
> I propped myself up between the mast & the table today and went on with Fol's *Etudes sur les Appendicularia* [*sic*]. As I write she is rolling the usual 6 to the minute and lurching ominously so that standing is impossible, but it is a comfort she is perhaps safe – she would be more comfortable if she was less bottom heavy.[5]

According to some later accounts, neither the officers nor the crew were happy with the performance of *Atalanta* in heavy weather, and one can imagine the fear and consternation among the young trainees when Able Seaman McClure was hurled to his death off the main topgallant yard by the sudden lurching of the ship as she jerked upright after a roll. In naval parlance *Atalanta* was officially referred to as "lively," but some seamen aboard said she was "crank," a pejorative nautical adjective used to describe a ship that was unstable and liable to capsize if given half a chance. The opinion that she was more than just "lively" was apparently shared by Captain Stirling. Many years later Edward Moss's son wrote to his mother that a contemporary of his father and Stirling had told him that before the November cruise, the captain had applied to the Admiralty for permission to shorten his cross-spars because he found the ship "too lively."[6]

By nature and by experience, the nineteenth-century sailor, so visibly at the mercy of forces beyond his reckoning or control, tended towards superstition. From *The Ancient Mariner* to *Moby Dick* to the mysteries of the Bermuda Triangle, myth and legend have always been present in the lives of men facing peril on the sea. It would not have been very surprising if some of those aboard *Atalanta* had a sense of uneasiness or foreboding as they made their way to what they hoped would be more benign southern waters. By all accounts they experienced a hard and troublesome westward crossing, and the young trainees were often terrified during the journey. Was it any wonder that when ordered aloft to reef or change sails some young trainees tried to hide, risking punishment in preference to climbing up onto the yards to face the very real prospect of being pitched overboard? Life and work aboard a forty-year-old sailing frigate in 1880 during a gale may have been better than it was rounding the Horn of South America as described in Dana's classic *Two Years Before the Mast*, but it was not for the faint of heart or weak of body. It was oftentimes a mental and physical ordeal that could only be fully understood by those who have lived through such experiences.

Before *Atalanta* left Tenerife on December 2, Stirling advised the Admiralty that they had been forced to lay-to during a gale that developed on November 19, and that they continued to experience heavy seas for the next ten days. It appears as if the weather was somewhat better after leaving the Canary Islands, but even so the second leg of the journey (to Barbados) took another thirty-one days. In all, including the three-day stopover at Tenerife, the trip had taken fifty-two days, considerably longer than was expected. On Christmas Day, when they were still on the high seas, Edward began a long letter to his mother, the first since leaving the Canary Islands. By that time he seems to have come to terms with the rough seas and the constant rolling of the ship as the NE Trades filled her sails to drive her steadily forward towards her destination.

My Dear Mother,

I like the old plan of a family gathering at Christmas. It seems suitable that the children & their children should gather at the parent's home to celebrate the feast. I would like to be with you today, to be at home is my general wish, but then I have so many homes. Chardville [Southsea] is (at present) my own, but where you are living is home too, and part of home is with Willy and Richard. It is 5 PM. (it is after 7 with you). We have been sliding along all day with more than 1/3 an acre of canvas (exactly 2,085 square yards) spread to the north east trade wind. You would think it rough enough, for the *Atalanta* rolls greatly. She is the reverse of being top-heavy and so she is what sailors call lively.

She keeps a steady swing, six to the minute 12 each side. The wind is neither warm nor cool, it is 75 degrees and the sea is a degree warmer. We had service on deck. Our parson, Rev. R. Nimmo, preached from 'glad tidings of great joy' then the men went to dinner and we had lunch – a small slice of mutton (we have 3 English sheep left yet) and a potato with a glass of lime juice. The men have had no fresh meat since we left Tenerife on 2nd Dec. We hope to get to Barbados about 3 or 4 Jan. – alas too late to send this letter, or Senie's, by the mail leaving on 30th Dec. The mails are only fortnightly and our letters will hardly be delivered before first week in Feb. So there will have been no news of us from about 12th Dec. to first week in Feb. We fear there may be the usual groundless reports of [our] loss. This ship being the successor to the *Eurydice* has already been reported lost more than once, but she is a totally different make of ship. There are only three of us worried, the Captain, the Navigating Lieutenant and myself. Mrs. Stirling lives in Southsea and Captain S. will be especially anxious to hear how she gets through February. This he won't hear till we arrive in Portsmouth.

After lunch I read the *Apocrypha*, or at least *2nd Maccabees* and the *Book of Tobias* – I had never read either before. They are in a Donay Bible[7] Nimmo lent me. Reading entails rather severe exercise, you have to hold the book with one hand and the table to steady yourself with the other, and all the time sway sideways or port-ways with the small of your back.

8:20 p.m. 31st Dec.

The old year has just gone out with you. I wish you a happy new one now, when perhaps your other children and perhaps grandchildren even, are wishing you it too.

We are 90 miles off Barbados. It is sweltering hot. The perspiration is running off me and my hands and head throbbing. Letters will be welcome tomorrow, but I look forward to a little fresh vegetable food especially. I can't keep in order without it. This however is medical. Tell the girls I wished them a happy '80 at the exact time it crept in.

Barbados, 8 Jan. 80

The mail goes tomorrow and I have worked for 4 days getting ready. I wrote for 4 hours in my cabin today. The thermometer was 84 degrees, but it felt hotter than I can ever remember. I had to take off everything. The terrible wet atmosphere makes the difference, towels won't dry your skin and clothes get sticky. We sail for Tobago tomorrow. Then St. Vincent, Grenada, Trinidad etc. Mails still addressed to Barbados up to *14th February*. We visit here to get that mail and leave for home on 2nd March, hoping to arrive (if there is fair wind) on or about 31st March.[8]

It is difficult to know what to make of Edward's remark that only the captain, the navigating lieutenant, and himself were worried. The comment was almost certainly intended to be ironic, but even so it is not entirely clear what message he meant to convey. Similar examples of irony in some other letters to his mother might suggest that it was a literary device he enjoyed using. But what did he really mean? If it was intended to be ironic, the comment can still have suggested concern about the safety of the ship, for if he was suggesting that the trio was not worried, it would mean that the crew and trainees were fearful. On the other hand, he could well have been using the ironic form to allay his mother's fears about his safety. In the context of the preceding sentence, "This ship being the successor to the *Eurydice* has already been reported lost more than once, but she is an entirely different kind of ship," that would seem to be the most logical conclusion. But if this were the case then Captain Stirling and some of his officers *were* concerned, perhaps less for the time they would be in the West Indies than for the return journey home.

In the meantime the weather was fair in spite the unaccustomed heat and humidity. *Atalanta* dropped anchor at Bridgetown, Barbados, on New Years Day, nine days later than had been anticipated when they left England. During their eight-day stay there, the ship was provisioned and the men were granted one or two days of welcome leave. Unfortunately, while they were at Barbados, two of them contracted yellow fever, though it was not diagnosed until they were back at sea.

On January 4 Edward penned a letter to six-year-old Ada, written on a small piece of flimsy paper and sealed in a tiny two- by three-inch envelope. In the light of what was to come, it is almost as painful to read today as it must have been for Thomasina and Ada in the days and months and after Edward's death.

> My Dear Ada,
>
> Nearly all the people here are black. They have very white teeth and are always laughing. It is hot here and I am writing with my coat and waistcoat off. The sun is nearly overhead, that is why it is so hot. I had a flying fish for breakfast this morning. The cook cut its wings off before it came to the table. There is plenty of fruit here, such as bananas and oranges and avocado pears. I saw some cocoa nuts on shore yesterday and if you will try to learn to read I will bring you one and also one for Beatrice. There are plenty of the canes they make sugar out of here. I do not know whether they would keep till the ship got home, but I will try. After you get this letter we will be some four weeks before the ship starts for home. This is to be on the 1st of March and the men will pull up the anchor and the band will play 'homeward bound' or 'the girls we left behind us' and the white sails will spread out, and the ship will lean over and glide away from the white sand and the palm trees and the black people in the boats, then for three or four long weeks there will be nothing but water and sky and at last we will see Southsea, and the ship will stop at Spithead and Captain Stirling will go and tell the Admiral, and then I will come to the pier in a boat and soon be at home with you and Mama and the rest of the family.
>
> Your affectionate Papa,
> Edward L. Moss[9]

20: London, April to June 1880

"*Atalanta* Feared Lost"

The story of the mysterious disappearance of HMS *Atalanta* and the death of Edward Lawton Moss begins with the discovery of the yellow fever after leaving Barbados. Edward viewed the appearance of the dreaded "Yellow Jack" aboard ship as an extremely serious development and immediately initiated measures that he believed would minimize the risk of an epidemic aboard the ship. At the time, there were a number of competing theories about the origins and treatment of yellow fever. Some medical authorities thought the disease arose out of unsanitary conditions; others that it was an airborne (miasmic) disease; and still others that it might be transmitted through contact with infected individuals. He intended to cover all three possibilities.

The actual cause of the disease would not be identified with certainty for another twenty years, in the wake of the 1898 Spanish-American War. During that conflict, far more American soldiers died from yellow fever, dysentery, and malaria than through military action. Cuba was considered to be the worst place in the hemisphere for the disease, and when a severe epidemic broke out during the three-year American occupation of the island after the war, a team of four doctors was appointed to study the disease. The Reed Commission, led by Dr. Walter Reed, was able to clearly establish that the viral disease was carried by the *Aides egypti* mosquito. Only about 20 per cent of those stricken with its most virulent form survived more than a few days. Moss himself had survived Yellow Jack when he was aboard *Bulldog* fifteen years earlier, and he moved quickly to deal with the situation. First the patients were isolated, at least to the extent that was possible on the crowded ship. They were then treated with the usual nostrums of the day: Their clothing was burned and a heavy dose of carbolic disinfectant was applied to their hammocks and living space with the intent of preventing the disease from spreading. These procedures covered two of the main medical theories, but Edward also believed that safety lay in going north to cooler weather as quickly as possible, for it was known that the disease was generally confined to sub-tropical or tropical regions. On January 31, when they arrived at Bermuda, he jotted down a hasty note to his brother William outlining the recommendations he had made to the captain and the preventative measures he had taken.

> Dear Willy,
>
> I got your letter at Barbados but could not reply to it there. Three days after leaving Barbados and before touching at Tobago a case of malignant yellow fever occurred and proved fatal on the 5th day.
>
> I know the disease too well to run any risk on a ship like this. She is in fact just the sort of craft to be swept with it as ships used to be long ago. 280 men in a space of less than 100 cubic feet each. No steam power to get away into cold weather. No room on deck to isolate more than one or two cases.
>
> Within half an hour of making my report to the captain we put the helm up and altered course for the north. Two volunteers and myself looked after the man. When he died we buried him at once and destroyed all clothes etc., etc. and I believe I have been able to prevent any secondary case. A man who slept [in the same bed] with the deceased on shore at Barbados had some feverish symptoms and I isolated him also. We could not get back to Barbados for water and provisions – the wind was too strong and foul – and we were beaten back on the Grenadine reefs, and had to run through. Then we made for St. Kitts where we could get nothing in consequence of the terrible flood, and here we are in strict quarantine, getting [only] water and food. No newspapers or letters. Last news from Senie at Xmas. We hope to leave today and get home about 1st March.

Although Edward did not mention it, he must have given some thought to Thomas Colan's experience during the scurvy inquiry three years earlier. Not for him a verbal report and verbal recommendation to his commanding officer, as Dr. Colan had done on the Nares expedition. He had no intention of leaving himself open to an accusation of negligence or dereliction of duty if there were more deaths, and decided to protect himself with a formal letter to Captain Stirling stressing the need to cut the cruise short and head for cooler regions. When the ship arrived at St. Kitts on January 22, Stirling wrote to the Secretary of the Admiralty, advising them of the situation, Moss's advice, and his own decision to abort the cruise and sail for England as soon as possible. In the letter he observed that yellow fever had been reported at several of the West Indian islands and suggested that risking a major outbreak aboard ship by remaining in the region was not justified in the light of his sailing orders.[1]

Both Stirling and Moss were probably happy enough to head back early anyway, for both of their wives were now well along in their pregnancies. Edward's Christmas letter had hinted that Mrs. Stirling was due sometime in February. Although the captain would have been unaware of it, she gave birth to a son on January 31, the very day *Atalanta* left Bermuda for England. In April, Thomasina Moss would also give birth to a boy who would never know his father.

Another reason for Stirling's decision to return early might have been that he was none too confident about the seaworthiness of the ship or the competence of some of his crew. However, most of the officers – eleven of the seventeen aboard – had sailed with him the previous year and all were experienced men, even if most of their time on sailing ships had been in the early stages of their careers. The service records of these officers show that almost all of them had been assigned to large steam or combination steam/sail vessels or to shore establishments much of the time during the past decade or more.[2]

The ordinary seaman trainees of course were still relative greenhorns, and Stirling probably did not have much faith in their competence in a tight situation. There are also indications that some of the regular crew and the 170 trainees were worried about the safety of the ship. In fact three men apparently chose to go AWOL (Absent Without Leave) rather to risk the return voyage aboard *Atalanta*. Stirling also left three other seamen ashore because of illness, so he was about to sail back to England with six fewer trained seamen than he had on the trip over. As things turned out, all six of these men were fortunate to have been left behind.

As Edward's letter indicated, *Atalanta* stopped briefly at Bermuda on January 29 to replenish food and water for the journey home. The quarantined ship was forced to anchor at Grassy Bay outside of the main harbour and the supplies were ferried out to her, for nobody was allowed to go ashore. Three days later, *Atalanta* set forth on the journey home. With reasonable weather and fair winds, the trip home could take less than a month, but Stirling knew it was much more likely to be longer. Plenty of foul weather could always be expected in the North Atlantic during the winter months, but they would probably be home by the middle of March. He could not have foreseen or expected the extent and duration of the gales that swept unrelentingly across the North Atlantic shipping lanes between February and April 1880. The first of a series of savage gales – some of them driven by hurricane force winds – did its most deadly work around the second week of February, and another at least equally malevolent storm hammered the Azores region between the 11th and 16th of April. Nor was there much respite in between according to newspaper reports and published weather records.

Stirling sailed straight into the first of these terrible weather systems, and if *Atalanta* survived its ferocious onslaught, she might have caught the full force of the second one. According to one experienced merchant captain, the February storm was the worst he had ever experienced.[3] On the 12th his ship was thrown onto its beam-ends for nineteen hours in the very locality where *Atalanta* was likely to have been at the time. Lloyd's of London later issued a report that eighteen vessels sailing for England from North American ports in January and February 1880 were listed as missing after this destructive February storm.[4]

The loss of the average merchant vessel usually merited only a sentence or two – a paragraph at most – in the "Missing or Lost" column of *The Times*, but the *Atalanta* was different. Between April 13, 1880, when the paper first revealed that there had been no news of the vessel for seventy-two days, and June 10, when she was officially declared lost, *The Times* published at least three dozen reports and letters relating to her probable fate. Initially every effort was made by the Admiralty (and also by *The Times*) to maintain a discrete air of confidence in the safe return of the ship. In an official news release on April 12, the Admiralty tried to put the best face possible on the situation with the suggestion that Stirling might have decided to follow his original orders, and if that was the case the ship was still not seriously overdue. This was patently misleading for there was absolutely no justification for such a suggestion. No fear or concern was expressed about the ship itself, which was claimed to possess "unusual stability." Nevertheless, three days earlier, the Channel Fleet, about to head home from Gibraltar, was ordered to search for the ship on the way.

If the authorities were much more concerned than they cared to admit, the relatives and friends of those aboard *Atalanta* became frantic once the news was out. On April 15 the Admiralty offices were besieged by 150 telegrams and two hundred personal inquiries from concerned relatives desperate for some word of hope.[5] Unfortunately, officialdom had no news, good or ill, to offer them. Beyond periodic observations about vessels that had taken up to ninety days to make the crossing from Bermuda or New York, the authorities continued to adopt a wait and see attitude. In this information vacuum, rumour and speculation flourished mightily. Some thought that *Atalanta* had probably been dismasted and driven far off course and out of the regular shipping lanes, which would explain why there had been no sightings of her. Others believed that she might have slowly beaten her way north in an effort to catch the Gulf Stream and the Westerlies and was overdue on that account. Still others thought Stirling might have been driven onto one of the many reefs around Bermuda, or that the ship was limping homeward with jury-rigged sails after losing her topmasts to the fury of a gale. Ominously, there had been no reported sightings of the ship since it had left Bermuda, and some suspected she might have been thrown over onto her beam-ends before turning over to go down with all hands. Still others (once again raising the spectre of the *Eurydice*) thought that she might have been "pooped," that is overwhelmed from astern by a huge rogue wave. All of these and many other equally speculative scenarios, along with others more bizarre, were bruited about in the pubs and drawing rooms of the country.[6]

There was only one fleeting moment of hope. A report that the missing ship had arrived safely at Falmouth was posted in newspaper offices and store windows at Portsmouth on April 13, prompting anxious relatives to flock to the dockyard for confirmation. At the gates their hopes were dashed when they found a notice stating that a ship named *Atalanta* had indeed arrived at Falmouth, but it was a merchant ship, not a naval vessel. In the face of this discouraging news, family members and friends turned away even more anxious and distressed.

Thomasina Moss, probably still abed after giving birth to a son six days earlier, would not likely have been among those who thronged to the dockyard. At Chardville the happiness of the blessed event must have been overwhelmed by the sombre realization that her husband was unlikely to be coming home. What a chaotic mixture of emotions must have kept Senie in a state of turmoil during the final days of her pregnancy and the months that followed! At one extreme was the joy of a healthy newborn son. At the other was fear and grief that accompanied the growing possibility, and then the cruel certitude, that *Atalanta* was gone, and with it her beloved Edward. They had enjoyed such a brief time together, really only four of their seven years of marriage when absences on the polar expedition and other service afloat are taken into account. Amidst this mixture of grief and happiness was Thomasina's growing realization that she was destined to raise her three children alone, and in greatly reduced circumstances.

Fortunately Edward had always been careful with his money, so at least there would be a bit of a cushion against unforeseen emergencies. She would also receive a modest widow's pension from the Navy – enough to at least ensure that she would not become dependent on the goodwill and charity of others. This, however, must have been small comfort, and Thomasina would have known only too well how much her future had been changed because of her husband's untimely death. The comfortable middle class lifestyle the family had been enjoying would soon be replaced by one of gentile frugality.

After the false April 13 report, there was nothing to buoy the hopes and hearts of those with relatives or friends aboard *Atalanta*. The Admiralty continued to offer up the opinion that she might still turn up, but as ship after ship arrived in England without news of her fate, that proposition became more tenuous with each passing day. A week later, Admiral Sullivan wrote to *The Times* to again correct "the erroneous opinion" that *Atalanta* and *Eurydice* were sister ships. Although he noted that the Vestal class of Symondite frigates were "very stiff, the stiffest under sail that we ever possessed," Sullivan claimed that they were only dangerous if they were short of water or provisions. No Vestal class ships had ever been lost according to the Admiral, who stated that he had sailed fourteen years in a Symonds brig and that the Admiralty had made the right choice when they refitted the old *Juno*.

By the end of the month, in spite of the natural reluctance to admit otherwise, the fate of the ship had become almost impossible to deny. *The Times* put the case succinctly:

> There is no news to report with reference to the *Atalanta*, and even those most sanguine are beginning to lose heart. The Channel Squadron is on its way to Bantry Bay, its searches at the Azores having evidently proved fruitless.... The public will probably not rest satisfied until an examination of Greenland and Iceland has been made.

One day later, the troopship HMS *Tamar* arrived at Portsmouth with Able Seaman John Verling aboard. Verling was one of the three sick men who had been left at Barbados. As soon as his presence became known, the press rushed to interview him, and upon publication of his comments the focus began to shift away from the fate of the ship to speculation and debate about why *Atalanta* had not survived the gales. Was it because of serious flaws in either the design or the refitting of the ship? Had she had been sent out with too few trained seamen and officers with insufficient experience under sail? Was the Admiralty, through failures of omission or commission, culpable in any way? Finally, should there be an independent inquiry to answer these and other questions related to the mysterious disappearance of *Atalanta*?

Some of these matters had already been raised of course, but Verling's remarks to the press really put the cat among the pigeons, sending the Admiralty into damage control mode. "Verling's account of the performance of the training ship is far from reassuring" opined *The Times*; "though the question will of course arise as to the value of his opinion." And Verling certainly had opinions. He judged the ship to be "exceedingly crank, overweighed, and ship-rigged instead of being fitted out like a Bark" (which would have had a different sail and mast configuration). The Able Seaman also claimed that the condition and performance of the ship had aroused Captain Stirling's mistrust. He stated that on one occasion after leaving Tenerife the ship had rolled over as much as thirty-two degrees, and Stirling had been heard to remark that "had she gone over one more degree she would have gone [completely] over and foundered." Verling also described the crew as "weak" and, except for two officers, badly out of training. For that reason, or so he believed, Captain Stirling "hardly left the deck." The vocal seaman also claimed that some of the young trainees, either too seasick or desperately fearful of going aloft, "hid themselves and couldn't be found when wanted."[8] However, these disturbing revelations or allegations were discounted immediately in an anonymous letter from "a late officer of *Atalanta*," published in the same edition of the paper.

The writer began by pointing out that the ship was not the same as *Eurydice*, as some people believed. He then stated that many false statements were being made about *Atalanta*, and denied Verling's claim that she was overmasted or unseaworthy, noting that during the refit six feet had been taken off the masts to reduce straining. He also claimed that after the first cruise Stirling had often remarked to him that the ship behaved well, and he (the writer) was also sure the other senior officers aboard had every confidence in the seaworthiness of the ship. Two days after this exchange of views, the Admiralty sent Post-Captain Culme-Seymour to question Verling, who was recuperating at Haslar Naval Hospital. On the strength of Culme-Seymour's report, they announced that the seaman had retracted a number of the statements he had made to the press. This apparent attempt at damage control failed to satisfy the Portsmouth reporter who had originally interviewed Verling, and in another *Times* article on May 1 he defended Verling and alleged that

Culme-Seymour had pressured the seaman into changing his story. This was almost certainly correct.

"Through no fault of his own," the reporter wrote, "Able Seaman John Verling, late of the *Atalanta*, has had distinction thrust upon him. Had his testimony been in favour of the behaviour and trustworthiness of the ship, the probability is that the Admiralty would not have troubled themselves about him, and he would have been saved a visit by a Flag-Captain while [he was] in hospital." The reporter was extremely sceptical about the motives of the naval authorities, referring to his earlier statement that questions would likely arise about the value of Verling's opinions since he had only recently received his rating as an Able Seaman.

> As such he was not expected to sit in judgement upon the professional advisors to My Lords [of the Admiralty] or to pronounce with authority as to the stability of the vessel – but if his censure [of the ship] be worth nothing, his praise must be equally valueless, and it is difficult to imagine why the Admiralty was so anxious to obtain his favourable opinion of the ship. That Verling has been, intentionally or otherwise, frightened into revoking his former testimony is clear; but the public will draw their own conclusions as to which expression of opinion is the more worthy of belief – the one that was voluntarily repeated on three separate occasions to three separate correspondents, or that which has been extracted from him by a Flag-Captain acting on instructions.[9]

It was a point well made. The reporter also refused to criticize Verling for "failing to use the term 'crank' with the precision of a naval architect who attaches special meaning to such expressions," noting that the seaman had based his remarks on what he believed to be the words or actions of the captain or the common belief among the crew. It was not, he believed, just the testimony of an ignorant seaman, but "the embodiment of the common belief of the crew." As for the Admiralty claim that Verling had retracted his remarks, and that "the petty officers and ships company thought well of the *Atalanta*," it was pointed out that the seaman's testimony had been taken down verbatim by a shorthand writer who recorded that Verling had clearly stated that he did not think the men had a high opinion of the ship, and that she laboured so much in rough water that they were all afraid of her.

Pressure on the government had been building steadily, and on May 12 the Admiralty announced that an official inquiry would be held "to determine if the ship, officers, and crew were all fit for the service in which she was employed" – a mightily obscure statement. Some people felt that a departmental inquiry was not good enough, and public demands for an independent inquiry were beginning to emerge. When Member of Parliament E. J. Reed (a former naval officer himself) called for an independent inquiry,[10] Admiral Sir William King Hall took offence at the inference that the Navy could not be trusted, and attacked Reed and other critics, labelling their demands "irresponsible." Reed replied in

The Times on May 27, attempting to smooth the Admiral's ruffled feathers by claiming no slur was intended. He expressed confidence that there had been no neglect "on the part of the officers, dockyards etc.," but nevertheless believed a departmental inquiry wasn't sufficient. He also observed that the MP from Falmouth (another ex-navy type) had protested the use of old sailing ships as training vessels even before *Juno* was chosen for a refit.

Three days after the opening of the new session of Parliament, a small group of MP's pressed for an independent, not Navy-dominated, tribunal. On May 25 the government (now led by Prime Minister Gladstone's Liberals, who had defeated the Conservatives two months earlier) named Admiral A. P. Ryder, Commander-in-Chief, Portsmouth, as the Inquiry Chairman. He was to be assisted by Vice-Admiral Randolph; Staff-Captain Robert B. Batt, the Harbour Master at Chatham; Mr. H. C. Rothery, the government Wreck Commissioner; and Mr. Bernard Waymouth, noted clipper ship designer and Secretary to the Chief [ship] Surveyor at Lloyds of London, the great maritime insurers. In 1868 Waymouth had designed one of the fastest clipper ships in the world, the *Thermopylae*, second only to the famous *Cutty Sark* in speed and fame. The critics were not satisfied with the proposed composition of the committee, and on the 28th, Mr. Jenkins (the MP for Falmouth) presented the House with the following private member's resolution.

> Resolved that in the opinion of this House, the proposed inquiry into the loss of the *Atalanta* will not be satisfactory if the committee does not partake less of a departmental character than that proposed by the government.

Jenkins motion prompted a brief but spirited debate among a half dozen or so members. Lord Henry Lennox, a former Secretary of the Admiralty, supported the motion even though he thought there was really no need for an investigation in the first place. A Mr. Norwood thought that the best and most balanced committee would be one led by the Wreck Commissioner, Mr. Rothery, plus two naval officers and an eminent shipbuilder. Unsurprisingly, retired Admiral Egerton, MP (another former Secretary of the Admiralty), thought naval officers would be preferable to civilians. Mr. Holmes favoured a civilian majority and E.J. Reed reiterated Norwood's view that Rothery should be Chair and that another civilian should be included to give better balance. The Right Honourable Robert Shaw le Fevre, Secretary of the Admiralty (1871–74) during the first Gladstone ministry, suggested that there was no need for an independent inquiry. He said that the existing process was the same as that which had been used for the HMS *Eurydice* and HMS *Captain*[11] investigations and believed naval officers were quite capable of acting independently. Moreover, there were two civilians among the five-member committee, and Admiral Ryder, a member of the Committee of [ship] Designs, was both knowledgeable and conscientious. As the debate began to falter Mr. Jenkins asked, and was given permission, to withdraw the motion. Jenkins must have known very well that it had no chance of success, but at least his motion served to put into the record the objections to an "in house" investigation dominated by naval men rather than civilians. To the critics it smacked too much of putting the fox in charge of the hen house.

On June 10 *The Times* reported that the Accountant-General of the Navy had been ordered to close the books of the missing ship as of June 4, and to remove the name of the ship from the Navy List. Widows of officers were to receive the special pensions they were entitled to in consequence of their husbands being drowned in the performance of their duty. On the same date, Permanent Secretary of the Admiralty Robert Hall opened the official investigation. The committee mandate was to inquire into the efficiency of the ship; was she "sound, stable, and seaworthy" and was her "rigging, equipment, officers, and crew sufficient and suitable to provide for her safety." These questions carefully limited the parameters of the investigation in a manner that did not call for an explanation of why the ship had been lost. Since there were no survivors of the actual event or any information about how she had met her fate, such a finding would of course have been impossible in any case. However, in spite of the narrowness of the mandate, it was at least implicit that the cause could be postulated on the basis of the evidence that would be presented to the committee.

21: Whitehall, London

"The Last Inquiry"

The hearings opened on July 7 with an overview of *Juno*'s history prior to becoming a floating police station in 1861. Some officers who had served on her during the 1850s and others who had left the ship after *Atalanta*'s first training voyage were then called to testify as to the character of the ship. All gave her a clean bill of health, though it was made quite clear that she was lively, as were other sailing ships of the same class designed by Sir William Symonds. None of the men who had sailed on *Juno* during her first two commissions (1845–49 and 1853–57) recalled any concerns about her seaworthiness or stability.

With these preliminaries out of the way, the Committee began the difficult task of attempting to establish the facts surrounding the choice of the ship and the extent of the repairs and alterations that were made between March 1877, when the Admiralty decided another deep sea training ship was needed, and November 1879, when *Atalanta* set forth on her final voyage. Should the forty-three-year-old *Juno* have been chosen for refit in the first place? Was she sound, stable, and seaworthy when she left on her second winter cruise? If not, why not? These questions went to the heart of the matter.[1]

Admiral Ryder, who led most of the questioning at the hearings, began by trying to establish the cost of the refit and the condition of the ship both before and after the work was done. It was revealed that the original repair estimate had been a modest £11,589, later amended to £19,294 after *Juno* had undergone a more thorough examination. However, by October 1879 the final tab for all the repairs and modifications reached £27,132, a far cry from the original estimate. According to a foreman from Pembroke Shipyards, at the going rate of £36/ton a brand new ship would only have cost another £5,000. The repairs to the old sailing ship were obviously very comprehensive and significant. Almost one-third of the ship was completely rebuilt. Perhaps that was not too surprising for a forty-three-year-old wooden ship that had languished most of her life dockside without the regular maintenance given to active vessels. However, given a final cost that was two and one-half times the original estimate, choosing to refit *Juno* instead of designing and building a new and more suitable ship appears to have been a grave error in judgment.

The original inspection of the ship had been carried out in April 1877, when some borings were taken to check the condition of the hull and determine if *Juno* was worth repairing. The Chief Constructor and his assistants at Portsmouth testified that they had not found any reason why the vessel could not be satisfactorily repaired, at least as far as they could determine. Most of the ship was considered to be sound, though it was admitted that the inspection had been "a bit superficial." After passing this first and apparently most important test, *Juno* was towed to Pembroke Dockyard in April for a more thorough examination. At Pembroke several thousand borings were taken to check virtually every timber in the vessel. Some parts of the hull must have been in terrible shape, for when the shipwrights opened her up, places were found that they described as "punk" – areas so soft that a finger could easily be pushed through the wood. Outright replacement of structural timbers in both the fore and aft sections of the hull, along with other major structural repairs was required to make the ship seaworthy. Yet in spite of this unexpectedly bad news – and the obvious extra cost that could be anticipated – there was no thought of abandoning the project.

For all practical purposes the die had already been cast, if not on the day it was decided *Juno* was the only available candidate, then after the first inspection. There is no evidence of any second thoughts by Admiralty officials. Repair work actually started in August 1877, five months before official approval for the estimated repairs was finally granted on December 21. Sixteen thousand of the £19,000 second estimate was allocated for repairs to the hull alone. A month later *Juno* was given a new name, HMS *Atalanta*.

As the inquiry proceeded, it was established that even before Stirling's first West Indies cruise, additional repairs and alterations had been ordered in an effort to reduce the "uneasiness" of the ship and remedy various defects that had been identified during a short sea trial. Bilge keels had been attached to the ship's bottom in an effort to make her less lively. These extra keels, positioned at an angle of roughly forty-five degrees off vertical, were bolted to the hull and ran seventy feet along each side of the ship to act as stabilizers. They were attached as an experiment – the Navy had never before put them on a pure sailing vessel, though they had been used on steam-driven ships. In September, Captain Marcus Hare had been ordered to send the design drawings for *Eurydice* to the Pembroke shipyard for guidance, even though the two vessels were not really identical and had different designers. He had also been asked to propose modifications to *Juno*, presumably based on his experience with *Eurydice*. Apparently Hare recommended shortening the mizzen-mast, the main-mast and the bowsprit, and suggested the addition of a forecastle on the main deck. Somewhere along the line – it is not clear when or upon whose recommendation or authority – approval was also granted to install the experimental bilge keels. After this work was completed, *Atalanta* was commissioned and left for the West Indies in November 1878. Once out in the Atlantic, it soon became apparent to Captain Stirling that he was in command of a ship that still had some serious problems.

On March 29, 1879, the day of his return from Bermuda, Stirling presented his superiors with a very extensive list of defects and required repairs. He reported, and it was confirmed by testimony at the inquiry, that the ship had taken on at least two inches of water an hour on the return trip from Barbados. Needless to say this was a major concern. Straining, particularly at the masts, had opened up seams, raising and opening up the upper deck and, (according to Stirling) twisting or breaking nearly all the pipes in the ship. Moreover, in spite of the six feet that had already been taken off the top-masts the previous summer, he still considered the ship to be too heavy topside. It was his opinion that the weight of the spars and rigging exacerbated the Symondite tendencies of the ship. The bilge keels had also been a real problem when the wind was up. When *Atalanta* heeled over by twenty-five degrees or more (to port, for example) the opposing bilge keel would come right out of the water, and with the sudden and sharp return movement of the ship it would strike the surface of the sea with tremendous force, causing the vessel to shudder and shake both fore and aft. Stirling believed this had strained the hull, causing it to leak.

However, when the ship was put into dry dock and examined at Portsmouth, it was noted that the hull was "much strained from the effects of the recent gale" rather than by the keels. The engineers claimed Stirling was wrong about the source of the straining and leaks, because when the copper sheathing on the ship's bottom had been examined it was found to be smooth, not warped, concluding that the leaking was not due to straining of the hull. They also denied that the ship was overmasted, and that the "lifting" at the upper deck was simply due to the masts being wedged too tightly where they met the planks of the deck. Their inspection had also revealed only five broken pipes and minimal twisting of others. No one at the inquiry thought to ask if any broken or twisted pipes might have been repaired or replaced during the first winter voyage – which was very probable.

After the April 1879 inspection, approval was given to remove the bilge keels, but Stirling was advised that there would be no further changes to the spars or the rigging. He was told that he had calculated their weight incorrectly and that the ship was not really ten tons too heavy topside as he believed. Surprisingly, in view of that judgment, he was given permission to remove four sixty-four-pounder guns from the gun deck. After a brief sea trial in September, he reported the ship was "very much more easy" with the experimental bilge keels removed. However, still believing *Atalanta* was top-heavy, and being denied any change in the rigging or spars, he asked and received permission to add ten tons of extra cement ballast to offset what he still saw as excessive weight topside. By that time the patience of his superiors had been exhausted, and it had been made clear to him that there would be no further alterations. Testimony was given that Stirling had signed the ship off as satisfactory following her inspection before taking the ship on her fatal final voyage. Stirling probably felt that he had little choice. If he continued to complain he would probably have been summarily removed from command. Many years later, a contemporary of

both Moss and Stirling told a family member that when the captain asked permission to shorten his cross spars because he found the ship too lively, the request was refused, and he was dismissed with the allegation that he had "cold feet."[2] No doubt he was stung by such a charge and in the end simply accepted the inevitable with the hope that the most recent repairs and modifications would be enough to make the ship safe.

During the hearings the chief financial overseer, Controller of the Navy Vice-Admiral Sir William Houston Stewart was questioned about the wisdom of choosing to refit an old ship that had been in Ordinary for seventeen years. Were not static ships on harbour duty as police hulks really just vessels that had been condemned as either obsolete or unfit for sea? Stewart answered that he "was not prepared to say that they are" – a reply that was evasive to say the least. Overall, his testimony on other matters did not sit well with the committee members either.

As the inquiry progressed, considerable time was devoted to the critical issue of *Atalanta*'s stability, and from the testimony it was evident that the movements of the ship under sail exactly matched those described by Edward Moss in his November 11 letter to Senie. One entry from the ship's log (during the first voyage) stated that the ship heeled over as much as forty degrees and then lurched back to windward twenty-two degrees, making twelve or thirteen oscillations a minute, a very lively performance indeed. Given that situation, in only a matter of seconds, a man standing on one of the topgallant spars would move through the air more than 127 feet at a speed of over seventeen miles an hour. Was it any wonder why one seaman was pitched overboard on the trip to the West Indies, or why some young trainees were afraid to go aloft?

The question of exactly how far *Atalanta* actually lurched or rolled was crucial, for if the ship really did go over as far as forty-three degrees, as Stirling was reported to have entered in the ship's log during the first voyage, then she may well have capsized in a storm and gone to her grave as a result. The C-in-C at Pembroke, Admiral Hood, refused to believe it, adding that if he knew that she had really lurched forty or more degrees he would have had her destroyed. However if it was really true that she rolled and lurched that much he wondered if the ship had simply "rolled herself to pieces" during one of the gales she encountered.

Rear-Admiral Charles T. Curme, who knew Francis Stirling very well, testified as to his character and competence, describing Stirling as a "cool man" who was not easily spooked. However, he also questioned the validity of the log entry that stated the ship had lurched over almost forty-five degrees during the first voyage. He thought it was most likely that someone other than Stirling, probably one of the junior officers, had just recorded his own estimate of how much the ship had heeled over. Perhaps that was so, but Lieutenant Alexander E. Bethell, who had been on the first voyage, also testified that he believed the ship had heeled over more than forty degrees. Curme, in what seemed to be an attempt to downplay the claim that the ship heeled excessively, pointed out the difficulty of getting an accurate measurement under adverse conditions and with the instruments available on the ship. Yet the fact remains that even if Stirling did not make the log entry himself, he was an experienced officer, and it was his evident belief – as well as the belief of others on the ship – that *Atalanta* was capable of heeling over by at least forty degrees in some circumstances.

On June 10 the last five Ordinary Seamen from *Atalanta* arrived at Portsmouth on HMS *Plover* and, like seaman Verling, were interviewed by the press. Generally speaking, their comments confirmed Verling's opinion of the ship. One man (McCormick), an Ordinary Seaman who had been sent ashore as a prisoner at Barbados, and who had been in the Navy since 1876, stated that he "had never liked the ship from the day he joined her," but it was "impossible to sail with a better captain."[3] He said that Stirling seemed to feel the ship couldn't be trusted and that in a gale she couldn't right herself readily if she went over too far. In July each of these men were called to testify at the inquiry, where McCormick's testimony was contradictory. He reiterated that while he didn't like the look of her, he thought *Atalanta* was "a very good sailing ship." He then added that she was leaky, and that her seams had opened up at the ports in heavy weather causing the caulking to work out on the way to Tenerife.

Thomas Jessup, who also claimed to have liked the ship, said that Stirling had allowed men to sleep on a topsail on deck when they were afraid to sleep below – which certainly suggests some crew members didn't want to be caught below if the ship foundered. He had nothing but praise for his commanding officer: "I know one thing," he said, " and that is that the Captain was up there whenever I was on watch. I never saw the Captain but when he was on deck. It seemed like this to me, that the Captain never had any faith in the officers, because he was always on deck, even in fine weather." Elmer Ellis, another fairly experienced seaman, described the ship as "a little crank," and OS Alfred Stansel confirmed that she was leaky and needed to be pumped out every two days, and in bad weather sometimes every night.

The Chief Carpenter's Mate on the first cruise was also called to testify, confirming once more that there was straining and leaking. The pumps were his responsibility and he stated that the bilges were usually pumped every four hours. He claimed that in bad weather the ship took on as much as three inches of water an hour and when they arrived at Barbados he estimated that they had about fifteen inches (about twenty tons) of water in the bilges. Sub-Lieutenant Harry Rivers, who had been on the first voyage to the West Indies, also claimed *Atalanta* had leaked more than any of his four previous ships.

Able Seaman Verling was not called to testify during the proceedings – it was claimed he was still too ill. Although it is true that he was still recuperating at Haslar Naval Hospital, given his original story to the newspapers it is astonishing that no effort was made to at least have a committee member question him in person. The serious discrepancy between the newspaper version and the report tabled by his interrogator, Post-Captain Culme-Seymour, should have been looked into, but it was totally ignored. At the very least Verling should have been asked the same questions that were posed to the other surviving seamen. Instead, Culme-Seymour's report was entered into the appendix of the final report without either comment or challenge. In it Culme-Seymour stated that Verling had denied virtually everything that had he had been quoted as saying to the press. Stirling's remark about sinking if the ship rolled another degree was described as "entirely fictitious"; the ship only rolled sixteen degrees each way, not over forty, and he (Verling) "could not say anything at all against the ship." Nor, according to his interrogator did he make any remarks about the officers, though he claimed the petty-officers thought well of the ship. It is very difficult to avoid the conclusion that the Admiralty authorities were not at all anxious to have Verling testify either in front of the committee or by deposition.

During the inquiry there was much discussion about the decision to refit *Juno* as a training ship. The basic reason, or so it was claimed, was that she was the only sailing ship available that was deemed suitable to the task, presumably because of her size and class of vessel. However, the Committee was unable to elicit important information about the decision from the officers who had served on the Admiralty Board that had chosen the *Juno*. In 1877, Rear-Admiral William Acland Hood was a Junior Lord of the Admiralty, and Admiral George Grenville Wellesley was First Sea Lord. During their testimony both men indicated they were willing to turn over the minutes of the meeting where the inspection of *Atalanta* was discussed. When they failed to do so, a formal request for the minutes was sent to Naval Secretary Robert Hall. He responded that the Admiralty was willing to grant the request, providing Hood and Wellesley wished it to be done. According to his letter, Hood and Wellesley claimed they had no objection but "declined to express any wish to do so."[4] The phrase accurately summed up Hood's response to Hall, but Wellesley flatly stated by letter that he was not prepared to make an exception to the practice of treating such minutes as confidential. Naval Secretary Hall had not ordered the two officers to comply with Ryder's request, so there the matter rested. Once again, it is virtually impossible to avoid the inference that something was being covered up.

Admiral of the Fleet Sir Thomas Symonds, who was C-in-C at Devonport in 1877, admitted that he had seen the June report on the condition of *Juno* after the second examination of the ship and testified that at the time he saw no reason why she couldn't be repaired, as he believed she was "sufficiently sound." However, it is clear from his remarks and later correspondence with the Committee secretary, that he did not approve refitting the old frigate as a training ship. This was not because of safety concerns but because he thought the ship was inadequate from the standpoint of health and space. On October 25, 1878, in his report to his superiors after a final inspection of the refitted ship, he recommended a reduction in the number of trainees to be carried and suggested a number of other changes before the ship left on its first transatlantic cruise.[5]

During the inquiry the Committee dwelt briefly with rumours that the ship was inadequately manned, but the evidence did not appear to support such a claim. The total number of crew members was 113: eleven executive officers, four civilian officers (Edward was one), six petty officers, twenty-six first-class petty officers, four second-class petty officers, six leading seamen, two shipwrights, twenty-one able seamen, nineteen domestics, and fourteen marines. In addition, there were 170 ordinary seamen trainees. Merchant ships regularly worked three- and four-masted sailing ships with far fewer seamen. How much recent experience many of the officers and seamen had on sailing vessels was another matter. None of the executive officers had less than nine years of service and the two most senior officers, Stirling and his second-in-command, Lieutenant Blackett, had served for nineteen and twenty-eight years respectively.[6] The service records do indicate that most of the executive officers did not have much recent experience in older wind-driven wooden vessels. However, for most of the crew, the 1879–80 winter voyage would have been their second high-seas voyage on the ship, and one might expect that they would have learned or re-learned the sailing-ship skills essential for their survival. As for Ordinary Seaman Jessup's statement that Captain Stirling seemed to always be on deck, seemingly because he didn't trust his officers, a competent and responsible commanding officer would expect to be visibly in charge whenever there was the slightest chance that his ship and crew might be in serious danger, particularly when he was responsible for a shipload of trainees.

After the formal hearings ended, the Committee continued to request further information to assist them in drawing their conclusions. For example, the Admiralty was asked to provide a list of naval sailing ships that had been lost since 1840. The results certainly give pause for thought. Of the nine sailing ships that had vanished without a trace during the previous forty years, five had been Symondites. Four of them were lost between 1856 and 1861, though with the exception of *Atalanta* all had been smaller sloop-rigged ships of between four hundred and six hundred tons.[7]

Probably through the urging of Bernard Waymouth it was agreed to have Mr. William Johns, Assistant to the Chief [ship] Surveyor at Lloyds, carry out an independent assessment of *Atalanta*'s stability. Mr. Nathaniel Barnaby, the Director of Naval Construction, was also asked to conduct a similar review, based on the design plans and other pertinent information. Barnaby concluded that *Atalanta* had a high degree of stability, although he did not entirely rule out the possibility that the ship had capsized during a storm. Johns agreed up to a point, but with an important caveat. His report stated that: "The vessel had an insufficient righting movement at large angles [of heel], and that it was by no means improbable that she would capsize if caught in a squall of wind unless carefully handled."

Nautically speaking, there are two kinds of stability, "initial stability" and "reserve or ultimate stability." A sailing ship that is wide, flat, and heavy will have a high degree of initial stability and will be "stiff" under sail. *Atalanta* fitted that description. However, the reserve stability must also be considered. A ship with a high degree of reserve (or ultimate) stability will be able to heel over farther before passing the point of no return but would take a longer time to right itself again, making it more likely to capsize if the degree of list became too great.[8] It will be recalled that there was testimony (from McCormick) that *Atalanta* did not right herself readily in a gale, and Edward Moss had referred to the ship as "bottom heavy." Stirling's addition of the extra ten tons of ballast before he left for the

West Indies in the fall of '79, was undoubtedly intended to increase *Atalanta*'s degree of reserve stability. Ultimately, Johns report placed a good portion of the blame for the loss of *Atalanta* at the doorstep of the designer, Sir William Symonds, stating that: "The ability of Symondite vessels to right themselves if thrown on their beam ends is greatly wanting in vessels of the Symondite type." He believed this characteristic accounted for the "early losses of such vessels, as well as that of *Atalanta*."

The Inquiry Committee released its report on December 29, 1880, and *The Times* published excerpts and comment the following day. The paper noted that after observing that they were not asked "to what cause the loss of *Atalanta* may be attributed the Committee conjectured on a number of possible causes."

> But it is to the section of the report that deals with the 'stability' of the ship that the public will turn to for such information as may be afforded as to the probable cause of the disaster. On this important question we need only call attention to the 34th paragraph, which states "... the ship was on the whole a very stable ship except at large angles of heel. In those few words lies the gist of the matter."

The paper suggested the Admiralty should have foreseen the large angles of heel that were likely to occur in serious storms and implied that the earlier loss of four Symondites should have influenced the decision of those who were responsible for sending the ship to sea on a winter cruise after Captain Stirling's report of her "alarming tendency to roll and lurch so much." The testimony of Admiral Wellesley was attacked as "remarkable for its tone of levity and indifference." Wellesley had testified that he couldn't even recall seeing Stirling's report after the first cruise, and if he did see it had only looked it over generally. He was taken to task for failing to recognize the need to inquire about the repairs or the stability of the ship before she was sent back to sea. This was seen as "a serious oversight in view of a report so alarming as to be unbelievable to some, and yet not so remarkable as to be disbelieved by the Controller [of the Navy]." Finally, the differing views of the two naval constructors, Johns and Barnaby, were noted, and *The Times* concluded: "A grave responsibility rests with those who allowed [*Atalanta*] to depart – a conclusion that the Committee certainly justifies, though it shrinks from openly stating it."

Although the matter was over and done with as far as the Admiralty was concerned after the report was made public, the controversy over the loss of the ship has never entirely gone away. A few years ago, in *Solved! The Greatest Sea Mystery of All*, Bermuda author David Raines postulated a loose conspiracy reaching as high as Prime Minister Gladstone himself, to "whitewash the royal decks" during the *Atalanta* Inquiry. Unfortunately, Raine failed to provide the documentation that would be needed to bring real credibility to many of his claims and allegations, and at times his book reads much more like a historical novel than a genuine attempt at scholarship.[9]

That said, there is little doubt that Wellesley and Hood (respectively First and Second Naval Sea Lords of the Admiralty in 1877) did their best to cover their backsides during the examination of their respective roles in the decisions that ultimately led to the loss of *Atalanta*. Both men were members of the Admiralty Board from January 1877 until December 1879 – dates that encompass the entire period when the ship was under reconstruction or repair. Neither officer was really called to account during the inquiry or in the final report. As Raine points out, the inquiry lacked credibility from the beginning, chaired and co-chaired as it was by two admirals, and weighted in favour of naval personnel. The public interest would have been better served if Henry Rothery or Bernard Waymouth had been placed in charge of a more balanced committee, as had been suggested in Parliament at the time the inquiry was announced.

Strangely, the First Lord of the Admiralty from August, 1877, until May 12, 1880, the Right Honourable William Henry Smith, Conservative MP for Westminster, was never called to testify. As First Lord, he was a ranking cabinet minister in Disraeli's government, and the person who should have been ultimately responsible for the decisions that had been made by his subordinates. It can hardly have been an oversight that he was omitted from the list of people who were being questioned. However, Smith, a wealthy businessman (W.H. Smith Books) was a politician and bureaucrat who had never served in the Navy and almost certainly left most practical matters relating to ships in the hands of his subordinates among the Admiralty Sea Lords. As an interesting aside, Smith (as well as the Royal Navy and the Victorian class system) was satirized brilliantly in Gilbert and Sullivan's 1878 comic opera HMS *Pinafore*. Apparently the character of Rt. Hon. Sir Joseph Porter, KCB, First Lord of the Admiralty, was based on Smith, and everyone knew it. It was not long before he was being publicly referred to as "Pinafore Smith."

In the song "*When I was a Lad*," Sir George Porter explains how he rose to his exalted position, belting out such memorable lines as "I cleaned all the windows and swept up the floor, and I polished up the handles on the big front door [and I] copied all the letters in hand so free, that now I am the ruler of the Queen's Navee." Although satire is not usually the type of evidence historians cite, irreverence for the Powers That Be is generally rooted in some aspect of reality, and HMS *Pinafore* undoubtedly reflected public opinion about the state of the Senior Service's leadership in 1878. It is highly probable that the First Lord was never called to testify at the inquiry because it was understood that he would know next to nothing about most of the subjects that were under review.

To sum up, the decision to refit *Juno* was a tragic error in judgment, and well before the end of the inquiry everyone realized it. Admiral Symonds, who knew more than most about the ships his father had designed, had from the beginning argued for an entirely different class of vessel. In a letter to then First Naval Lord Admiral Sir Hastings Reginald Yelverton, G.C.B., dated March 16, 1877, Symonds had suggested a screw frigate rather than a pure sailing vessel, but his advice was ignored. Eighteen months later, he conducted the final inspection of the rebuilt ship, and while he pronounced her to be fit, it is obvious that he had reservations about her as a training ship. His October 25, 1878, report, written about a fortnight before *Atalanta* left for the West Indies on her first cruise was forthright. In Symonds view, the new forecastle was too heavy, the masts were overstayed, and the ship was too small and unhealthily overcrowded. He recommended the removal of the four upper deck guns, and a reduction of the ship's complement to 250. Once again he maintained that a steam frigate would be better and more useful, stating that *Atalanta* was more likely to be wrecked than a steam frigate and would be useless in wartime. He recommended using ships like HMS *Ariadne* or *Galatea* as deepwater training ships. The former was a 4,426 ton, 3,350 HP sail and screw frigate designed by Sir. Baldwin Walker, then the Chief Surveyor for the Navy. *Galatea*, built in 1859, could carry a complement of 450 and Symonds thought such a ship could serve double duty as a training vessel in peacetime or a ship of war in times of trouble.

On July 21, 1880, right after he testified before the Ryder Committee, Admiral Symonds clarified his opinion about *Atalanta* in a letter that was later included in the appendix of the inquiry report. With commendable candour he modified his earlier statements about the soundness of the ship and gave his views about the probable reason for her demise.

> I could not pronounce *Atalanta*, 36 years old, sound. Who can say what hidden defect may have caused her loss, by springing a leak, etc., etc., although thoroughly repaired? If it is true, as I believe is stated, that she worked and broke pumps, very old age I should pronounce to be the cause, as her sister ship *Spartan* never worked, below or aloft, and I, who have stood at dockside when many an old ship of such a date was being broken up, would not put young men in such a ship.

Symonds belated judgment about the fundamental reason for the loss of the *Atalanta* rings true; she should never have been chosen in the first place. However, during the spring of 1877, the war drums were rolling ominously in the Balkans. On April 24 Russia declared war on Turkey, and who could say that Britain would not be drawn into the fray? The Navy needed more seamen, and the order was sent out to find another training ship similar to the *Eurydice*. To design and build one from scratch could take two or more years and would also be more costly than a refit. Still, there were those who did advocate such a course – Liberal MP Jenkins from Falmouth, and MP Sir Thomas Brassey, for example. Brassey, who had the reputation as an outstanding yachtsman, believed that if the Navy was determined to use a sailing ship to train seamen, at least they should go with a modern design and not refit some obsolete frigate. At the time no one appeared to be listening, but it is significant that Prime Minister Gladstone appointed Brassey to the position of Civil Lord of the Admiralty on May 12, 1880, when he replaced all but one of the Disraeli-appointed Admiralty Commissioners just a month before the hearings. Brassey served for three years as one of the Civil Lords and then became Secretary of the Admiralty. He represented a new and younger generation of naval administrators who would ultimately prod the Senior Service reluctantly away from its Nelsonian fixation and towards a twentieth century dominated by steam and steel. To once again quote James Morris, "slowly, creakily, the Royal Navy adapted to modernity. It progressed in a welter of argument, admiral against admiral, newspaper critic against naval spokesman, and if its professional ideas changed slowly, its gnarled, stubborn and ornate style was more resistant still."[10] All of this was apparent in both the story of the loss of the *Atalanta* and that of the earlier Nares Arctic Expedition.

Thomasina Moss, along with others who lost loved ones on *Atalanta*, never really accepted the conclusions of the Ryder Inquiry. Many of them must have had information, particularly in the form of family letters, which could have been useful to the committee, but of course their testimony was never solicited or considered. Yet dead men sometimes can tell tales and may do so with much more honesty and truthfulness than those who might have reason to cover up their negligence or culpability. However, like the other grieving mothers and wives, Senie had to put all this behind her and move on with her life as best she could. One of the first things she had to do was to try and secure a measure of financial security for herself and her children. In this she had the support, and hopefully the influence of a number of Edward's acquaintances. Thomas Huxley, Secretary of the Royal Society, along with almost two score of Edward's friends in the scientific and medical communities, appealed directly to the Lords of the Admiralty in an effort to induce them to increase the normal widows and children's pension Thomasina was entitled to receive. In a petition to the Lords, they pointed out "in the strongest possible way" their opinion of Moss's scientific accomplishments, noting his professional abilities on the Arctic Expedition, his scientific writings, and his Arctic sketches and paintings, which they rightly deemed "invaluable as an Arctic record" of the expedition – which was certainly true. Finally they pointed out that some of the most distinguished scientists had begun their careers as medical officers in the Navy and that "the work already done by him gave great promise of a distinguished future."[11] Admiralty records tersely record that while Senie was recommended for special consideration, the government could "only grant a special pension." This meant that she would receive an extra £30 a year, bringing her income up to £100 plus an allowance of £14 per child, for an annual income of £142. It was not much, and she deserved more, but at least it was enough for her to maintain her independence.

Epilogue

Thomasina Moss did not return to Ireland after Edward's death, remaining in southern England for the rest of her life, finally passing away in 1932 at the age of eighty-eight. Neither Ada nor Beatrice ever married. Edward, born shortly after his father's death, was educated at Dover College, a public school in Kent. In his unpublished biography, he wrote that "as a small child I used to be very frightened by stormy nights and I would lay awake wondering if my father would suddenly return from some desert island like the shipwrecked sailors I had heard of." He followed his father and grandfather into the medical profession, receiving his medical education at Guy's and St. Thomas' Teaching Hospital in London before entering the Royal Army Medical Corps in 1905.

During the Great War, Edward Moss served with distinction in France and Salonika (Greece). He was mentioned in dispatches three times and awarded the Military Cross and the CMG – Companion of the Order of St. Michael and St. George. In 1919 he volunteered for service as a medical administrator with the British "Syren Force" that briefly supported the White Army in the Murmansk region during the ongoing Bolshevik Revolution. After retiring from the Army in 1925, Colonel Moss began a second career as Administrator of the Louise Margaret Hospital for Women at Aldershot, the British Army training base in Hampshire. He died in February 1975 at Donaghmore, County Leix, Eire. Edward junior had two sons, Peter Dugdale Moss and Robert Edward Moss. The latter joined the Royal West Kent Regiment and retired with the rank of Major. Robert Moss died in Hampshire at the age of eighty-two, leaving his wife Mary and two sons – Nigel Robert Dugdale Moss and Jeremy Michael Edward Moss. It is through the generosity of Mary Moss and her sons that the author was given access to the letters and other family information that has been important in linking together the threads of Edward's life story.

Edward Lawton Moss may not have been a major figure in the fields of nineteenth-century medicine, art, or polar exploration, but his life and career exemplified the best traditions of the Royal Navy Medical Branch during the Victorian Era. His untimely death – the victim it would seem of bad luck as well as incompetence and negligence at the highest levels of the Navy – obviously cut short what should have been a much longer and ultimately rewarding life. The apex of Edward's naval career (and probably also of his life) was obviously the 1875–76 polar expedition, which he entered into with the utmost enthusiasm and pride. His abilities were very much in evidence in all aspects of his work, both in the field and aboard ship, and they gained him high praise from Captain Nares and Commander Markham.

This book has been written in his honour and in memory of the many other Royal Navy medical officers who contributed to the advancement of science and medicine, explored the High Arctic and other remote regions of the world, or simply served faithfully far from home during war or peacetime. It is also written in remembrance of the countless sailors who met untimely deaths at sea.

> There are no roses on sailors' graves,
> Nor wreaths upon the storm tossed waves,
> No last post from the Royal Band,
> So far away from their native land,
> No heartbroken words carved in stone,
> Just shipmates bodies then alone,
> The only tributes are the seagulls sweeps,
> And the teardrops when a loved one weeps.
>
> (Royal Lifeboat Society)

Colour Plates

St. Mark's church, Blue Mountains, Jamaica, February 1867.

Sea-cliffs, Trinidad , undated.

Ruined temple , Aiyina Island, near Athens, undated.

Part of the ramparts of Maiden Castle, Dorset, the largest Iron Age hill fort in Europe, dawn, 2 July 1871.

One of Moss's hunting camps near Comox, Vancouver Island, September 1872.

Alert and *Discovery* at Godhavn, Disko Island, on their way north, 10 July 1875.

Alert in winter quarters, seen from among the grounded floes on her seaward side, March 1876.

Alert in winter quarters, seen from astern; the rudder has been unshipped and hung across the stern to prevent it from being damaged by ice pressures. December 1875.

Morning prayers and inspection under the tent housing on the deck of HMS *Alert*; the deck has been covered with snow for insulation.

At Floeberg Beach, northern Ellesmere Island, the officers of HMS *Alert* enjoy the companionable warmth and comfort of the ship's wardroom, in striking contrast to the winter cold and darkness outside.

Alert in winter quarters, soon after the sun returned, March 1876; in case the ice moves out the ship is moored by chains to anchors embedded in the beach.

The combined western and northern sledge parties (Markham's and Aldrich's) struggling through chaotic pressure ridges on their way to Cape Joseph Henry, 8 April 1876.

Markham and the other three members of his northern party still capable of walking, on their return to *Alert*, 14 June 1876.

Alert and *Discovery* in Kennedy Channel, homeward bound, off Cape Constitution, 20 August 1876.

Landscape at Hisarlik (Troy), November 1878.

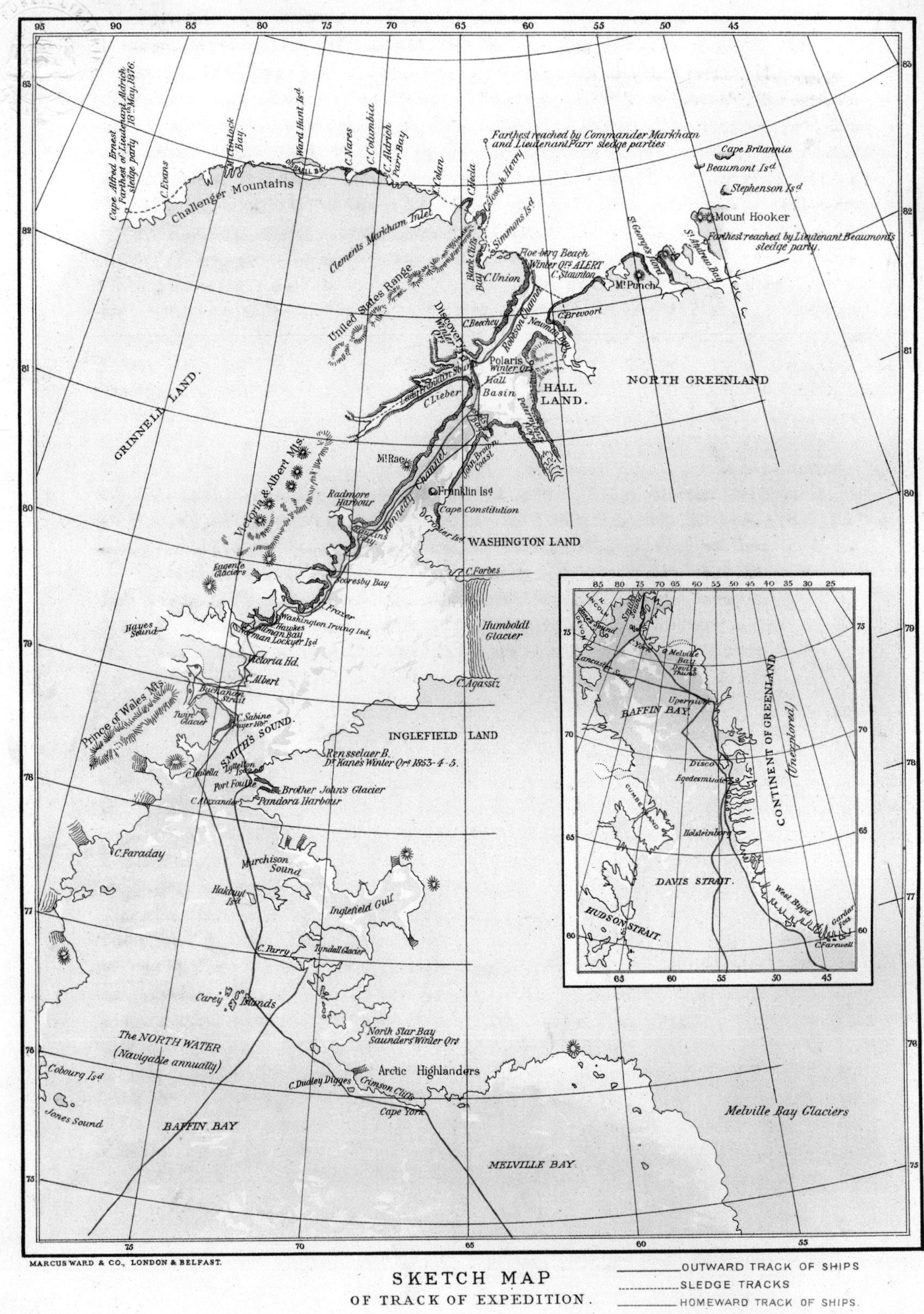

Map of the area of operations of the British Arctic Expedition, 1875–76.

1: Guildford, Surrey – "The Letter"

1 University of British Columbia Special Collections. R.L. Reid Fonds: Correspondence, Incoming Letters: T.M. Moss; Photographs.

2 British Columbia Archives, Vertical Files, reel 96, item 0557. Edw. L. Moss RN, by J.R. Anderson. Also *Victoria Daily British Colonist*, 12 August 1875, p. 3. Anderson and Moss were both members of the local Natural History Society.

3 R.L. Reid Fonds: T.M. Moss to R.L. Reid, 1927, n.d.

4 British Columbia Archives, Clipping File, reel 96, item 0689. T.M. Moss to R.L. Reid, 9 January 1929.

2: Dublin, Ireland – "Edward"

1 Moss family records: "*Memories and Legends*," typescript, p. 13. Dictated by Teresa Moss in 1906.

2 Ibid., p. 10.

3 Davis Oakley, *The Irish School of Medicine* (Dublin: Town House Press, 1988), pp. 89–90. "In 1840 an epidemic of typhus swept through [Ireland] and many doctors died. In 1842 the British House of Commons began preparing a Bill which would become known as the Medical Charities Act. This bill, which was passed the following year, dealt with the provision of support for dispensaries and fever hospitals, the remuneration of medical officers and the administration of the system."

4 Ibid., p. 90.

5 Ibid., p. 96.

6 Moss family records: "*Memories and Legends*," p. 14.

3: Portsmouth – "The Royal Navy"

1 In the summer of 1848, Dr. Richardson, accompanied by Dr. John Rae of the Hudson's Bay Company, travelling by boat, searched the mainland coast from the Mackenzie Delta to the mouth of the Coppermine River. After wintering at Fort Confidence on Great Bear Lake, Richardson returned to England, but Rae continued the search in 1849 and 1851; travelling by sledge then boat, he searched most of the south and east coasts of Victoria Island. John Richardson, *Arctic Searching Expedition* (London: Longman, 1851); E.E. Rich, ed., *John Rae's Correspondence with the Hudson's Bay Company on Arctic Exploration 1844–1855* (London: Hudson's Bay Record Society, 1953). – WB

2 Christopher Lloyd and Jack S. Coulter, *Medicine and the Navy*, Vol. IV: *1815–1900* (London: Livingstone, 1963), pp. 17–50.

3 James Morris, *Heaven's Command* (London: Penguin, 1979), p. 312. Chapter 21, "By the Sword," brilliantly sums up the role and state of the Royal navy during the mid-Victorian period.

4 For a thorough analysis of the changing landscape of medical care and the medical profession in Britain, see chap. 4, "Health and Medicine," by Virginia Berridge, in vol. 3 of F.M.L. Thompson, ed., *The Cambridge Social History of Britain, 1750–1950* (Cambridge: Cambridge University Press, 1990). For the Navy specifically, see Lloyd and Coulter, *Medicine and the Navy*.

5 Cited in Donald McNair, *Surgeons and Seapower*, part 3, p. 11. Surgeon Alexander Rattray was attached to HMS *Topaze* at Esquimalt in 1861–62.

6 Lloyd and Coulter, *Medicine and the Navy*, p. 114.

7 See Berridge, in *Cambridge Social History of Britain*, pp. 191–200.

4: Haiti – "For the Honour of the Flag"

1 Morris, *Heaven's Command*, p. 414.

2 Anthony Preston and John Major, *Send a Gunboat: 150 Years of the British Gunboat* (London: Brasseye Publications, 1975), p. 75.

3 Moss family papers.

4 *Punch*, 27 January 1866.

5 Robert D. Heinl and Nancy G. Heinl, *Written in Blood: The Story of the Haitian People 1492–1971* (Boston: Houghton Mifflin, 1978), pp. 226–35.

5: HMS *Simoom* – "Service Afloat"

1 Adm53/9563, extracts from the Log Book of HMS *Simoom*, February 1866 to April 1870.

2 No date, 1866, Moss family papers.

3 The Washington Treaty involved more than the *Alabama* claims. It also covered navigation of rivers, including the Yukon, fisheries, and trade. It meant that the United States implicitly recognized Canada, including the new Northwest Territories, as a separate entity. – WB

4 F. Lee Benns, *European History Since 1870* (New York: Appleton-Century-Crofts, 1955), p. 160.

5 Moss family papers. Between 1865 and 1868 Joseph Lister was actively promoting the use of carbolic acid as an antiseptic and it is possible that Moss was an observer during operations where carbolic spray was used. Unfortunately, in spite of Lister's efforts the medical community in general was very slow to accept the idea that bacteria, which could be killed by antiseptics, were responsible for many diseases. It was not until about 1880 that Lister and Pasteur's germ theory were universally accepted in the medical profession.

6 Moss family papers.

7 Byron Farwell, *Queen Victoria's Little Wars* (New York: Norton, 1972), chap. 15, pp. 170–76.

8 Moss family papers.

6: Portland, Dorset – "Service Ashore"

1 Reg Perry, *A History of the Royal Naval Hospital Portsmouth* (1997). This short pamphlet describes the Portland Sick Quarters as they existed in 1903 and later. The buildings listed and described at that time match Moss's description many years earlier, though the history of the Portland Hospital complex deserves a more thorough investigation.

2 Edward to his mother, 4 December 1870, Moss family papers.

3 Moss family papers.

4 Ibid.

5 Ibid.

6 Edward to his mother, 21 July 1870, Moss family papers.

7 Edward to his mother, 2 August 1870, Moss family papers.

8 Edward to his mother, 14 August 1870, Moss family papers.

9 Barbara Tuchman, *The Guns of August* (New York: Macmillan, 1962), p. 29.

10 Moss family papers.

11 Ibid.

12 Edward to his mother, 23 October 1870, Moss family papers.

13 Edward to his mother, 15 June 1871, Moss family papers.

14 Edward was referring to his younger sister, nineteen-year-old Phoebe Anna, whose artistic talents were considerable. In 1873 Phoebe married paleontologist Dr. Ramsay Heatley Traquair, a professor of Zoology at the Royal College of Science in Dublin. Shortly after their marriage the couple moved to Scotland where Traquair became the Keeper of Natural History at the Royal Scottish Museum and widely recognized as Britain's leading authority on fossil fish. After her marriage Phoebe Anna Moss (Traquair) continued to develop her talents throughout a long life (1852–1936) and today is recognized as one of the most important women artists of the late nineteenth and early twentieth century Arts and Crafts movement. Her eldest son, Ramsay Traquair, became an architect and the influential first Director of the School of Architecture at McGill University in Montreal (1886–1903).

15 Moss family papers.

16 R.S. Allison, *Sea diseases: The Story of a Great Natural Experiment in Preventative Medicine in the Royal Navy* (London: John Bale Medical Publications, 1943). See chap. 11, "The Nineteenth Century."

17 Moss to his mother, 15 January 1871, Moss family papers.

18 Moss family papers.

19 *Cambridge Social History of Britain*, pp. 195–97.

20 Moss family papers.

7: British Columbia – "A Change of Course"

1 Moss family papers.

2 Harry Gregson, *A History of Victoria 1842–1970* (Victoria: Victoria Observer Publishing, 1970), p. 82. This boundary dispute between the United States and Britain arose from the ambiguous wording of the treaty of 1846 that established the northern boundary of the Oregon Territory. It identified the boundary as the midline of the channel be-

tween Vancouver Island and the mainland, and of Juan de Fuca Strait. The channel breaks into several channels, however, and between the two principal ones, Haro Strait and Rosario Strait, lie the San Juan Islands. The dispute over the ownership of the San Juan Islands came to a head in 1859 when U.S. troops occupied the islands. No armed conflict developed, however, since General Winfield Scott (Commander-in-Chief of the United States Army) arranged with the British for joint occupation of the islands. Finally Kaiser Wilhelm I, acting as mediator, settled the dispute by selecting Haro Strait as the boundary in 1872, thus placing the San Juan archipelago in the United States (Gregson, 1970; Vouri, 2004). – WB

3 Moss family papers.

4 Edward to his mother, 2 April 1872, Moss family papers.

5 Edward to his mother, 21 May 1872, Moss family papers.

6 *Victoria Daily Colonist*, 27 May 1872.

7 Ibid.

8 Mechanics' Institutes were educational institutions established in the nineteenth century to provide adult education, especially in technical subjects, for working men. In many cases they also functioned as libraries. They were particularly popular in Britain, Canada, the United States, and Australia. – WB

9 William Alexander Smith was born in Windsor, Nova Scotia, on 20 August 1825. Lured by the California Gold Rush, he moved to California in 1853 and in 1854 legally changed his name to Amor de Cosmos. Moving north to Victoria, B.C., in 1858, he founded the newspaper *The Daily British Colonist* (now the *Victoria Times-Colonist*). Entering politics, he played a leading role in the negotiations leading to British Columbia's entry into Confederation in 1871 and became premier of British Columbia in 1872 for a term of two years. R. Wild, *Amor de Cosmos* (Toronto: Ryerson Press, 1958). – WB

8: Esquimalt – "His Own Master"

1 The eldest of Edward's two brothers, William Richardson Moss (Willy), moved to England where he was apprenticed to a cotton manufacturer at Bolton, near Chester. He married Martha Waddington, a daughter of the owner, and eventually became a wealthy and prominent businessman.

2 Moss family papers.

3 The basic history of Esquimalt Naval Base, replete with myriad details about the ships and naval activities as well as the ongoing development of the Base prior to WW II can be found in Longstaff, *Esquimalt Naval Base: A History of Its Work and Defences* (Victoria: Victoria Book and Stationery Co., 1941).

4 Cited from Moss's "General Remarks" section of the 1872 Medical and Surgical Journal of Esquimalt Naval Hospital – Pacific Station. During the narrative of this work there will be frequent references to the Moss Medical Journals. The Medical Journals are unpaginated and will hereafter be referred simply by the surgeon's name and date, and where appropriate by the name of the ship.

5 Moss, Medical Journal, 1872.

6 Ibid.

7 Ibid.

8 Moss, Medical Journal, 1873.

9 Moss, Medical Journal, 1874.

9: Esquimalt Hospital – "Do No Harm"

1 Loyd and Coulter, *Medicine and the Navy*, pp. 83–87. As a matter of interest, the medical journals that were submitted annually by every British naval surgeon, afloat or ashore, between roughly 1758 and 1880, comprise a remarkable and unparalleled longitudinal compilation of medical practice, statistics, and geographic or ethnographic information. Although not all of them have survived, thousands of these documents can still be located through the operational records of the Royal Navy at the National Archives of the United Kingdom in Kew.

2 Moss, Medical Journal, 1872, Case 18.

3 Berridge, in F.M.L. Thompson, ed., *Cambridge Social History of Britain* (Cambridge: Cambridge University Press, 1990), Vol. 1, p. 203.

4 Matthew Coates, Medical Journal, 1875.

5 Berridge, in *Cambridge Social History of Britain*, Vol. 1, p. 203.

6 Moss, Medical Journal, 1872, Case 2.

7 Ibid., Case 21.

8 Moss, Medical Journal, 1873.

9 Moss, Medical Journal, 1874.

10 Ibid.

11 Moss, Medical Journal, 1872, Case 6.

10: Vancouver Island – "The Best of Times"

1 Sir William Laird Clowes, *The Royal Navy: A History From the Earliest Times to the Death of Queen Victoria*, Vol. VII (London: Chatham, 1903).

2 Edward to sister-in-law Marie Malone, 24 January 1873, Moss family papers.

3 Edward to his mother, 18 March 1873, Moss family papers.

4 Moss family papers.

5 Ibid.

6 *Victoria Daily Standard*, 18 December 1873.

7 Chinook jargon was the *lingua franca* of the west coast from Alaska to California. It was a mixture of English, French, and the language of the Chinook Indians ("Tsinuk" was the name given to them by their neighbours, the Chehalis). The Chinook Indians' territory embraced the lower Columbia River and the coast for some distance north of that river. Lewis and Clark estimated their number at four hundred; they have now merged completely with the Chehalis and their original language is extinct. – WB

8 Moss family papers.

9 Dr. John Helmcken (1824–1920), son-in-law of Governor James Douglas of the Colony of Victoria, was both a medical doctor and a prominent figure in the operations of the Hudson's Bay Company on Vancouver Island. Entering politics, he played a major role in the negotiations leading to British Columbia's entry into Confederation in 1871. Retiring from politics in that year, he returned to his medical practice. W.P. Marshall, "Helmcken, John Sebastian." In *Dictionary of Canadian Biography*, Ramsay Cook, ed. (Toronto: University of Toronto Press, 1998), vol. 14, pp. 472–74). – WB

10 Edward to his mother, 22 August 1874, Moss family papers.

11 Edward to Marie Malone, 30 August 1874, Moss family papers.

12 Edward to his mother, 18 November 1874, Moss family papers.

13 Edward to his mother, 17 December 1874, Moss family papers.

14 Thomasina to "Mama," 20 December 1874, Moss family papers.

15 National Archives of the United Kingdom, Adm 1/6346, "Arctic Officers Appointments and Records."

11: England – "The Arctic Expedition"

1 Pierre Berton, *The Arctic Grail: The Quest for the Northwest Passage and the North Pole, 1818–1919* (Toronto: McClelland and Stewart, 1988), pp. 411–12.

2 For the Hall Expeditions, see Chauncey Loomis and M.A. Wilson, *Weird and Tragic Shores: The Story of Charles Francis Hall, Explorer* (New York: Alfred Knopf, 1971) and (C.H. Davis, *Narrative of the North Polar expedition, U.S. Ship Polaris, Captain Charles Francis Hall commanding*. Washington, DC: Government Printing Office, 1876; E.V. Blake, ed., *Arctic experiences* (New York: Harper & Brothers, 1874).

3 It is very clear from Captain Nares' May 25, 1875, sailing orders, that he was expected to "attain the highest possible latitude, and if possible reach the North Pole." During the expedition he was also ordered to carry out a large number of scientific duties. In *The Arctic Grail*, Berton downplayed the scientific goals of the expedition by stating that the scientific tasks were relegated to paragraph 26 of the instructions. However, almost all of the previous paragraphs in the sailing orders were related to logistical matters that were crucial if the expedition was to accomplish the many other tasks that had been assigned. The scientific and exploration goals were certainly viewed as extremely important by the luminaries of the Royal Geographic Society and the Royal Society.

4 Sir George Strong Nares, 1831–1915, entered the Navy in 1845. In 1852 he served with the Belcher polar expedition seeking to discover the fate of Sir John Franklin. In 1872 he was placed in command of the *Challenger* oceanographic expedition but was recalled in 1875 to lead the new polar expedition. He was considered the best choice for the task because of his extensive scientific and surveying qualifications and experience in both the north and south polar regions. He retired in 1892 with the rank of Vice-Admiral.

5 The reference to Lieutenant Albert Markham being a zealot is explained as follows. In the spring of 1873, in anticipation of an expedition to reach the North Pole being mounted, Markham volunteered, and was granted leave, to join the Dundee whaling ship *Active* on its regular voyage to Davis Strait, in part to gain arctic experience (which no serving officer of his rank had) and in part to make arrangements to buy sledge dogs for the impending expedition. On his return he published a book on his experiences (Markham, 1874) and thus was a natural choice to command HMS *Alert* when the expedition, under the leadership of Capt. George Nares, was approved in 1874. – WB

6 *Lancet*, 29 May 1875, p. 763.

7 Moss family papers.

8 Ibid.

9 Pierre Berton, *Arctic Grail*, p. 420. According to Berton as many as 200,000 people gathered to bid farewell to the ships. Even allowing for press exaggeration the turnout was astonishing, demonstrating how the general public had been caught up in the Arctic fever.

12: Greenland – "To the Shores of the Polar Sea"

1 For this detail and a general account of the expedition, see Nares (1878). – WB

2 Forty-one-year-old Hans Hendrick, a Greenland Eskimo and experienced Arctic traveller, had previously served on Elisha Kane's 1853 expedition and most recently with Charles Hall as a hunter, sled driver, and interpreter in 1871–73. Hans Island, located roughly in the middle of Nares Strait

between Northern Ellesmere Island and Greenland was named after Hendrick. It has recently been in the news because of conflicting claims about sovereignty over the small island, both Denmark and Canada asserting ownership.

3 *Pandora* was the ship of Sir Allen Young's private expedition whose aim was to reach the North Magnetic Pole and, if possible, to complete a transit of the Northwest Passage. Due to heavy ice, neither objective was attained (see A.W. Young, *Cruise of the "Pandora"* (London: William Clowes, 1876)). – WB

4 Lieutenant W. Henry Pullen was chaplain on board *Alert*. – WB

5 "Loons" – a mis-hearing of "looms," the then common name for various members of the *Alcidae*, i.e., cliff-nesting sea-birds. – WB

6 A misspelling of Vaigat, otherwise known as Sullorsuaq, the strait between Disko and the mainland of Greenland. – WB

7 The allusion to Gilbert à Beckett is to Thomas à Beckett's father, or more precisely to his wife's methods of locating the latter. While fighting in the Holy Land, Gilbert was captured by a Saracen chief; the latter's daughter fell in love with him and helped him to escape to England. Following him, but knowing only two words of English, "London" and "Gilbert," on reaching a Mediterranean port, she allegedly wandered the waterfront shouting "London" until she found a ship bound for England. Then on reaching London, she wandered the streets, shouting "Gilbert" until she found him. They were soon married and Thomas à Beckett was born shortly thereafter. – WB

8 Moss family papers.

9 An ice-quartermaster was a sailor experienced at navigating a ship through the dangerous pack ice. Usually the Navy hired men who had many years of service in the whaling fleets that operated in far northern waters during the summer months. *Alert* and *Discovery* each had three of them.

10 Lieutenant May was Fourth Lieutenant on board *Alert*. – WB

11 So called because of "red snow" on the cliffs west of Cape York, first recorded by Captain John Ross in 1818; he examined it under a microscope and deduced that the red particles were of vegetable origin. J. Ross, *A voyage of discovery* (London: John Murray, 1819). Red snow is caused by a number of species of criobont algae, the commonest being *Chlamydomonas nivalis*, found in snow in both polar regions. – WB

12 Henry Feilden was naturalist on board *Alert*. – WB

13 Moss family papers.

13: Floeberg Harbour – "Polar Winter"

1 Sailing and ice master on board Hall's ship, *Polaris*. – WB

2 Berton, *Arctic Grail*, pp. 389–90.

3 The description of the fall explorations as well as the daily activities aboard ship has been gleaned from several sources. The most important of these have been the official journals and reports of Albert Markham, Captain Nares, and Edward Moss, and the books the three men wrote about their experiences. See Moss, *Shores of the Polar Sea: A Narrative of the Arctic Expedition of 1875* (Belfast: Marcus Ward, 1878); Nares, *Narrative of a Voyage to the Polar Sea during 1875–76 in HM Ships* 'Alert' and 'Discovery,' (2 vols.) (London: Sampson Low, Marston, Searle & Rivington, 1878), and Markham, *The Great Frozen Sea: A Personal Narrative of the 'Alert'* (London: Daldy Isbister & Co., 1878). For more easily accessed sources, see also: Fergus Fleming, *Ninety Degrees North: The Quest for the North Pole* (London: Granton Books, 2001), chap. 19, Berton, *Arctic Grail*, chap. 11, John Maxton-Graham, *Safe Return Doubtful*, chap. 3.

4 Lieutenant Pelham Aldrich was First Lieutenant on board *Alert*. – WB

5 Fleming, *Ninety Degrees North*, p. 340.

6 Berton, *Arctic Grail*, p. 416.

7 Third Lieutenant on board *Alert*. – WB

8 Captain Nares coined the term "palaeocrystic" to describe the ancient Arctic ice that had been formed over thousands of years.

9 Lieutenant Adolphus W. Greely, Fifth U.S. Cavalry, led the United States expedition to Lady Franklin Bay, Ellesmere Island, as part of the First International Polar Year, in 1881–84. He and his men carried out detailed meteorological and other scientific observations for two years and also achieved some impressive feats of exploration, and then, in the summer of 1883, following orders, started south by boat. Forced to winter at Cape Sabine on Pim Island, only seven men of the original twenty-five were still alive when a relief ship reached them. One of the seven men died on board the ship. See A.W. Greely, *Three years of arctic service* (New York: C. Scribner's, 1886). – WB

10 See Loomis and Wilson, *Weird and Tragic Shores*, for the details.

11 Moss, *Shores of the Polar Sea*, chap. 6.

12 Nares was Mate on board Captain Henry Kellett's *Resolute*, which wintered once at Dealy Island (1852–53) off the south coast of Melville Island, and again off Cape Cockburn, Bathurst Island (1853–54). The play *Charles II* was performed on 23 February 1852; on 1 February 1853, Nares also played the Queen in the farce *King Glumpus* (W. Barr, *A Frenchman in Search of Franklin* [Toronto: University of Toronto Press, 1992]). – WB

14: Markam and Parr – "Daring to Do All …"

1 Great Britain, Parliament, *Journals and Proceedings of the Arctic Expedition, 1875–76* (1875 C-1153; 1876 C-1560 and 1877 C-163). These extremely detailed documents, covering the period from 1875 to 1878, total 1,280 pages. They are now available online through the University of Manitoba at http://www.umanitoba.ca/faculties/arts/anthropology/bluebooks/. They have been one of the primary sources of information about the spring sledging parties. However official records, such as the sledge party journals, seldom tell the whole story, and the private journals of expedition leaders such as Nares and Markham have also been examined, along with Nares' and Markham's books.

2 Third Lieutenant on board *Alert*. – WB

3 First Lieutenant on board *Discovery*. – WB

4 Alberta Hastings Markham Papers (notebooks and journals 3 April – 8 May 1876), MG 29 B20, Library and Archives Canada. Microfilm, reel 822. Referred to in the text as "diary" or "personal journal." In the absence of Markham's personal record of the return journey to the ship, the present narrative of that trek is based primarily on his official journal and the Nares and Markham books about the expedition. The writer has not come upon other narratives that cite Markham's second notebook, and it is possible that the Markham family has it but have chosen to not open it to public scrutiny.

5 Captain Sir William Edward Parry, leading a party hauling boats on runners, reached a latitude of around 82° 45' N on 23 July 1827, from a base at Treurenburg Bay (now Sorgfjorden) in northern Spitsbergen, Svalbard. See W.E. Parry, *Narrative of an attempt to reach the North Pole* (London: John Murray, 1828). – WB

6 Clive Holland (ed.), *Farthest North: A History of North Polar Expeditions in Eye-witness Accounts* (London: Robinson Publishing, 1994), p. 83.

7 Prior to his Greenland expedition of 1870, Nils Adolf Erik Nordenskiöld had participated in, or led, four expeditions to Svalbard. He is best known to history for making the first transit of the Northeast Passage in *Vega* in 1878–79. See George Kish, *North-East Passage* (Amsterdam: N. Israel, 1973). – WB

8 Great Britain, Parliament, *Journals and Proceedings* (C1636), HMSO London. Refer also to the Arctic Blue Books, 1877a, pp. 161–64.

9 A hot beverage made from eggs, sugar, milk, and brandy. One assumes that Moss had to have recourse to powdered milk and eggs. – WB

10 Feilden reports finding the first nest with eggs on 21 June 1876 and that the birds "afforded a most valuable change of diet to our sick" (H. Feilden, in G.S. Nares *Narrative of a Voyage* (London: Sampson Low, Marston, Searle and Rivington1878), vol. 2, p. 217. – WB

11 Great Britain, Parliament, *Journals and Proceedings*, p. 124.

15: Aldrich and Beaumont – "Hearts of Oak"

1 Pelham Aldrich Journals, Library and Archives Canada, MG-29 B12.

2 Great Britain, Parliament. *Journals and Proceedings*, p. 351.

3 Great Britain, Parliament, *Journals and Proceedings*, Captain Nares' official report, p. 24.

4 G. Hattersley Smith, "The British Arctic Expedition, 1875–76," *Polar Record*, Vol. 18, No. 113, 1976, p. 124.

5 John Maxton-Graham, *Safe Return Doubtful: The Heroic Age of Arctic Exploration* (New York: Scribner, 1988), p. 70.

6 *London Times*, 8 December 1876.

16: London – "Feet of Clay"

1 *London Times*, 30 November 1876.

2 *London Times*, 1 December 1876.

3 *Illustrated London News*, 16 December 1876.

4 *Lancet*, 29 November 1876.

5 *London Times*, 4 December 1876.

6 *The Navy*, 9 December 1876. See also Fleming, *Ninety Degrees North*, p. 186; Berton, *Arctic Grail*, p. 431.

7 *London Times*, 5, 8, 12 December 1876.

8 Ibid., 2 May 1877.

9 Ibid., 7 December 1876.

10 Ibid., 1 December 1876.

11 Medical Director-General Alexander Armstrong was himself fully cognizant of the dangers of scurvy in the Arctic, having served as surgeon on board Robert M'Clure's *Investigator*, 1850–54. – WB

12 Edward Augustus Inglefield had commanded *Isabel*, searching Smith Sound and Jones Sound in 1852 and then, as captain of HMS *Phoenix*, had made two voyages from Britain to Beechey Island to resupply Belcher's squadron in 1853 and 1854. As events turned out, he helped to evacuate the personnel from that squadron in 1854. – WB

13 James Donnet had been Surgeon on board Horatio Austin's *Assistance* in 1850–51. – WB

14 *Report of the Committee appointed by the Lords Commissioners of the Admiralty to enquire into the causes of the outbreak of scurvy in the recent Arctic Expedition* (C-1722), HM Stationery Office, London, pp. 1–11.

15 Ibid., pp. 12–25.

16 Ibid., pp. 26–32.

17 Ibid., pp. 46–54.

18 Ibid., pp. 33–39.

19 Ibid., pp. 59–64.

20 Ibid., pp. 59–82.

21 Ibid., pp. 290–309.

22 Ibid., Appendix 2, pp. 321–23.

23 Ibid., p. 301.

24 Ibid., p. 309.

25 Ibid., pp. 309–16.

26 Sir George Richards had commanded HMS *Assistance*, under Sir Edward Belcher in 1852–54. – WB

27 *Report of the Committee...*, p. iv.

28 *Tragedy and Triumph: The Journals of Captain R.F. Scott's Last Polar Expedition* (New York: Prospero Books), pp. 301.

29 Berton, *Arctic Grail*, p. 418.

30 E. J. C. Kendall, "Scurvy During Some British Polar Expeditions, 1875–1917," *Polar Record* 7, no. 51 (1955): 474.

31 Dr. Frederick Cook, who had served as medical officer on board Adrien de Gerlache's *Belgica* during that ship's Antarctic wintering (1897–99), claimed to have reached the North Pole in April 1908, a year before Peary, and announced his claim a few days before Peary did so in 1909. The debate as to which man has the prior claim still continues. The majority view appears to be that neither claim is valid: according to Cook's Inuit companions, Cook was never out of sight of land, while Peary's navigation techniques were so inadequate that he could not have known whether he had reached the Pole but was probably within a few tens of kilometres of that spot. W. Herbert, *The Noose of Laurels* (London: Hodder and Stoughton, 1990; R. Bryce, *Cook and Peary* (Mechanicsburg, PA: Stackpole Books, 1997). – WB

17: Kingston, Ireland – "Brief Interlude"

1 *Illustrated London News*, 27 July 1878.

2 As near as can be determined, Edward Moss published about a dozen scientific articles or "notes" in journals between 1873 and 1880.

18: Beshika Bay, Turkey – "Letters from Troy"

1 The "Great Powers" were Germany, Austro-Hungary, Russia, Great Britain, and France. L.S. Stavrianos, *The Balkans since 1453* (London: C. Hurst & Co., 2000). – WB

2 F.L. Benns, *European History since 1870* (New York: Appleton-Century-Crofts, 1955), pp. 223–24.

3 Otto Eduard Leopold von Bismarck, as Minister-President of Prussia, had engineered the unification of the numerous states of Germany. As Chancellor of the North German Confederation from 1867, in 1871, he became the first Chancellor of the German Empire. E. Eyck, *Bismarck and the German Empire* (New York: W.W. Norton, 1964); O. Pflanze, *Bismarck and the Development of Germany* (Princeton: Princeton University Press, 1963). – WB

4 More correctly: Heinrich Schliemann. For further details, see David A. Traill, *Schliemann of Troy* (New York: St. Martin's Griffin, 1995). – WB

5 *Archaeology*, January/February 2002, pp. 54–58.

6 Moss family papers.

7 *Archaeology*, January/February 2002, p. 56.

8 Edward to Maria Malone, 10 December 1878, Moss family papers.

9 Rudolf Ludwig Karl Virchow (1821–1902) was a German pathologist whose cell research helped establish the germ theory of disease. He helped found the Berlin Society for Anthropology, Ethnology and Pre-history. He became a close friend of Schliemann, visiting his field site at Hissarlik (Troy) and participating in his excavations. It was largely due to his support that Schliemann gained a degree of recognition by the archaeological community, and it was certainly due to Virchow that Schliemann's treasures went to the Berlin Museum of Ethnology. E. H. Ackenberger, *Rudolf Vichow* (Madison: University of Wisconsin Press, 1953). – WB

10 Moss to Schliemann, 20 July 1879. Courtesy of Schliemann Archive, Gennadius Library, American School of Classical Studies, Athens.

11 Ibid., 5 November 1879.

12 Schliemann to Moss, 22 November 1879. Courtesy of David A. Trail.

13 Heinrich Schliemann, *Ilios: The City and Country of the Trojans* (New York: Arno Press, 1976 reprint), p. 268. Edward's sketch of the Troy excavation site is also included on page 325.

14 Moss family papers.

15 Publisher of his book, *Shores of the Polar Sea*. – WB

16 Moss family papers.

19: HMS *Atalanta* – "The Perils of the Deep"

1 It is highly probable that the decision to commission another training ship was the troublesome situation in the Balkans. If war broke out with the Russians, the navy was going to need more seamen.

2 According to an introductory statement at the parliamentary enquiry into the loss of HMS *Atalanta* (formerly *Juno*), the vessel was chosen for a second training ship in October 1877. In fact, testimony would later establish that the decision to examine the old frigate to see if she was worth refitting was made at the Admiralty Board level on 20 March 1977. Some work on the vessel was already underway in August, five months before estimated costs were finally approved.

3 Unless otherwise cited, the information about the refitting and later repairs or modifications to *Atalanta* has been taken from the official report and evidence given at the inquiry into the loss of HMS *Atalanta*. See Parliamentary Papers, *Report of the Committee Appointed by the Lords Commissioners to Enquire into the Loss of HMS Atalanta*, 1881, Vol. XXII (C2739), pp. 1–233.

4 The full story of the sinking of *Eurydice* may be found in the *London Times*, 26 March 1878.

5 Moss family papers.

6 Ibid.

7 This is a misreading of "Douay Bible." The Douay version of the Bible, on which nearly all English Catholic versions are still based, was translated from Latin by members of the English College at Douai in Northern France; the Old Testament appeared in 1582 and the New Testament in 1609. The bulk of the translation was by Father Gregory Martin. – WB

8 Moss family papers.

9 Ibid.

20: London – "*Atalanta* Feared Lost"

1 Inquiry, op. cit., p. 195. Stirling to Adm. E.G. Fanshaw, C-in-C Portsmouth. The letter was written at St. Kitts but mailed from Bermuda on 29 January.

2 David F. Raine, *Solved! The Greatest Sea Mystery of All* (St. Georges, Bermuda: Pompano Publications, 1997), appendix 1, pp. 283–89. Strangely, Raine wrongly identifies the staff surgeon as a Dr. George Beale and even attributes conversation to Beale – who was not even on the ship during the 1879 cruise. Beale was the senior medical officer on the 1878 cruise but was replaced by Edward Moss in September 1879.

3 *London Times*, 18 May 1880, in a letter to the editor from "Old Arctic" explorer Sir Allen Young.

4 *Hansard*, 22 May 1880.

5 *London Times*, 15 April 1880.

6 Ibid., 16, 17, 18, 20, 21, 27 April, 1 May, 11 June. Also *Saturday Review*, 24 April 1880, p. 527 and *Illustrated London News*, 24 April, p. 394.

7 *London Times*, 26 April 1880.

8 Ibid., 27 April 1880.

9 Ibid.

10 Ibid., 27 May 1880.

11 HMS *Captain* was an experimental screw-driven battleship built in 1869. In September 1870, she turned turtle and went down during a gale while undergoing sea trials off the coast of Spain. Only eighteen of her crew of five hundred survived.

21: London – "The Last Inquiry"

1 Unless otherwise cited, the factual information and testimony included in this chapter is all taken from the official inquiry into the loss of *Atalanta*. Specific testimony by individuals may be easily accessed through the comprehensive index to the report.

2 Undated note by E.L. Moss Jr., Moss family papers.

3 *London Times*, 10 June 1880.

4 Inquiry. The correspondence between George Martin, Committee Secretary, and Naval Secretary Robert Hall, included in the Index took place in September, some months after the inquiry adjourned. Presumably the reason Martin requested the minutes of the Admiralty Board meeting was because he hoped to find out if there had been a discussion of Admiral Symonds October 25, 1878, report.

5 After his final inspection of the refitted ship, Admiral Symonds suggested that the ship's complement be reduced to 250 because of overcrowding. His recommendation was not accepted, and the ship sailed with over 280 men aboard, apparently a reduction of twenty trainees.

6 Raine, *Solved!*, appendix 1, pp. 283–89.

7 *London Times*, 29 December 1880.

8 David Gerr, *The Nature of Boats: Insight and Esoterica for the Nautically Obsessed* (Camden, ME: International Marines, 1992).

9 Raine did not include any notes or bibliography and much of his narrative, including his main conclusions, is highly speculative to say the least. Moreover, the inclusion of spurious dialogue and events, such as a description of discussion between Captain Stirling and Staff Surgeon Beale (who was not even on the ship) is fatal. This is unfortunate, given that there is also considerable evidence that Raine also conducted serious research into his subject.

10 Morris, *Heaven's Command*, p. 312.

11 Copy in Moss family memorabilia

Bibliography

Unpublished Manuscripts, Letters, Diaries, Unpublished letters and miscellaneous documents belonging to the Moss family

Albert Hastings Markham Papers (notebooks and journals 3 April–8 May 1876), MG 29 B20, LAC.

Correspondence between Edward L. Moss and Henry Schliemann: David A. Trail, University of California.

Correspondence between Robie Louis Reid and Thomasina Moss, R.L. Reid Collection, University of British Columbia, Special Collections, Vancouver, BC.

George Strong Nares Papers (journals, logbooks, correspondence) 1875–76, MG 29-B12. LAC.

Lentz, Florence K., et al., *Historical Furnishings Report: British Camp Hospital, San Juan Island National Historical Park, WA, U.S.A.* Seattle, WA: Department of the Interior National Park Service, 1990.

McIntyre, Kyle, *A Canadian 'Old Arctic,' Lieutenant Wyatt Rawson, R.N., and the Nares Polar Expedition of 1875–76*, unpublished MS.

Pelham Aldrich Journals, MG 29-B21, Library and Archives Canada.

Government Documents

HOUSE OF COMMONS, PARLIAMENTARY PAPERS

Great Britain, Parliament 1877. *Report of the Committee appointed by the Lords Commissioners of the Admiralty to enquire into the causes of the outbreak of scurvy in the recent Arctic Expedition* (C-1722) HM Stationery Office, London.

Journals and Proceedings of the Arctic Expedition, 1875–76 (1875 C-1153, 1876 C-1560, 1877 C-1636) HM Stationery Office, London.

Papers and Correspondence Relating to the Equipment and fitting out of the Arctic expedition of 1875 (C-1153) HM Stationery Office, London.

Report of the Committee Appointed by the Lords Commissioners to Enquire into the Loss of HMS Atalanta, 1881, Vol. XXII (C-2739). HM Stationery Office.

ADMIRALTY PAPERS

ADM 101/279, *Medical and Surgical Journal of Esquimalt Naval Hospital – Edward L. Moss, Assistant-Surgeon, Pacific Station between 29 May and 31 December 1872* (copy at Esquimalt Naval and Military Museum, Esquimalt, BC).

ADM 101/281 15450, *Medical and Surgical Journal of Esquimalt Naval Hospital – Edward L. Moss, Surgeon between 1 January and 31 December 1873* (copy at ENMM, Esquimalt, BC).

ADM 101/281 15450, *Medical and Surgical Journal of Esquimalt Naval Hospital – Edward L. Moss, Surgeon, between 1 January and 31 December 1874* (copy at ENMM, Esquimalt, BC).

ADM 101/281 (ref.149) *Medical and Surgical Journal of Esquimalt Naval Hospital, Mathew Coates, Staff Surgeon, between 1 January and 31 December 1875* (copy at ENMM, Esquimalt, BC).

ADM 101/228 (ref. 106) *Assistant Surgeon E.L. Moss 1865: "Actions and Destructions at Hayti,"* National Archives of the United Kingdom, Kew, UK.

ADM53/9563, Extracts from the Log books of HMS *Simoom*, February 1866–April 1870, PRO.

Miscellaneous unpublished Admiralty documents related to the naval career of E.L. Moss, 1864–1880, NAUK.

Newspapers and Periodicals

Illustrated London News, 1865, 1875–1880.

Lancet, 1875–1877.

Punch, January 26, 27, 1866.

The Graphic (London), June 1876, Nov. 1876.

The Times (London) 1875–1880.

Victoria Daily British Colonist, 1872–1875.

Secondary Sources

Ackenberger, E.H. *Rudolf Vichow: Doctor, Statesman, Anthropologist.* Madison: University of Wisconsin Press, 1953.

Allison, R. S., *Sea Diseases: The Story of a Great Natural Experiment in Preventative Medicine in the Royal Navy.* London: John Bale Medical Publications, 1943.

Barr, W., ed. *A Frenchman in Search of Franklin. De Bray's Arctic Journal, 1852–54.* Toronto: University of Toronto Press, 1992.

Berton, Pierre, *The Arctic Grail: The Quest for the Northwest Passage and the North Pole, 1818–1919.* Toronto: McClelland and Stewart, 1988.

Blake, E.V., ed. *Arctic experiences: containing Capt. George E. Tyson's wonderful drift on the ice-floe, a history of the Polaris expedition, the cruise of the Tigress and rescue of the Polaris survivors.* New York: Harper & Brothers, 1874.

Bryce, R. *Cook and Peary: The Polar Controversy Resolved.* Mechanicsburg, PA: Stackpole Books, 1997.

Caswell, John. "The R.G. S. And the British Arctic Expedition, 1875–76," *Geographical Journal* 143 (1977).

Clowes, Sir William Laird, *The Royal Navy: A History from the Earliest times to the death of Queen Victoria*, Vol. VII. London: 1903.

Coakley, Davis. *The Irish School of Medicine: Outstanding Practitioners of the 19th Century.* Dublin: Town House, 1988.

Davis, C.H., ed. *Narrative of the North Polar expedition, U.S. Ship Polaris, Captain Charles Francis Hall commanding.* Washington, DC: Government Printing Office, 1876.

Deacon, Margaret, and Ann Savours. "Sir George Strong Nares (1831–1915)," *Polar Record* 18, no. 113 (1976).

Eyck, E. 1964. *Bismarck and the German Empire.* New York: W.W. Norton & Co., 1964.

Farwell, Byron, *Queen Victoria's Little Wars.* New York: W. W. Norton, 1972.

Feilden, H. Appendix III, Ornithology. In: Nares, G.S. *Narrative of a voyage…*,1878, Vol. 2, p. 217.

The Geographical Magazine (January 1, 1877), "The Outbreak of Scurvy," pp. 3–5, (April 1, 1877), pp. 89–90, "The Moral Scurvy."

Gerr, David, *The Nature of Boats: Insight and Esoterica for the Nautically Obsessed.* Camden, ME: International Marine, 1992.

Gosset, W. P., *The Lost Ships of the Royal Navy.* London: Mansell, 1986.

Gough, Barry M., *The Royal Navy and the Northwest Coast of North America 1810–1914: A Study of British Maritime Supremacy.* Vancouver: University of British Columbia Press, 1971.

Greely, A.W. *Three years of arctic service: an account of the Lady Franklin Bay expedition of 1881–84.* New York: C. Scribner's Sons, 2 vols., 1886.

Gregson, Harry, *A History of Victoria, 1842–1970.* Victoria: Victoria Observer, 1970.

Hattersley-Smith, Geoffrey. "The British Arctic Expedition, 1875–76," *Polar Record* 18, no. 113 (1976).

Heinl, Robert D., and Nancy G. Heinl, *Written in Blood: The Story of the Haitian People 1492–1971.* Boston: Houghton Mifflin, 1978.

Herbert, W. *The Noose of Laurels: Robert E. Peary and the Race to the North Pole.* London: Hodder and Stoughton, 1989.

Hocking, Charles, *Dictionary of Disasters at Sea During the Age of Steam.* London: Lloyds Register of Shipping, 1969.

Holland, Clive, ed., *Farthest North: A History of North Polar Expeditions in Eye-witness Accounts.* London: Robinson, 1994.

Kendall, Dr. E.J.C. "Scurvy during Some British Polar Expeditions, 1875–76," *Polar Record* 7, no. 51 (1955).

Kish, George. *North-East Passage: Adolf Erik Nordenskiöld – his life and times.* Amsterdam: N. Israel, 1973.

Kusche, Lawrence David, *The Bermuda Triangle Mystery Solved*. New York: Harper and Row, 1975.

Lloyd, Christopher, and J.L.S. Coulter, *Medicine and the Navy 1200–1900*: vol. IV, *1815–1900*. London: Livingstone, 1963.

Longstaff, Major F. V., *Esquimalt Naval Base: A History of its Works and Defenses*. Victoria: Victoria Book and Stationery, 1941.

Loomis, Chauncey, and M. A. Wilson, *Weird and Tragic Shores: The Story of Charles Francis Hall, Explorer*. New York: Alfred Knopf, 1971.

Markham, Albert H., *The Great Frozen Sea: A Personal Narrative of the Voyage of the 'Alert.'* London: Daldy, Isbister, 1878.

Markham, Albert H., *A Whaling Cruise to Baffin's Bay and the Gulf of Boothia. And an Account of the Rescue of the Crew of the "Polaris."* London: Sampson Low, Marston, Low & Searle, 1874.

Markham, Clements. *A history of the Abyssinian expedition*. London: John Murray, 1869.

Marshall, W.P. "Helmcken, John Sebastian." In *Dictionary of Canadian Biography*, Ramsay Cook, ed. Toronto: University of Toronto Press, Vol. 14 (1998), pp. 472–74.

Maxton-Graham, John, *Safe Return Doubtful: The Heroic Age of Arctic Exploration*. New York: Scribners, 1988.

McNair, Donald. "Surgeons and Seapower." Parts 1, 2, 3. *West Coast Boat Journal* (March–May 1985).

Morris, James, *Heaven's Command: An Imperial Progress*. London: Penguin, 1979.

Moss, Edward Lawton, *Shores of the Polar Sea: A narrative of the Arctic Expedition of 1875*. Belfast: Marcus Ward, 1878 (copy at PABC).

Moss, Edward Lawton, "Sport in British Columbia," *The Graphic*, London (June 1876).

Nares, Capt. Sir George Strong, *Narrative of a Voyage to the Polar Sea during 1875–76 in H.M. Ships 'Alert' and 'Discovery'* (2 vols.). London: Sampson Low, Marston, Searle and Rivington, 1878.

Parry, W.E. *Narrative of an attempt to reach the North Pole in boats fitted for the purpose, and attached to H.M. Ship "Hecla" in 1827*. London: John Murray, 1828.

Perry, Reg., *A History of the Royal Naval Hospital Portland*. Portland, UK: Artsmiths, n.d.

Pflanze, O. *Bismarck and the Development of Germany*. Princeton: Princeton University Press, 1963.

Preston, Anthony, and John Major, *Send a Gunboat: A Study of its Role in British Policy, 1854–1904*. London: Longmans Green, 1967.

Raine, David F., *Solved: The Greatest Sea Mystery of All*. Georgetown, Bermuda: Pompano, 1997.

Reid, Robie Louis, "Memories of an Esquimalt Pioneer" October 28, 1928, in *Vancouver Province*, PABC 96-0685.

Rich, E.E., ed. *John Rae's Correspondence with the Hudson's Bay Company on Arctic Exploration 1844–1855*. London: Hudson's Bay Record Society, 1953.

Richardson, John. *Arctic Searching Expedition: a Journal of a Boat-voyage through Rupert's Land and the Arctic Sea, in Search of the Discovery Ships under Command of Sir John Franklin*. London: Longman, Brown, Green & Longmans, 1851.

Ross, J. *A voyage of discovery, made under the orders of the Admiralty, in His Majesty's ships Isabella and Alexander …* London: John Murray, 1819.

Schliemann, Heinrich, *Ilios the city and country of the Trojans: The results of researches and discoveries on the site of Troy and throughout the Troad in the years 1871, 72, 73, 78, 79*. London, 1881.

Scott, Robert F. *Tragedy and Triumph: The Journals of Captain R.F. Scott's Last Polar Expedition*. New York: Prospero Books, 1993.

Stavrianos, L.S. *The Balkans since 1453*. London: C. Hurst & Co., 2000.

Thompson, F. M. L., ed., *The Cambridge Social History of Britain 1750–1950*, Vol. 3, 'Social agencies and institutions.' Cambridge: Cambridge University Press, 1990.

Traill, David A., *Schliemann of Troy: Treasure and Deceit*. New York: St. Martin's Griffin, 1977.

Traill, David A., and Paul. C. Appleton, "Letters from Troy," *Archaeology* (January/February 2002).

Trotter, Wilfred Pym, *The Royal Navy in Old Photographs*. London: J.M. Dent, 1975.

Vouri, Mike, *Outpost of Empire: The Royal Marines and the Joint Occupation of San Juan Island*. Seattle: Northwest Interpretive Association, 2004.

Wild, R. *Amor de Cosmos*. Toronto: Ryerson Press, 1958.

Young, A.W. *Cruise of the "Pandora." From the private journal kept by Allen Young*. London: William Clowes & Sons, 1876.

Index

A

Abyssinian Expeditions, 24–25
Admiralty, 2, 10, 12, 16, 40. *See also* Royal Navy
  Arctic Expedition, 93–94, 120, 138–39, 145, 152
  Esquimalt Hospital, 56, 59, 61
  HMS *Atalanta,* 175, 180, 186, 188–91, 195–96, 200–203
  satirized in HMS *Pinafore,* 203
  widows' pensions, 205
ague. *See* malaria
Aides egypti mosquito, 185
air quality, 146–47, 154
  ventilation, 11, 66, 147
Alabama business, 22, 46
alcohol, 56, 58
  Esquimalt Hospital, 62
  grog, 56, 114, 125
  port wine, 129
  rum, 120, 146, 148, 152
  rum *vs.* tea, 144, 146, 148–49, 152
  sledging parties, 142, 144, 149–50
  "spirits of wine," 120
  whisky punch, 114
alcohol abuse, 66, 72–74
Aldrich, Pelham, 113–14, 120, 122, 126, 136. *See also* Western Party
  abstinence and, 142
  forced to turn back, 127, 133
  knowledge of scurvy, 135
  orders (intended route), 118
  scouting party, 108
  sled dogs, 110
  testimony before inquiry, 146–47
Alexandra (sledge), 118, 122–23
Alsace-Lorraine, 36
America, 46
  Moss's opinion on, 50
  polar ambitions, 93–94
American expansionism, 22
American flag, 136
amputations, 16, 126
Anderson, James, 3
Anglican funeral liturgy, 30
Antarctic (Scott) expedition, 153–54
Antarctic voyage of 1839-43 (James Ross), 9
antiscorbutic. *See* lime juice
Apocrypha, 182
Appleton, Paul C., xv, xvi
Archaeology, 164
Arctic Expedition (Franklin) (1825-27), 10
Arctic Expedition (Nares), xv, 111. *See also* HMS *Alert;* HMS *Discovery*
  and British claim to High Arctic, 136
  British naval discipline, 111–12
  clothing and equipment, 111, 114, 120
  contributions to science and geography, 108, 136, 143
  criticism by *Navy,* 145
  deaths, 124, 126, 128–29, 131, 135, 138
  Eastern Party, 120, 127, 134–35, 141
  emergency rescue teams, 128–29
  Floeberg Harbour, 105, 108–15
  inquiry, 144, 146–47, 150, 152
  medical check-ups, 114–15

medical supplies, 127, 129, 148
Middle pack route, 101–3
Moss's participation (*See* Moss, Edward Lawton)
national pride, 93–94, 97–98 (*See also* "Polar Fever")
Northern Party, 114, 117–18, 122–25, 127–31, 143
pride, 135
public debate, 141–42, 145 (*See also* "Old Arctics")
scientific emphasis, 94–95, 154
scurvy, 138, 152–54 (*See also* diet; lime juice)
voyage to Greenland, 99–101
weather and climatic observations, 108
welcome home banquets, 141–43
Western Party, 114, 116, 118, 122, 126, 133, 142
winter harbour, 105, 108, 111–14
Arctic expedition (Parry), 10, 90, 112–13, 125, 129
Arctic Grail, The (Berton), 98, 111
Armstrong, Alexander, 46, 95, 104, 146, 152
authority on scurvy, 149
memorandum to Nares (May 1875), 149–51
"Naval Hygiene and Scurvy," 151
testimony before inquiry, 150
arsenic, 12
astronomy, 136
Atkinson, E. L., 153
atmospheric theory. *See* "miasmic" or atmospheric theory
attempted murder, 66, 72–74
Austrians, 93
Ayles, Adam, 133, 142
Azores, 21

B

bacterial theory, 58
Baffin Bay, 101
Balkans, 161, 204
Russo-Turkish War, 162
Treaty of Berlin, 162
Treaty of Stefano, 162
Barbados, 21, 181–82
Barnaby, Nathaniel, 201
Batt, Robert B., 192
bear hunts, 84–87, 159
Arctic Expedition, 102–3
Beaumont, Lewis, 120, 134–36. *See also* Eastern Party
forced to turn back, 127
knowledge of scurvy, 135
return trip, 138
testimony before inquiry, 146
Belcher, Sir Edward, 90
Belize (British Honduras), 21
Bell, John, 73–74
belladonna, 69
Bermuda, 186–87
Berrie, James, 122, 155
Berton, Pierre, 144, 153
Arctic Grail, The, 98, 111
on British naval routine, 112
Beshika Bay, Turkey, 159, 162, 167–68
British naval flotilla, 162
Bethell, Alexander E., 198
Bible, 30
Donay Bible, 182
infallibility of scripture, 32
"birdcages" (Victoria legislative buildings), 51
Bismarck, Otto Eduard Leopold von, 162
Bloodhound (sledge), 118, 122
Blue Books. *See* Navy Blue Books
botany, 136
brachiopods, 127
Brading, Charles, 73–74
Bramberly House, 97
Brassey, Thomas, 204
Brent geese, 129
British Columbia, 51
British Trans-Arctic Expedition (1968–69), 154
bronchitis, 66
Budington, Captain, 105, 108, 112, 136
"*Bulldog* Affair," 13–14, 18
E. Moss's description, 14–19
inquiry (1866), 147
public opinion in Britain, 16–17
Bulldog (sledge), 118, 122, 127
Butler, Josephine, 68

C

cabbage, 149
Calvert, Frank, 163, 167–68
Canadian Alert Bay weather station, 108
Canadian colonies, 22
Canadian Forces Bay Alert, 105
Canadian sovereignty in polar region, 136
Canary Islands, 181
Cape Dudley Diggs, 102–3
Cape Haitien, 14–16. *See also* "*Bulldog* Affair"
Cape Joseph Henry, 118, 122, 126, 131, 133
Cape York, 102–3
carbolic acid, 11, 185
Carey Islands, 101–2
"Case of the Brutalised Bandsman, The," 73
Cator, Post-Captain, 53, 55, 59
Challenger (sledge), 118
Chambers Journal, 36
child-birthing practices, 88–89
children
  contagious diseases, 41
  smallpox vaccination, 71
Chinamen (servants), 3, 54–55, 80, 88
Chinese cooks, 54
Chinese medicinal recipes, 87–88
chloral hydrate, 72
chloroform, 11
cholera, 7, 24
Cholera Hospital, Dublin, 7
Christmas, 113, 181
Civil War (U.S.), 22
cleanliness and sanitation, 11, 58, 66
clothing and equipment
  Stephenson's complaints, 111, 120
Coates, Matthew, 66–68, 71–72, 74
Colan, Thomas, 94–95, 104, 113–14, 126, 151, 186
  on abstinence, 142
  Armstrong's testimony, 150
  promotion (following Arctic Expedition), 155–56
  testimony before inquiry, 146–47
cold sores, 122
Congress of Berlin, 162
Constantinople, 162
Contagious Diseases Act, 68
Contemporary Review, 32
Cook, Frederick, 154
Cooksworthy, Mrs., 37
coots, 100
Coppinger, Dr. Richard, 134–35, 138
Coppinger, William, 95
Cosmos, Amor de (formerly Bill Smith), 51
Craig, Peter, 135
Crimean War, 58, 144
crimson cliffs, 102–3
Crystal Palace, 94
Cuba, 185
Culme-Seymour, Post-Captain, 190–91, 199–200
Curme, Charles T., 198
Cusack, James, 6
Cutty Sark, 192

D

Dana, Richard Henry, *Two Years Before the Mast,* 181
Dardanelles, 162
Darwin, Charles, 9–10
Darwinian theory, 30, 70
Day, Captain, 63–64
Depot Point, 123
diet, 11, 58, 63. *See also* medical theory; provisions
  Arctic Expedition, 70, 103, 108, 146–49 (*See also* lime juice; scurvy)
  eggs (loon and duck), 101, 103
  fresh meat, 108, 125, 128–29, 144, 146, 148–49, 152–53
  fresh vegetables, 146, 149, 153, 182
  HMS *Alert,* 153
  recovery from alcoholism and, 72
  uterine rejuvenation and, 71
digitalis, 69
Discovery Bay, 105
Discovery Harbour, 136
Disko, Greenland, 99
Disraeli, Benjamin, 90, 94, 162
doctors. *See* medical doctors
dogsledges, 111, 118
Doidge, James, 133
Donay Bible, 182
Donnet, James, 146, 150
Dublin, 5–8, 93
Dugdale, Thomasina Mary, 46, 49–50. *See also* Moss, Thomasina Mary
Dumbbell Bay, 109
dysentery, 63, 66, 185

E

Eastern Party (Arctic Expedition), 141
  death, 135
  forced to turn back, 127
  hardships, 134
  orders (intended route), 120
  scurvy, 134–35
Edmunds, James, 144
Edward, Prince of Wales, 97, 143
"Edward's Preserved Potatoes," 149
Egerton, Algernon F., 101, 109, 126, 145–46, 192
egg flip, 129
eggs (loon and duck), 101, 103
Ellesmere coast, 118, 133
  absence of game, 109
Ellesmere Island, 94, 105, 108, 110
Elliot, Wm., 178
Ellis, Elmer, 199
emergency rescue teams, 128–29
enteric fever. *See* dysentery
epilepsy, 66
Episcopalian Church, 79
Eskimo dog handlers, 99, 109–10
Esquimalt, 3, 45, 81
  climate, 54
  cost of provisions, 54
  "grog shops," 56
  house at, 79–80
  Moss's quarters, 53–54
  Naval Reading Room, 81, 84
  servants and labor, 54–56, 59
  smallpox vaccination, 71
  Thomasina's description, 81
Esquimalt appointment, 45–46, 49
  advantages, 51
Esquimalt Hospital, 2, 46, 51
  alcoholism, 72
  deaths, 66
  dysentery, 63
  fire protection, 62–63
  garden, 61, 63
  heart disease, 69
  journals, 65–67, 69
  latrines, 58
  liquor control, 56, 62
  medical treatments, 65–74
  patients, 59, 61, 66–67
  renovations, 56–64
  scarlet fever, 63
  scurvy, 70, 127
  small boat, 62–63
  staffing, 59, 61, 63–64
  treatment of injuries, 66, 71
  venereal diseases, 66–68
Esquimalt Naval and Military Museum, 56
Esquimalt Naval Hospital. *See* Esquimalt Hospital
Esquimaux [sic] dress, 114
Etudes sur les Appendicularia, 180

F

fall sledging parties, 109
Feilden, Henry, 103, 108, 128, 138, 154
female patients, 70
feminist reformers, 68
Fenian Raids, 22
Floeberg Harbour, 105, 108–15
  absence of game, 109
  departure from, 136
  exploration parties, 109
  ice-houses, 108
  preparation for spring expeditions, 114
fossils, 100, 127
Fountain, James, 73
France, 36, 41
  British enmity towards, 35
Franco-Prussian War, 34–36
Franklin, Jane Griffin, Lady, 118
Franklin (1825–27) Arctic expedition, 10, 90, 93
Fraser, Thomas R., 146, 151
Fraser's Magazine, 163
Freethinkers, 30, 80
fresh meat, 108, 135, 144, 146, 148–49, 152–53
  Arctic hare, 125, 128–29
fresh vegetables, 146, 149, 153, 182
Friend, The, 81
frostbite, 109, 122, 126

G

gallbladder (bear), 87–88
Gambia, 21
Garde, Stuart, 73
gardens (kitchen), 53, 80
    Esquimalt Hospital, 61, 63
Geffard, Fabré, 14, 18–19
geology, 136
Germany, 36, 41
Gibraltar, 21, 24
Giffard, George, 118, 126
Gladstone, William Ewart, 23, 192, 204
gold pin (copied for Thomasina), 166, 170
gonorrhea, 66, 68
Good, Joseph, 122
Good Words, 36
goose hash, 129
Graphic, The, 84, 159
Greely Arctic expedition, 112
Greenland, 94, 120, 134. *See also* Eastern Party (Arctic Expedition)
    Moss's description of, 99–100
    scurvy, 148
Greenland Expedition (1870), 127
Greenland sled drivers, 99, 109–10
Greenwich (igloo), 108
grog, 114, 125
"grog shops," 56
gunboat diplomacy, 13. *See also* "*Bulldog* Affair"
gunnery, changes in, 10
Guns of August, The (Tuchman), 36
gunshot wounds, 66, 71
Guy Fawkes Day, 113

H

Haiti, 12
    British intervention, 18
    Fabré Geffard, 14, 18–19
    Sylvain Salnave, 14, 16, 18–19
Halifax, N.S., 21
Hall, Charles Francis, 94, 99, 145
    grave, 136
Hall, Robert, 193, 200
Hall, William King, 191
Hall Basin, 105
Hall expedition
    conflict, 112
    lemon juice, 136
Hamilton, Vesey, 45
Hand, James, 134, 136
Hare, Marcus, 196
Hare, Richard, 71, 92, 178
Hart, Henry Chichester, 136
heart disease, 66, 69
Heaven's Command (Morris), 10
Heinl, Roberta and Nancy, *Written in Blood,* 18
Hendrick, Hans, 99, 135
Henry VIII, King, 29
"Higher Criticism," 30
Hill, Elias, 122–23, 155
Hills, George, 2, 79
Hillyar, Charles Farrel, 53
Hisarlik, 160, 162–64, 168, 171
Hissalik. *See* Hisarlik
History of European Morals (Lecky), 169
HMCS *Naden,* 56
HMS *Achilles,* 41
HMS *Alert,* 10, 94, 96, 113, 123, 178. *See also* Arctic Expedition (Nares)
    air quality, 147
    arrival at Discovery Harbour, 136
    daily routine, 111–12
    departure for Arctic Expedition, 98–99
    departure from Floeberg Bay, 136
    departure of spring sledgers, 117
    diet, 153
    library, 113
    medical responsibility for, 95
    Middle pack route, 101–3
    Moss's living quarters, 97
    passage through Robeson Channel, 105
    refitting for polar mission, 93
    return to Valencia, 138
    scurvy, 126, 129
    welcome home, 141
    winter harbour (*See* Floeberg Harbour)
HMS *Ariadne,* 204
HMS *Atalanta,* xvi, 3, 175, 178, 183, 189, 191. *See also* HMS *Juno*
    competence of crew, 180, 187, 190, 199, 201
    continuing controversy, 202–3
    cover up and damage control, 188, 190–91, 200, 202

design, 202
experimental bilge keels, 196–97
Moss's concerns about, 198, 201
official inquiry, 191, 193
performance in heavy weather, 179–81, 191, 198
quarantine, 187
reported missing, 176, 182, 187
rumour and speculation, 188
Ryder Inquiry, 195–205
seaworthiness, 187, 190–91, 195, 199
stability, 198, 201–2
Stirling's criticism of, 176, 197–98
suitability as training ship, 175, 195, 204
yellow fever, 185
HMS *Boscawen,* 29, 34, 36, 42
HMS *Boxer,* 50
HMS *Bulldog,* 10, 12–15, 19, 185. *See also* "*Bulldog* Affair"
scuttling of, 16
HMS *Cameleon,* 69–70
HMS *Captain,* 192
HMS *Discovery,* 95, 102–3, 109, 114, 120, 136
Arctic Expedition, 93, 98–99
fresh meat, 153
scurvy, 126
welcome home, 141
winter harbour, 105
HMS *Duke of Wellington,* 97
HMS *Eurydice,* 182–83, 188–89
design drawings for, 196
inquiry, 192
loss of, 175–76, 178
HMS *Excellent,* 142
HMS *Galatea,* 19, 204
HMS *Inconstant,* 42
HMS *Iron Duke,* 157
HMS *Juno,* 175. *See also* HMS *Atalanta*
decision to refit, 189, 196, 200, 203
seaworthiness, 195
HMS *Lily,* 19
HMS *Myrmidon,* 71
HMS *Pinafore* (comic opera), 203
HMS *Plover,* 199
HMS *Prince Arthur,* 50
HMS *Princess Royal,* 41
HMS *Repulse,* 69, 71–73
HMS *Research,* 162, 164, 169, 171–72, 178
HMS *Scout,* 50–51, 53, 61, 63–64, 69, 78
HMS *Simoom,* 21–27, 34, 43, 178–79
HMS *Sparrowhawk,* 72
HMS *Tamar,* 190
HMS *Tenedos,* 64
HMS *Topaze,* 157
HMS *Victory,* 12
HMS *Warrior,* 10
Hodgson, Charles, Chaplain, 138–39
Hoggin, William, 73
Holland, Benjamin, 67
Homer, *Iliad,* 160
Hood, William Acland, 198, 200, 203
Hooker, Joseph, 9, 40
Hope, James, 16, 146
Hornby, Admiral, 162
Hudson's Bay Company, 51, 54, 56, 111
Hunt, John, 32
hunting expeditions, 84–85
bear hunts, 84–87, 102–3, 159
in British Columbia, 84–87
Carey Islands, 103
from Floeberg Harbour, 108–9
Greenland, 100
Huxley, Thomas, 10

I

ice-boats, 123, 128
ice hummocks. *See* "Paleocrystic Sea"
ice-masters, 102
ichthyology, 10
Iliad (Homer), 160
Ilios (Schliemann), 163
Illustrated London News, 16, 36, 158, 162
Indian hunting guide (Skupac), 85–88
infallibility of scripture, 32
infectious diseases, 42–43, 71. *See also* smallpox
Inglefield, E. A., 146
Innes, Mr., 2
[Irish] Fenians, 16
Irish Times, 138, 155

J

jagged pack ice. *See* "Paleocrystic Sea"
Jeffrey, Gwyn, 101
Jenkins, William, 135, 204
Jessup, Thomas, 199, 201
Johns, William, 201

K

Kane Basin, 136
Kendall, Richard, "Scurvy During Some British Arctic Expeditions, 1875–1917," 153
Kennedy Channel, 105, 136
Kew (igloo), 108
King's College, 23
Kingstown, Ireland, 21, 157–60
Kip, William, 79
Knights of St. John, 23

L

Lady Franklin Bay, 105
Lancet, The, 66, 95, 142, 144, 151
  reporting on inquiry, 146
Lawton family, 5
Lecky, William Edward Hartpole, *History of European Morals,* 169
lemon juice, 11, 135–36. *See also* diet; lime juice
Lennox, Henry, 192
Lethbridge, Thomas, 21, 24, 45
"Letters from Troy" (Moss), 164
Lewis, Robert, 69
Lick House, San Francisco, 49, 78
Lievely, Greenland, 99
Limacina, 103
lime juice, 128–29, 153. *See also* diet; scurvy
  Moss on, 148
  Richards' view of, 152
  sledge crews, 120, 127, 144–46, 149
Linnean Society, 155, 159
Lister's germ theory, 11
Lloyd's of London, 187, 192
London, 42
London Telegraph, 98
Lyttleton Island, 103

M

malaria, 70, 169, 185
Malone, Marie, 77, 81, 88
Malta, 21, 23–24
Marco Polo (sledge), 118, 120, 123, 143
Marcus Ward & Co., 157, 159, 172
marine botany, 95, 112
Markham, Albert Hastings, 100–101, 123–24, 147, 150. *See also* Northern Party
  bear hunt, 102
  exploration and depot provisioning, 108–9
  lime juice and, 120, 125, 144
  on Moss's helpfulness, 122
  personal ambition, 125, 129–31
  polar fever, 95
  on possibility of reaching the Pole, 114
  responsibility for Porter's death, 131
  sledge motto, 117–18
  speech on sledge travelling (to Royal Geographical Society), 143
  testimony before inquiry, 146
  withheld scurvy information, 124–25, 129, 135
  writing, 158–59
Markham, Clements, 93, 95, 99, 101, 143, 145, 154
  "*To the Threshold of the Unknown,*" 94
Markham Hall, 108
marriage, 25, 37–39, 46, 49–50, 55, 74, 78, 80–81
  arranged marriages, 46
Mason, Dean, 79
May (Lieutenant), 102, 109, 128–29
McClintock, Francis Leopold, 110
McClintock, Lady, 117
McCormick (ordinary seaman), 199, 201
McCreight, Mr., 74
McKenna, Arthur, 21
measles, 41
Mechanics Institute, 51
Medical Charities Act, 6
medical doctors (Irish)
  compensation and health risks, 6–7
medical officers (Navy). *See* Royal Navy medical officers
medical principles
  "do no harm," 65
medical research, 40. *See also* scientific research

medical supplies, 58
Arctic Expedition, 127, 129, 148
Navy, 58, 66
medical theory
childbirth, 88–89
on cholera, 7
cleanliness and sanitation, 11, 58
"era of scientific medicine," 11
on scurvy, 152–53
on yellow fever, 185
medicine as a "science," 65
Mediterranean, 21
Mediterranean Fleet, 162
meeting houses. *See* Quakers
Melville Bay, 102
"Memories of an Esquimalt Pioneer" (Reid), 3
mercury, 12, 68
Métis unrest, 22
"miasmic" or atmospheric theory, 58, 150
Middle pack route, 101–3
Mitchell, David, 122
"Modernism," 30
Montreal, 24
morphine, 127
Morris, James, 13, 205
Heaven's Command, 10
Moss, Ada Dugdale, 88, 90, 93, 157, 207
last letter from her father, 183
Moss, Amelia Jane, 6
Moss, Beatrice Mary, 157, 207
Moss, Edward Jr., 207
Moss, Edward Lawton, 19, 154
on abuse of alcohol, 58, 72
advice (written) re yellow fever, 186
Arctic Expedition, 90–96, 113, 120, 122–23, 126–29, 154–55 (*See also* Arctic Expedition (Nares))
Arctic Medal, 155
art (sketches, watercolours), xv, 3, 16, 101, 113, 157–58, 162, 204
at Beshika Bay, 162
Bulldog (sledge), 118, 122–23, 127
cabin on the *Alert,* 97
career ambitions and prospects, 9, 35, 40, 46, 49, 77, 91, 104, 154–55, 159
children and descendents, 88, 157, 207
on cleanliness and sanitation, 58
colleagues and superiors respect for, 101, 122, 129, 143, 154
conscientiousness, 66
created Naval Reading Room, 81, 84
death, xvi, 183
discontent and unhappiness, 37–38, 40, 43, 178
early life, 5–8, 80
engagement to Thomasina Mary Dugdale, 46
Esquimalt appointment, 45–46, 49, 51, 53–74, 77
family background, 5–8
family reunion (after Arctic Expedition), 138
father's death, 8
finances (money and living expenses), 32, 34–35, 45, 49, 54–55, 79, 89, 97, 157, 179
financial assistance to mother, 9, 22, 33–34, 37, 81, 97
under fire (HMS *Bulldog*), 14–16
found scurvy in Northern Party, 129
on Franco-Prussian War, 34–36
on friends and friendship, 30, 39
happiness in marriage, 74, 79, 90
HMS *Atalanta,* 175, 178, 182, 185–86, 198, 201
HMS *Bulldog,* 12–16
on HMS *Simoom* (troopship), 21–27
humour, 25, 79, 89, 182–83
hunting and exploration sorties, 84–88, 100–103, 108, 125, 159
interlude in Ireland, 157–60
joined HMS *Research,* 162
joined Royal Navy, 9–10, 12
lodgings at Southsea, 97
marriage, 46, 49, 74, 79, 90
marriage preparations and wedding, 78–79, 81
on matrimony, 37–39, 46, 50, 55, 81
medical practice (Arctic Exhibition), 113, 120, 122–23, 127, 129, 154–55
medical practice *(Atalanta),* 185–86
medical practice *(Bulldog),* 16
medical practice (Esquimalt), 55–56, 65–74, 77
medical practice (female patients), 70–71
medical practice (Portland), 36, 38, 41–43
melancholy (or pessimism), 37–38, 43
on naval life, 40
"On Specimens of *Osteocela Septentrionalis*", 159
at Portland Sick Quarters, 26, 29–43
on prevalent diseases (Pacific Coast), 70

promotion examinations, 26, 33
Quaker family roots, 80
relationship (bond) with mother, 6, 29
religious affiliation, 80–81
religious views, 25–26, 29–31, 79–80
renovations to Esquimalt Hospital, 56–64
rheumatism, 39
on safety of *Atalanta,* 198, 201
scientific interests and accomplishments, 9, 34, 40, 77, 95–96, 101, 112, 127, 154, 159, 204
on scurvy outbreak, 127, 148, 154
Shores of the Polar Sea, xv, 3, 110–11, 155, 157, 159
on sled dogs, 109–10
sledge motto, 118
snowshoes (*See* snowshoes)
social life (Edward and Thomasina), 84
"Sport in British Columbia," 84, 159
testimony at *Bulldog* inquiry, 18
testimony before Arctic Expedition inquiry, 147–48
views on matrimony, 25
visit to King's College and St. Bartholomew's, 23
visits to Schliemann's dig, 163–65, 169–70
wit and irony, 25, 79, 81, 182–83
yellow fever, 13, 185
Moss, Jeremy Michael Edward, 207
Moss, Mary, 207
Moss, Mary Teresa, 6, 40
Moss, Nigel Robert Dugdale, 207
Moss, Peter Dugdale, 207
Moss, Phoebe Anna, 6, 38, 40, 80–81
Moss, Richard Jackson, 6, 26, 32–33, 40, 159, 163
Moss, Robert Edward, 207
Moss, Teresa (Richardson), 5, 37
children, 6
cholera, 7
education, 6, 32
husband's early death, 7
Moss, Thomasina Mary, 55, 78
after Edward's death, 189, 205, 207
on Arctic Expedition offer, 91, 96
birth of children, 4, 88–89, 157, 187, 189
correspondence with R. L. Reid, 1–4, 74, 84
description of domestic bliss, 90
description of Esquimalt, 81
marriage, 4, 78–79
Quaker family roots, 80
Moss, William, 5
Cholera Hospital, 7
death, 8
medical practice, 6
Moss, William Richardson, 6, 40, 45, 50, 55, 172, 180
Mullen, Mrs., 80
Murray, Peter, 72
Museum Square (Esquimalt), 56
Mushroom Point, 127
mutton, 129
Mycenae (Schliemann), 163

N

Napoleon III (Louis Napoleon), 35
Nares, George, 97, 113, 117, 123. *See also* Arctic Expedition (Nares)
awareness of scurvy, 126
censured (Inquiry Report), 152
choice of winter harbour, 105
criticism, 144–45
emergency rescue teams, 128–29
farewell to sledge crews, 118
knighthood, 142
lime juice issue, 120, 147, 149–51
order for night travel, 126
on possibility of reaching Pole, 114
reconnoitering party to View Point, 128
report to Admiralty, 138–39
request for tribunal to clear his name, 152
rescue party to Western Party, 134
skill and seamanship, 94–95, 101–2, 108
speech to Royal Geographic Society, 143
testimony before inquiry, 146, 151
writing, 158–59
natural sciences, 10
Nature, 33
"Naval Hygiene and Scurvy" (Armstrong), 151
Naval Reading Room (Esquimalt), 81, 84
naval surgeons, 77
family life and, 40
independence, 12
medicinal supplies, 58, 66
scientific research, 40

Navy. *See* Royal Navy
Navy, 144–45
Navy Blue Books, 34
  Moss's articles in, 27, 35, 37, 90
Nelson, Horatio Nelson, Viscount, 10, 19
"New Theology," 30
New Year, 113–14
New York, 78, 93
News of the World, 36
night travelling, 126–27
Nightingale, Florence, 58
Nimmo, R., 181–82
Ninnis, Belgrave, 95, 109, 149
Nordenskiöld, Nils, 127
Northern Party, 114, 117, 122, 143. *See also* Markham, Albert Hastings
  deaths, 124, 128–29, 131
  emergency rescue of, 128–29
  orders (intended route), 118
  return trip, 127–28
  scurvy, 124–25, 129
  sledge weights, 123–24, 130
  turning point celebration, 125

O

"Old Arctics," 93, 111, 143–46, 151
"On Specimens of *Osteocela Septentrionalis*" (Moss), 159
Opernivik. *See* Upernavik
opium, 72, 127, 129
O'Reilly, Mrs., 2–3
O'Reilly, Peter, 2, 50, 84
Osborn, Sherard, 93
oysters, 129

P

Pacific Station at Esquimalt. *See* Esquimalt
pack ice, 102, 105, 136
"Paleocrystic Sea," 109–11, 123–24
  unsuited to sledges, 110, 130
Pandora, 100
paralytic diseases, 70
Parr, A. A. Chase, 109, 114–15, 118, 120
  knowledge of scurvy, 124
  lone journey for help, 128
  snow-blindness, 122
Parry, Sir William Edward, 125, 129
Parry (1821–23) Arctic expedition, 90, 112
Parry (1818) first Arctic expedition, 113
Patrick, Mrs., 41, 46, 97
Paul, Charles, 134–36
Peary, Robert, 110, 145, 154
Petersen, Nels, 99, 126
phisitis. *See* TB
Piblokto (hysterical fits), 110
Piraeus, Greece, 171–72
pneumonia, 66
Point Ellice House, 50, 84
Point Moss, 110
"Polar Fever," 93
"Polar Virus," 145
Polaris Bay, 136
Polaris Bay Depot, 134–35
Polaris (ship), 94, 105
Pole, the, 90, 103, 114, 118, 150
  impractical over Paleocrystic Sea, 130
  Robert Peary, 154
  South Pole, 154
  Times, The, on, 139
  ultimate goal, 94
Poor Relief (Ireland) Act, 6
Poppie (sledge), 118, 126
port wine, 129
Porter, George, 124
  death, 128–29, 131
Portland, 33, 35
  contagious diseases outbreak, 41–42
  geology (Moss's description), 33–34
  smallpox, 41–42, 65
Portland Sick Quarters, 27, 29–43
  smallpox, 65
Portsmouth, 21, 26, 94, 96, 141
  Arctic Office, 97
  preparation for Arctic Expedition, 93
potato famine (Ireland), 7
prevention, 11
"Priam's Treasure," 164
pride, 134–35
Proceedings of the Zoological Society of London, 95
prostitutes, 68
Providence (schooner), 14

provisions, 95. *See also* diet; lime juice
- Arctic Expedition, 99, 103, 146
- *Atalanta,* 183, 186
- *Bulldog* (sledge), 127
- *Cameleon,* 69
- provision depots (Arctic), 108–9, 127–28
- sledging parties, 120, 146, 152

Pullen, Henry, 100, 113, 118, 126
Punch, 17, 36

Q

Quakers, 5–6, 34–35, 46, 79, 169
- marriage prerequisites, 80–81

Queenston, Ireland, 93
Quincey, Dr., 31
quinine, 11, 70, 127

R

race
- "deterioration of the race" theory, 70

Rae, John, 111, 145
Raines, David
- on credibility of Ryder Inquiry, 203
- *Solved! The Greatest Sea Mystery of All,* 202

Randolph, Vice-Admiral, 192
Rattray, Alexander, 11
Rawson, Wyatt, 111, 126, 134–35
"Recent Arctic Expedition, The" (paper), 155
Reed, E. J., 191–92
Reed, Walter, 185
Reed Commission, 185
Reid, Robie Louis, 74, 84
- correspondence with Thomasina Moss, 1–4
- "Memories of an Esquimalt Pioneer," 3

rheumatism, 39, 66, 70
Richards, Sir George, 145, 151–52
Richardson, John (grandfather), 6, 84
Richardson, Sir John, 40
- contribution to natural sciences, 10

Richardson, Teresa. *See* Moss, Teresa
Richardson family, 5–6
Rivers, Harry, 199
RMS *Jamaica Packet,* 18
Robertson, A. R., 74
Robeson Channel, 105, 120, 134
Ross, James, 9
Rothery, H. C., 192, 203
Royal Arctic Theatre, 113
Royal Canadian Navy, 56
Royal College of Physicians in London, 7
Royal College of Science (Dublin), 8
Royal College of Surgeons, 8
Royal Dublin Society, 155, 159, 172
Royal Geographical Society, 93, 99, 143–44
Royal Irish Academy, 155, 159
Royal Naval College at Greenwich, 142
Royal Navy. *See also* Admiralty
- British naval discipline, 111–12
- half pay, 42, 89, 157
- imperial role, 13
- leave regulations, 24, 38
- slow adaptation to modernity, 205
- smallpox inoculation, 41–42, 71

Royal Navy medical officers
- career expectations, 9–10
- cleanliness and ventilation, 11
- naval surgeons, 12, 40, 58, 66, 77
- scientific research, 9–10
- surgeons *vs.* physicians, 9

Royal Society, 93, 155, 159
rum, 120, 148
rum *vs.* tea, 146, 152
Ruskin, John, 94
Russia, 161–62
Russo-Turkish War, 162
Ryder, A. P., 192, 195
Ryder Inquiry, 195–205
- report, 202
- testimony of ordinary seamen, 199

S

Salnave, Sylvain, 14, 16, 18–19
San Francisco, 49, 78–79, 93
San Juan Island, 2, 46, 51
San Juan marines at Esquimalt, 62–63, 66–67
Sanitary Record, The, 144
sanitary reform, 11
Sanitary Review, The, 151
Saturday Athenaeum, 36
Scammander (river), 164–66, 168

scarlatina. *See* scarlet fever
scarlet fever, 41, 63, 71
Schliemann, Heinrich, 160
  Calvert's opinion of, 167
  credit to Moss, 163, 171
  excavation at Hisarlik, 160, 162–64, 171
  Ilios, 163
  Moss's assistance, 169–71
  Moss's criticism of, 163–70
  Mycenae, 163
  "Priam's Treasure," 163–64
  religious views, 167
  Troy and its Remains, 163
Schliemann of Troy (Trail), 163
scientific community (mid-Victorian)
  anti-Trinitarianism, 31
  seeking synthesis (biblical and science), 30
scientific research
  Moss's interest in, 9, 34, 40, 77, 95–96, 101, 112, 127, 154, 159, 204
  naval surgeons, 9–10
scorbutus. *See* scurvy
Scott, Robert (Expedition to Antarctic), 153–54
Scott Polar Research Institute, 113
scurvy, xv, 11, 66, 115, 122, 129, 136, 147, 150–51
  Aldrich's knowledge of, 135
  Armstrong on, 152
  Beaumont's knowledge of, 135
  Charlton Island on James Bay, 145
  Clements Markham on, 94
  Donnet-Fraser paper on, 152
  Eastern Party (Arctic Expedition), 134–35
  Esquimalt Hospital, 70, 127
  fresh meat and, 129, 135
  HMS *Alert,* 126, 129
  HMS *Discovery,* 126
  Inquiry's conclusions on, 152
  Kendall on, 153–54
  Markham's silence on, 124–25, 129, 135
  medical knowledge of, 152–53
  Moss's testimony (before inquiry) on, 148, 154
  Northern Party (Arctic Expedition), 124–25
  public interest, 144
  Western Party (Arctic Expedition)), 133
"Scurvy During Some British Arctic Expeditions, 1875–1917" (Kendall), 153
Sea of Marmora, 162
Sedan, 36
Self, James, 129
sewage disposal, 66
Shaw le Fevre, Robert, 192
sheep, 103
shingles, 66
Shirley, John, 124, 129
Shores of the Polar Sea (Moss), xv, 3, 110–11, 155
  artistic quality, 157–58
  compensation for, 159
  non-judgmental, 158
  review in *Illustrated London News,* 158
Sierra Leone, 21
skating, 81, 90
Skupac (Indian hunting guide), 85–88
sled dogs, 99, 110
  difficulties with, 109
  health problems, 110–11
sledge crew rations, 129. *See also* diet
  alcohol, 120, 125
  lime juice, 120, 125, 127–28
sledge crews, 108
  determination to succeed, 117–18
  difficulties, 110
  enthusiasm, 120
  night travelling, 127
  snowshoes and, 111
  training, 108
sledge mottos, 117–18
sledge weights, 123–24, 130, 146
  Armstrong's testimony, 150
  questions about, 142
sledges
  merits and shortcomings, 143
  suitability to terrain, 110, 130, 134
smallpox, 43
  Chinese residents of Victoria, 71
  Portland Sick Quarters, 65
  in ships at Portland, 41–42
smallpox vaccination, 11
  Esquimalt, 71
  Navy, 41–42, 71
Smith, Bill. *See* Cosmos, Amor de (formerly Bill Smith)
Smith, William Henry, 203
Smith Sound [Smith's Sound], 100–101
snow-blindness, 122